"THER … THE BEST TEXT OF THE … ABLE IN ENGLISH."
… e *Historical Bulletin*

"We … ner volume of Father Copleston's class… … phy. It is marked by solid learning, breadth of vie… … ntific objectivity and shrewd common sense."
The London *Tablet*

"Father Copleston continues his urbane and very readable account of philosophers and their systems. His book has the consecutiveness and unity of a novel . . . With the two volumes that preceded, it constitutes a remarkable achievement, the most considerable work of scholarship produced by English Scholasticism in our day, a work that has been received with respect by philosophy scholars everywhere."
Book Reviews

"The present volume may be warmly recommended not merely for those academically concerned with the history of philosophy, but for anyone aspiring to a clearer insight into the process by which the European mind cast off the tutelage of the Mediaeval doctors."
Avery R. Dulles, S.J.
Woodstock Letters

"For those who are familiar with the first two volumes of Father Copleston's *History of Philosophy*, it will be sufficient to say that this, the third volume, maintains the same standard of excellence. Father Copleston's work is already recognized as the standard Catholic history of philosophy."
The Catholic World

"In this volume, Father Copleston continues the fine scholarship and good style that characterized his previous two volumes."
Catholic Library World

"Father Copleston's work will rank as the most authoritative and outstanding study in this field by a Catholic scholar and second to none as a book of general reference on the subject."
Homilectic and Pastoral Review

A History of Philosophy

VOLUME III

Late Mediaeval and Renaissance Philosophy

PART I

Ockham to the Speculative Mystics

by Frederick Copleston, S.J.

IMAGE BOOKS
A Division of Doubleday & Company, Inc.
Garden City, New York

Image Books Edition 1963
by special arrangement with The Newman Press
Image Books Edition Published February, 1963

DE LICENTIA SUPERIORUM ORDINIS:
E. Helsham, S.J.
Praep. Prov. Angliae
NIHIL OBSTAT:
J. L. Russell, S.J.
Censor Deputatus
IMPRIMATUR:
✠ Joseph, Archiepiscopus Birmingamiensis
Birmingamiae die 4 Januarii 1952

Printed in the United States of America
Cover by Ronald Clyne

CONTENTS

APPENDICES

FOREWORD

This volume is concerned with the philosophy of the fourteenth century. A good deal in the history of the philosophical thought of this period is still obscure, and no definitive account of it can be written until we have at our disposal a much greater number of reliable texts than are at present available. However, in publishing the account contained in this volume I am encouraged by the thought that the learned Franciscan scholar, Father Philotheus Boehner, who is doing so much to shed light on the dark places of the fourteenth century, was so kind as to read the chapters on Ockham and to express appreciation of their general tone. This does not mean, of course, that Father Boehner endorses all my interpretations of Ockham. In particular he does not agree with my view that analysis discloses two ethics implicitly contained in Ockham's philosophy. (This view is in any case, as I hope I have made clear in the text, a conjectural interpretation, developed in order to account for what may seem to be inconsistencies in Ockham's ethical philosophy.) And I do not think that Father Boehner would express himself in quite the way that I have done about Ockham's opinions on natural theology. I mention these differences of interpretation only in order that, while thanking Father Boehner for his kindness in reading the chapters on Ockham, I may not give the impression that he agrees with all that I have said. Moreover, as proofs were already coming in at the time the chapters reached Father Boehner, I was unable to make as extensive a use of his suggestions as I should otherwise wish to have done. In conclusion I should like to express the hope that when Father Boehner has published the texts of Ockham which he is editing he will add a general account of the latter's philosophy. Nobody would be better qualified to interpret the thought of the last great English philosopher of the Middle Ages.

FOREWORD

This volume is concerned with the philosophy of [illegible] century [illegible] [illegible] of the [illegible] [illegible] of this period [illegible] [illegible] and [illegible] [illegible] we have [illegible] [illegible] number of [illegible] that [illegible] available [illegible] The [illegible] of this volume [illegible] [illegible] to whom [illegible] in writing the chapters on Ockham [illegible] [illegible] [illegible] [illegible] [illegible] the time the chapter [illegible] [illegible] I was unable to make [illegible] use of [illegible] [illegible] it was wiser to have done. In consequence I should like to express the hope that when [illegible] has published the [illegible] of Ockham which he is editing he will give us [illegible] account of the latter's [illegible]. Nobody would be better qualified to interpret the thought of the last great English philosopher of the Middle Ages.

Chapter One

INTRODUCTION

Thirteenth century – Fourteenth century contrasted with thirteenth – Philosophies of the Renaissance – Revival of Scholasticism.

1. In the preceding volume I traced the development of mediaeval philosophy from its birth in the pre-mediaeval period of the early Christian writers and Fathers through its growth in the early Middle Ages up to its attainment of maturity in the thirteenth century. This attainment of maturity was, as we have seen, largely due to that fuller acquaintance with Greek philosophy, particularly in the form of Aristotelianism, which took place in the twelfth century and the early part of the thirteenth. The great achievement of the thirteenth century in the intellectual field was the realization of a synthesis of reason and faith, philosophy and theology. Strictly speaking, of course, one should speak of 'syntheses' rather than of 'a synthesis', since the thought of the thirteenth century cannot legitimately be characterized with reference to one system alone; but the great systems of the period were, in spite of their differences, united by the acceptance of common principles. The thirteenth century was a period of positive constructive thinkers, of speculative theologians and philosophers, who might criticize one another's opinions in regard to this or that problem, but who at the same time were agreed in accepting fundamental metaphysical principles and the mind's power of transcending phenomena and attaining metaphysical truth. Scotus, for example, may have criticized St. Thomas's doctrines of knowledge and of analogy in certain points; but he criticized it in what he regarded, rightly or wrongly, as the interests of objectivity of knowledge and of metaphysical speculation. He considered

that St. Thomas had to be corrected or supplemented in certain points; but he had no intention of criticizing the metaphysical foundations of Thomism or of undermining the objective character of philosophic speculation. Again, St. Thomas may have thought that more must be allowed to the unaided power of the human reason than was allowed to it by St. Bonaventure; but neither of these theologian-philosophers doubted the possibility of attaining certain knowledge concerning the metaphenomenal. Men like St. Bonaventure, St. Thomas, Giles of Rome, Henry of Ghent and Duns Scotus were original thinkers; but they worked within the common framework of an ideal synthesis and harmony of theology and philosophy. They were speculative theologians and philosophers and were convinced of the possibility of forming a natural theology, the crown of metaphysics and the link with dogmatic theology; they were uninfected by any radical scepticism in regard to human knowledge. They were also realists, believing that the mind can attain an objective knowledge of essences.

This thirteenth-century ideal of system and synthesis, of harmony between philosophy and theology, can be viewed perhaps in relation to the general framework of life in that century. Nationalism was growing, of course, in the sense that the nation-States were in process of formation and consolidation; but the ideal of a harmony between papacy and empire, the supernatural and natural focuses of unity, was still alive. In fact, one can say that the ideal of harmony between papacy and empire was paralleled, on the intellectual plane, by the ideal of harmony between theology and philosophy, so that the doctrine as upheld by St. Thomas of the indirect power of the papacy in temporal matters and of the State's autonomy within what was strictly its own sphere was paralleled by the doctrine of the normative function of theology in regard to philosophy together with the autonomy of philosophy in its own sphere. Philosophy does not draw its principles from theology, but if the philosopher reaches a conclusion which is at variance with revelation, he knows that his reasoning is at fault. Papacy and empire, especially the former, were unifying factors in the ecclesiastical and political spheres, while the pre-eminence of the university of Paris was a unifying factor in the intellectual sphere. Moreover, the Aristotelian idea of the cosmos was generally accepted and helped to lend a certain appearance of fixity to the mediaeval outlook.

But though the thirteenth century may be characterized by reference to its constructive systems and its ideal of synthesis and harmony, the harmony and balance achieved were, at least from the practical standpoint, precarious. Some ardent Thomists would be convinced, no doubt, that the synthesis achieved by St. Thomas should have been universally accepted as valid and ought to have been preserved. They would not be prepared to admit that the balance and harmony of that synthesis were intrinsically precarious. But they would be prepared, I suppose, to admit that in practice it was scarcely to be expected that the Thomist synthesis, once achieved, would win universal and lasting acceptance. Moreover, there are, I think, elements inherent in the Thomist synthesis which rendered it, in a certain sense, precarious, and which help to explain the development of philosophy in the fourteenth century. I want now to illustrate what I mean.

The assertion that the most important philosophical event in mediaeval philosophy was the discovery by the Christian West of the more or less complete works of Aristotle is an assertion which could, I think, be defended. When the work of the translators of the twelfth century and of the early part of the thirteenth made the thought of Aristotle available to the Christian thinkers of western Europe, they were faced for the first time with what seemed to them a complete and inclusive rational system of philosophy which owed nothing either to Jewish or to Christian revelation, since it was the work of a Greek philosopher. They were forced, therefore, to adopt some attitude towards it: they could not simply ignore it. Some of the attitudes adopted, varying from hostility, greater or less, to enthusiastic and rather uncritical acclamation, we have seen in the preceding volume. St. Thomas Aquinas's attitude was one of critical acceptance: he attempted to reconcile Aristotelianism and Christianity, not simply, of course, in order to avert the dangerous influence of a pagan thinker or to render him innocuous by utilizing him for 'apologetic' purposes, but also because he sincerely believed that the Aristotelian philosophy was, in the main, true. Had he not believed this, he would not have adopted philosophical positions which, in the eyes of many contemporaries, appeared novel and suspicious. But the point I want to make at the moment is this, that in adopting a definite attitude towards Aristotelianism a thirteenth-century thinker was, to all intents and purposes, adopting an attitude towards *philosophy*. The significance of this fact has not always been realized by historians. Looking on mediaeval philosophers, especially those of the thirteenth century, as slavish adherents of Aristotle, they have not seen that Aristotelianism really meant, at that time, philosophy itself. Distinctions had already been drawn, it is true, between theology and philosophy; but it was the full appearance of Aristotelianism on the scene which showed the mediaevals the power and scope, as it were, of philosophy. Philosophy, under the guise of Aristotelianism, presented itself to their gaze as something which was not merely theoretically but also in historical fact independent of theology. This being so, to adopt an attitude towards Aristotelianism was, in effect, to adopt an attitude, not simply towards Aristotle as distinguished, for example, from Plato (of whom the mediaevals really did not know very much), but rather towards philosophy considered as an autonomous discipline. If we regard in this light the different attitudes adopted towards Aristotle in the thirteenth century, one obtains a profounder understanding of the significance of those differences.

(i) When the integral Aristotelians (or 'Latin Averroists') adopted the philosophy of Aristotle with uncritical enthusiasm and when they acclaimed Aristotle as the culmination of human genius, they found themselves involved in difficulties with the theologians. Aristotle held, for example, that the world was uncreated, whereas theology affirmed that the world had a beginning through divine creation. Again, Aristotle, as interpreted by Averroes, maintained that the intellect is one in all men and denied personal immortality whereas Christian theology maintained personal immortality. In face of these obvious difficulties the integral Aristotelians of the faculty of arts at Paris contended that the function of philosophy is to report faithfully the tenets of the philosophers. Therefore there was no contradiction involved in saying at the same time that philosophy, represented by Aristotle, taught the eternity of the world and the unicity of the human soul, while truth, represented by theology, affirmed the creation of the world in time and each man's possession of his individual rational soul.

This plea on the part of the integral Aristotelians or 'Averroists' that they were simply reporting the tenets of Aristotle, that is, that they were acting simply as historians, was treated by the theologians as a mere subterfuge. But, as I remarked in my second volume, it is difficult to ascertain what the mind of the Averroists really was. If, however, they really meant to do no more than report the opinions of past thinkers, and if they were sincere in affirming the truth of Christian revelation and theology, it would seem that their attitude must have been more or less this. Philosophy represents the work of the human reason reflecting on the natural order. Reason, personified by Aristotle, tells us that in the natural course of events time could have had no beginning and that the intellect would naturally be one in all men. That time had no beginning would thus be a philosophical truth; and the same must be said of monopsychism. But theology, which deals with the supernatural order, assures us that God by His divine power created the world in time and miraculously gave to each individual man his own immortal intellectual soul. It is not that something can be a fact and not a fact at the same time: it is rather that something would be a fact, were it not for God's miraculous intervention which has ensured that it is not a fact.

In regard to creative activity the position is, of course, exactly the same whether the integral Aristotelians of the faculty of arts at Paris were simply reporting Aristotle's teaching as they interpreted it, without reference to its truth or falsity, or whether they were affirming it as true. For in either case they did not add anything, at any rate not intentionally. It was the philosophers of the faculty of theology who were the productive and creative thinkers inasmuch as they felt compelled to examine Aristotelianism critically and, if they accepted it in the main, to rethink it critically. But the point I am trying to make is rather this. The position adopted by the integral Aristotelians implied a radical separation between theology and philosophy. If their own account of their activity is to be taken at its face value, they equated philosophy with history, with reporting the opinions of former philosophers. Philosophy understood in this sense is obviously independent of theology, for theology cannot affect the fact that certain opinions have been held by certain thinkers. If, on the other hand, the theologians were right in thinking that the integral Aristotelians really meant to assert the truth of the offending propositions, or if these propositions were asserted as propositions which would have been true, had not God intervened, the same conclusion concerning philosophy's complete independence of theology is implied. As the philosopher would be concerned merely with the natural course of events, he would be justified in drawing conclusions which conflicted with theological doctrine, since he would simply be asserting what would have been the case, had the natural course of events prevailed. Theology could tell us that a conclusion reached by philosophy did not represent the facts; but the theologian would not be justified in saying that the philosopher's reasoning was wrong simply because the conclusion at which he arrived was theologically unacceptable. We may learn from theology that the natural course of events has not been followed in some particular case; but that would not affect the question what the natural course of events is or would have been.

The most obviously salient features of the integral Aristotelianism or 'Averroism' of the thirteenth century were its slavish adherence to Aristotle and the rather desperate devices adopted by its adherents to square their position with the demands of theological orthodoxy. But implicit in integral Aristotelianism was a sharp separation between philosophy and theology, and an assertion of the former's complete independence. It is true that one should not over-emphasize this line of thought. The separation between theology and philosophy which was implicit in fourteenth-century Ockhamism did not derive from thirteenth-century 'Averroism'. But the appearance on the scene of the Aristotelian system in the thirteenth century was the factor which made it possible to give serious attention to the question of synthesis or separation, precisely because it led to the emergence of something which could be either synthesized or separated.

(ii) St. Thomas Aquinas recognized the distinction between philosophy and theology, in regard to both method and subject-matter. As I pointed out in the last volume, he took this distinction seriously. Though theology tells us that the world did not exist from eternity but had a beginning, no philosopher, according to St. Thomas, has ever adequately demonstrated this fact. The alleged proofs of the world's eternity are invalid, but so are the alleged proofs of the statement that the world did not exist from eternity. In other words, philosophy has not succeeded in solving the question whether the world was or was not created from eternity, though revelation does give us the answer to the question. This is an example of the real distinction which exists between philosophy and theology. On the other hand, St. Thomas certainly did not think that the philosopher could arrive, by valid rational argument, at any conclusion incompatible with Christian theology. If a philosopher arrives at a conclusion which contradicts, explicitly or implicitly, a Christian doctrine, that is a sign that his premisses are false or that there is a fallacy somewhere in his argument. In other words, theology acts as an external norm or as a kind of sign-post, warning the philosopher off a cul-de-sac or blind alley. But the philosopher must not attempt to substitute data of revelation for premisses known by the philosophic reason. Nor can he make explicit use of dogma in his arguments. For philosophy is intrinsically autonomous.

In practice, this attitude meant that the philosopher who adopted it philosophized in the light of the faith, even if he did not make formal and explicit use of the faith in his philosophy. The maintenance of this attitude was, moreover, facilitated by the fact that the great thinkers of the thirteenth century were primarily theologians: they were theologian-philosophers. At the same time, once philosophy was recognized as an intrinsically autonomous discipline, it was only to be expected that it should tend in the course of time to go its own way and that it should, as it were, chafe at its bonds and resent its position as handmaid of theology. And indeed, once it had become a normal proceeding for philosophers to be primarily, and even exclusively, philosophers, it was natural that philosophy's alliance with theology should tend to disappear. Furthermore, when the philosophers had no firm belief in revelation, it was only to be expected that the positions of theology and philosophy should be reversed, and that philosophy should tend to subordinate theology to herself, to incorporate the subject-matter of theology in philosophy or even to exclude theology altogether. These developments lay, indeed, well in the future; but they may be said, without absurdity at least, to have had their remote origin in the appearance of the Aristotelian system on the scene in the early thirteenth century.

These remarks are not intended to constitute an evaluation of the Aristotelian philosophy; they are meant to be a historical interpretation of the actual course of development taken by philosophic thought. No doubt, they are somewhat too summary and do not allow for the complexity of philosophic development. Once philosophy had been recognized as an autonomous discipline, that process of self-criticism which would seem to be essential to philosophy set in, and, not unnaturally, the criticism, as it grew, undermined the foundations of the synthesis achieved in the thirteenth century. That is one of the reasons why I spoke of that synthesis as 'precarious'. Whatever one may think of the truth or falsity of Aristotelian metaphysics, for example, it was not to be expected that philosophic thought should stop at a particular point: criticism was, from the practical standpoint, inevitable. But there is a second factor to bear in mind. Once a closely-knit theological-philosophical synthesis had been achieved, in which philosophical terms and categories were used for the expression of theological truths, it was not unnatural that some minds should feel that faith was in danger of being rationalized and that Christian theology had become unduly contaminated with Greek and Islamic metaphysics. Such minds might feel that the mystical rather than the philosophical approach was what was needed, especially in view of the wrangling of the Schools on points of theoretical rather than of primarily religious significance and interest. This second line of thought would also tend to dissolve the thirteenth-century synthesis, though the approach was different from that of thinkers who concentrated on philosophical problems and undermined the synthesis by extensive and far-reaching criticism of the philosophic positions characteristic of that synthesis. We shall see how both lines of thought manifested themselves in the fourteenth century.

(iii) To turn to a different field, namely that of political life and thought. It would obviously be absurd to suggest that there was ever anything but a precarious harmony and balance between the ecclesiastical and civil powers in the Middle Ages: no profound knowledge of mediaeval history is required to be well aware of the constantly recurring disputes between pope and emperor and of the quarrels between popes and kings. The thirteenth century was enlivened by these disputes, especially by those between the emperor Frederick II and the Holy See. Nevertheless, although both parties sometimes made extravagant claims in their own favour, the quarrels were, so to speak, family quarrels: they took place within that mediaeval framework of papacy and empire which found a theoretical expression in the writings of Dante. Moreover, as far as the commonly held political theory was concerned, the distinction between the two powers was recognized. St. Thomas Aquinas who, living in Paris, was more concerned with kingdoms than with the empire, recognized the intrinsically autonomous character of temporal sovereignty, though he naturally also recognized the indirect power of the Church in temporal affairs which follows from the recognition of the superiority of the supernatural function of the Church.[1] If one keeps to the plane of theory, one can speak, therefore, of a balance or harmony between the two powers in the thirteenth century, provided that one does not obscure the fact that in practical life the harmony was not so very apparent. The plain fact is that those popes who entertained grandiose ambitions in regard to temporal power were unable to realize those ambitions, while emperors who wished to do exactly as they chose without paying any attention to the Holy See were also unable to fulfil their desires. Triumphs on either side were temporary and not lasting. A certain balance, of a somewhat precarious nature, was therefore achieved.

At the same time, however, national kingdoms were becoming consolidated and the centralized power of national monarchs gradually increased. England had never been subject, in any practical sense, to the mediaeval emperor. Moreover, the empire was primarily a German affair; France, for instance, was independent; and the course taken by the dispute between Boniface VIII and Philip the Fair of France at the close of the thirteenth century showed clearly enough the position of France in relation both to the Holy See and to the empire. This growth of national kingdoms meant the emergence of a factor which would eventually destroy the traditional balance of papacy and empire. In the fourteenth century we witness the reflection, on the plane of theory, of the civil authority's growing tendency to assert its independence of the Church. The emergence of the strong national States, which became such a prominent feature of post-mediaeval Europe, began in the Middle Ages. They could hardly have developed in the way they did without the centralization and consolidation of power in the hands of local monarchs; and the process of this centralization and consolidation of power was certainly not retarded by the humiliation to which the papacy was exposed in the fourteenth century through the 'Babylonish captivity', when the popes were at Avignon (1305–77), and through the succeeding calamity of the 'Great Schism', which began in 1378.

The Aristotelian theory of the State could be, and was, utilized within the framework of the two-powers scheme by a thirteenth-century thinker like St. Thomas. This facilitated the theoretical recognition of the State as an intrinsically autonomous society, though it had to be supplemented by a Christian idea of the end of man and of the status and function of the Church. This 'addition' was not, however, simply an addition or juxtaposition; for it profoundly modified, by implication at least, the Greek outlook on the State. Conversely, by emphasizing the Aristotelianism in mediaeval political theory the position of the State could be stressed in such a way as practically to reverse the typical mediaeval conception of the proper relation between the two powers. We can see an example of this in the fourteenth century in the political theory of Marsilius of Padua. To say this is not to say, however, that Marsilius's theory was due to the Aristotelian philosophy: it was due much more, as we shall see later, to reflection on concrete historical events and situations. But it does mean that the Aristotelian theory of the State was a double-edged weapon; and that it not only could be but was utilized in a manner foreign to the mind of a theologian-philosopher like Aquinas. Its use represented, indeed, the growing political consciousness; and the phases of its use expressed the phases of the growth of that consciousness in concrete historical development.

2. If the thirteenth century was the period of creative and original thinkers, the fourteenth century may be called, in contrast, the period of Schools. The Dominicans naturally tended to adhere to the doctrines of St. Thomas Aquinas: and a series of injunctions by various Dominican Chapters encouraged them to do so. A number of works on the texts of St. Thomas appeared. Thus, at the request of Pope John XXII, Joannes Dominici composed an *Abbreviatio* or compendium of the *Summa theologica*, which he finished in 1331, while another Dominican, Benedict of Assignano (d. 1339), wrote a *Concordance*, in which he tried to show how the doctrine of the *Summa theologica* harmonized with that of St. Thomas's commentary on the *Sentences*. Then there were the commentators on, or interpreters of, St. Thomas, Dominicans like Hervaeus Natalis (d. 1323), who wrote a *Defensa doctrinae D. Thomae* and attacked Henry of Ghent, Duns Scotus and others, or John of Naples (d. 1330). But it was the fifteenth century, with John Capreolus (c. 1380–1444), rather than the fourteenth century, which was distinguished for achievement in this field. Capreolus was the most eminent commentator on St. Thomas before Cajetan (1468–1534).

Besides the Thomists there were the Scotists, who formed a rival school to the former, though Duns Scotus was not, in the fourteenth century, the official Doctor of the Franciscans in the same way that St. Thomas was the official Doctor of the Dominicans. In addition, there were the Hermits of St. Augustine, who followed the teaching of Giles of Rome. Henry of Ghent also had his followers, though they did not form a compact school.

In the fourteenth century these groups together with those who followed other thirteenth-century thinkers more or less closely represented the *via antiqua*. They lived on the thought of the preceding century. But at the same time there arose and spread in the fourteenth century a new movement, associated for ever with the name of William of Ockham. The thinkers of this new movement, the *via moderna*, which naturally possessed all the charm of 'modernity', opposed the realism of the earlier schools and became known as the 'nominalists'. This appellation is in some respects not very apposite, since William of Ockham, for example, did not deny that there are universal concepts in some sense; but the word is universally employed and will doubtless continue to be employed. There is not much point, then, in attempting to change it, though a better name is 'terminists'. The logicians of the new movement gave great attention to the logical status and function of terms. It is true that they strongly opposed and criticized the realism of earlier philosophers, particularly that of Duns Scotus; but it would be an over-simplification of their anti-realism to say that it consisted in attributing universality to 'names' or words alone.

It would, however, be a grossly inadequate description if one contented oneself with saying that the fourteenth-century nominalists attacked the realism of the thirteenth-century philosophers. The nominalist movement possessed a significance and an importance which cannot be adequately expressed by reference to one particular controversy. It constituted the wedge which was driven between theology and philosophy, and which broke apart the synthesis achieved in the thirteenth century. The nominalist spirit, if one may so speak, was inclined to analysis rather than to synthesis, and to criticism rather than to speculation. Through their critical analysis of the metaphysical ideas and arguments of their predecessors the nominalists left faith hanging in the air, without (so far as philosophy is concerned) any rational basis. A broad generalization of this sort has, of course, the defects attaching to such generalizations; it does not apply to all thinkers who were influenced by nominalism; but it indicates the result of the more extreme tendencies in the movement.

Philosophy can hardly live without the analytic and critical spirit: at least, critical analysis is one of the 'moments' of philosophic thought, and it is natural that it should follow a period of constructive synthesis. As we have seen, the spirit was present, to a certain extent, in the thought of Duns Scotus, who maintained, for example, that the proofs of the soul's immortality are not absolutely conclusive and that a number of the divine attributes often held to be demonstrable cannot really be demonstrated. But it must be noted that Scotus was a metaphysician who argued as a metaphysician. It is true that he was, like other mediaeval metaphysicians, a logician; but the logician had not, with him, begun to take the place of the metaphysician: his system belongs to the group of thirteenth-century metaphysical syntheses. In the fourteenth century, however, a change can be observed. Metaphysics, while not abandoned, tends to give place to logic; and questions which were formerly treated as metaphysical questions are treated primarily as logical questions. When William of Ockham tackles the subject of universals, he places the emphasis on the logical aspects of the question, on the *suppositio* and *significatio terminorum* rather than on the ontological aspects. Ockham seems to have been convinced of his fidelity to the exigencies of the Aristotelian logic; and one can even say that it was in the name of the Aristotelian logic, or of what he regarded as such, that Ockham criticized the metaphysics of predecessors like Duns Scotus and Thomas Aquinas. One can, of course, devote oneself to logical studies without troubling about metaphysics, and some of the Oxford logicians of the fourteenth century seem to have done so. But one can also go on to criticize metaphysical arguments and proofs in the name of logic, and this is what Ockham did. As we shall see, he to all intents and purposes undermined the natural theology and metaphysical psychology of his predecessors. In his opinion, the alleged proofs or demonstrations of God's attributes or of the spirituality and immortality of the soul either rest on principles the truth of which is not self-evident or terminate in conclusions which do not strictly follow from the relevant premisses. Ockham admitted, indeed, that some metaphysical arguments are 'probable'; but this simply illustrates the tendency in the fourteenth century to substitute probable arguments for demonstrations.

This substitution of probable arguments was connected, of course, with the nominalist tendency to doubt or to deny the validity of inferring from the existence of one thing the existence of another. Ockham stressed the primacy of intuition of the existent individual thing. In regard to a thing's existence the first question to ask, then, is whether we intuit it as existent. In the case of the spiritual soul, for example, Ockham would deny that we have any such intuition. The question then arises whether we can argue with certainty to the existence of the spiritual soul from the intuitions we do have. Ockham did not think this possible. He did not indeed make a purely phenomenalistic analysis of causality: he used the principle himself in metaphysics: but the later 'extremists', like Nicholas of Autrecourt, did give such an analysis. The result was that they questioned our knowledge of the existence of material substance, and probably also of the spiritual soul. In fact, no logical inference from the existence of one thing to the existence of another could amount to a 'demonstration' or cogent proof. In this way the whole metaphysical system of the thirteenth century was discredited.

This thoroughgoing criticism of the preceding metaphysical systems obviously involved a breach in the synthesis of theology and philosophy which had been a characteristic of those systems. St. Thomas, for example, even if he treated the philosophical arguments for the existence of God in works which were only in part philosophical, as distinct from theological, was certainly convinced that valid metaphysical arguments can be given for God's existence. These arguments belong to the *praeambula fidei*, in the sense that the acceptance of divine revelation logically presupposes the knowledge that a God exists who is capable of revealing Himself, a knowledge which can be gained in abstraction from theology. But if, as a number of the fourteenth-century philosophers believed, no cogent proof or demonstration of God's existence can be given, the very existence of God has to be relegated to the sphere of faith. Two consequences follow. First of all, theology and philosophy tend to fall apart. Of course, this consequence might be avoided, were the whole idea of philosophic 'proof' to be revised, but if the choice lies between demonstration and faith, and if the demonstrability of the 'preambles' of faith is denied, the consequence can scarcely be avoided. Secondly, if the important problems of traditional metaphysics, problems which linked philosophy with theology and religion, are relegated to the sphere of faith, philosophy tends to take on more and more a 'lay' character. This consequence did not become very apparent with Ockham himself, since he was a theologian as well as a philosopher, but it became more apparent with certain other fourteenth-century thinkers, like Nicholas of Autrecourt, who belonged to the faculty of arts.

To say that a thirteenth-century philosopher like St. Thomas was preoccupied with 'apologetics' would be untrue and anachronistic. None the less, though not preoccupied with apologetics in the way some Christian thinkers of a later age have been, he was certainly concerned with the relation between philosophy and revelation. Alive to the contemporary currents of thought and to the controversies of his time, he was prepared neither to reject the new Aristotelian metaphysics in the name of Christian tradition nor to pursue philosophic reflection without any regard to its bearing on Christian theology. He was careful to synthesize dogmatic theology on the one hand with his philosophy on the other, and to show the link between them. When we come to William of Ockham in the fourteenth century however, we find a marked absence of any concern for 'apologetics'. We find, indeed, a theologian who considered that his predecessors had obscured or overlaid Christian truths with false metaphysics; but we find also a philosopher who was quite content to apply his principles in a logical and consistent manner, without appearing to care, or perhaps fully to realize, the implications in regard to the synthesis between theology and philosophy. Truths which he believed but which he did not think could be philosophically proved he relegated to the sphere of faith. By assigning to the sphere of faith the truth that there exists an absolutely supreme, infinite, free, omniscient and omnipotent Being, he snapped the link between metaphysics and theology which had been provided by Aquinas's doctrine of the provable *praeambula fidei*. By making the moral law dependent on the free divine choice he implied, whether he realized it or not, that without revelation man can have no certain knowledge even of the present moral order established by God. The best that man could do, unaided by revelation, would presumably be to reflect on the needs of human nature and human society and follow the dictates of his practical reason, even though those dictates might not represent the divine will. This would imply the possibility of two ethics, the moral order established by God but knowable only by revelation, and a provisional and second-class natural and non-theological ethic worked out by the human reason without revelation. I do not mean to say that Ockham actually drew this conclusion from his authoritarian conception of the moral law; but it was, I think, implicit in that conception. To make these observations is not of itself, of course, to make a statement either in favour of or against the validity of Ockham's philosophical arguments; but it is as well to draw attention to the lack of apologetic preoccupations in Ockham. He was a theologian and a philosopher and a political and ecclesiastical pamphleteer; but he was not an 'apologist', not even in the senses in which Aquinas can reasonably be called an 'apologist', and still less in the modern sense of the word.

Some philosophers in the fourteenth century endeavoured to bridge the threatening gap between theology and philosophy by extending Henry of Ghent's theory of 'illumination'. Thus Hugolino of Orvieto (d. 1373), a Hermit of St. Augustine, distinguished certain degrees of illumination, and maintained that Aristotle, for example, was enlightened by a special divine illumination which enabled him to know something of God and of certain of His attributes. Others, however, turned to mysticism and concentrated their attention on a speculative treatment of the relation of the world to God and, in particular, of the relation of the human soul to God. This movement of speculative mysticism, the chief representative of which was the German Dominican Meister Eckhart, was, as we shall see later, very far from being simply a reaction to the arid wranglings of the Schools or a flight from scepticism to the safe haven of piety; but it was, none the less, a feature of the fourteenth century, quite distinct from the more academic philosophy of the universities.

An important feature of fourteenth-century university life, particularly at Paris, was the growth of science. Something will be said about this later on, though only a brief treatment of this theme can be expected in a history of philosophy. The development of mathematical and scientific studies by such fourteenth-century figures as Nicholas of Oresme, Albert of Saxony and Marsilius of Inghen is generally associated with the Ockhamist movement; and thus it is regarded as a feature of the fourteenth, as contrasted with the thirteenth, century. There is certainly truth in this contention, not so much because William of Ockham showed any particular interest in empirical science or because the fourteenth-century scientists accepted all the Ockhamist positions as because the Ockhamist philosophy should, of its very nature, have favoured the growth of empirical science. William of Ockham had a strong belief in the primacy of intuition, that is, in the primacy of intuition of the individual thing: all real knowledge is ultimately founded on intuitive knowledge of individual existents. Moreover, the only adequate ground for asserting a causal relation between two phenomena is observation of regular sequence. These two theses tend of themselves to favour empirical observation and a fresh approach to scientific questions. And in point of fact we do find that the leading figures in fourteenth-century science were associated in some way, though sometimes rather loosely, with the 'modern way'.

At the same time one is not justified in asserting without qualification that a rudimentary appreciation of physical science was peculiar to the fourteenth century, as contrasted with the thirteenth, or that the scientific studies associated with the Ockhamist movement were the direct progenitors of Renaissance science. Already in the thirteenth century interest had been taken in the Latin translations of Greek and Arabic scientific works, and original observations and experiments had been made. We have only to think of men like Albert the Great, Peter of Maricourt and Roger Bacon. In the following century criticism of Aristotle's physical theories coupled with further original reflection and even experiment led to the putting forward of new explanations and hypotheses in physics; and the investigations of the physicists associated with the Ockhamist movement passed in the fifteenth century to northern Italy. The science of the universities of northern Italy certainly influenced the great scientists of the Renaissance, like Galileo; but it would be a mistake to think that Galileo's work was nothing but a continuation of 'Ockhamist' science, though it would be also a mistake to think that it was not influenced by the latter. For one thing, Galileo was able to achieve his results only through a use of mathematics which was unknown in the fourteenth century. This use was facilitated by the translation, at the time of the Renaissance, of works by Greek mathematicians and physicists; and Galileo was stimulated to apply mathematics to the solution of problems of motion and mechanics in a way for which the mediaeval scientists did not possess the necessary equipment. The use of mathematics as the special means of disclosing the nature of physical reality led to a transformation in physical science. The old way of common-sense observation was abandoned in favour of a very different approach. Though it may sound strange to say so, physical science became less 'empirical': it was set free not only from Aristotelian physical theories but also from the common-sense idea of an observational method which had tended to prevail among earlier physicists. It is true that some continuity can be observed between thirteenth- and fourteenth-century science, and between fourteenth-century science and that of the Renaissance; but that does not alter the fact that in the last period a revolution in physical science took place.

3. Mention of the Renaissance of the fifteenth and sixteenth centuries probably still conjures up for some minds the idea of a sudden and abrupt transition and awakening, when the learning and literature of the ancient world were made available, when education began, when men began to think for themselves after the intellectual slavery of the Middle Ages, when the invention of printing made the wide dissemination of books at last possible, when the discovery of new lands broadened men's horizons and opened up new sources of wealth, and when the discovery of gunpowder conferred an inestimable blessing upon mankind.

Such a view is, of course, a considerable exaggeration. As far as the recovery of ancient literature, for example, is concerned, this began centuries before the Italian Renaissance; while in regard to thinking for oneself, it does not require a very profound knowledge of mediaeval philosophy to realize that there was plenty of original thinking in the Middle Ages. On the other hand, one should not emphasize the element of continuous transition so much that one implies that the Renaissance does not form a recognizable period or that its achievements were negligible. It is a question of looking at the matter in the light of our present knowledge of the Middle Ages and of correcting false impressions of the Renaissance, and not a question of suggesting that the word 'Renaissance' is a mere word, denoting no reality. Something more on this subject will be said at a later stage; at the moment I wish to confine myself to a few introductory remarks on the philosophies of the Renaissance.

When one looks at mediaeval philosophy, one certainly sees variety; but it is a variety within a common pattern, or at least it is a variety set against a common and well-defined background. There was certainly original thought; but none the less one gets the impression of a common effort, of what one may call teamwork. The thirteenth-century philosophers criticized one another's opinions; but they accepted not only the same religious faith but also, for the most part, the same metaphysical principles. One thus obtains the impression of a philosophical development which was carried on by men of independent minds but which was at the same time a common development, to which the individual philosophers made their several contributions. Even in the fourteenth century the *via moderna* was so widespread a movement as to grow in the course of time into a more or less hardened 'school', taking its place along with Thomism, Scotism and Augustinianism.

When one looks at Renaissance philosophy, however, one is faced at first sight with a rather bewildering assortment of philosophies. One finds for instance Platonists, Aristotelians of various kinds, anti-Aristotelians, Stoics, sceptics, eclectics and philosophers of nature. One can separate the philosophies into various general currents of thought, it is true, even if it is rather difficult to know to which current one should assign a particular thinker; but the over-all impression is one of a pullulating individualism. And this impresson is, in many respects, correct. The gradual breakdown of the framework of mediaeval society and the loosening of the bonds between men which helped to produce a more or less common outlook; the transition to new forms of society, sometimes separated from one another by religious differences; the new inventions and discoveries; all this was accompanied by a marked individualism in philosophic reflection. The feeling of discovery, of adventure, was in the air; and it was reflected in philosophy. To say this is not to retract what I have already said about the inadequacy of regarding the Renaissance as without roots in the past. It had its roots in the past and it passed through several phases, as we shall see later; but this does not mean that a new spirit did not come into being at the time of the Renaissance, though it would be more accurate to say that a spirit which had manifested itself to a certain extent at an earlier date showed an outburst of vitality at the time of the Renaissance. For example, the recovery of the classical literature had started at a much earlier date, within the Middle Ages, as has already been remarked; but historians, while rightly emphasizing this fact, have also rightly pointed out that in regard to the Renaissance the important point is not so much that numbers of fresh texts were made available as that the texts were read in a new light. It was a question of appreciating the texts and the thought therein contained for themselves and not just as possible sources of Christian edification or disedification. The bulk of Renaissance thinkers, scholars and scientists were, of course, Christians; and it is as well to remember the fact; but none the less the classical revival, or perhaps rather the Renaissance phase of the classical revival, helped to bring to the fore a conception of autonomous man or an idea of the development of the human personality which, though generally Christian, was more 'naturalistic' and less ascetic than the mediaeval conception. And this idea favoured the growth of individualism. Even among writers who were devout Christians one can discern the conviction that a new age for man was beginning. This conviction was not due simply to classical studies, of course; it was due to the complex of historical changes which were taking place at the Renaissance.

It was at the time of the Renaissance that the works of Plato and Plotinus were translated, by Marsilius Ficinus; and in the earlier phase of the period an attempt was made to form a philosophical synthesis of Platonic inspiration. The Platonic philosophers were, for the most part, Christians; but, very naturally, Platonism was looked on as a kind of antithesis to Aristotelianism. At the same time another group of humanists, influenced by the Latin classical literature, attacked the Aristotelian logic and Scholastic abstractions in the name of good taste, realism and the feeling for the concrete, rhetoric and literary exposition. A new idea of education by means of classical literature rather than by abstract philosophy was taking shape. Polite and humanistic scepticism was represented by Montaigne, while Justus Lipsius revived Stoicism and Pierre Gassendi Epicureanism. The Aristotelians of the Renaissance, apart from the Scholastics, were meanwhile divided among themselves into the Averroists and those who favoured the interpretation of Aristotle given by Alexander of Aphrodisias. These latter favoured an interpretation of Aristotle's psychology which led to the denial of human immortality, even the impersonal immortality admitted by the Averroists. Pomponazzi, the chief figure of this group, drew the conclusion that man has a purely terrestrial moral end. At the same time he professed to be a believing Christian and so had to make a rigid division between theological and philosophical truth.

The philosophies which took the form of revivals of classical thought tended to accustom people to an idea of man which had no very obvious connection with Christianity and which was sometimes frankly naturalistic, even if the authors of these naturalistic pictures of man were generally Christians. An analogous process of development went on in regard to the philosophy of nature. Whereas certain forms of Oriental thought would scarcely favour the study of nature, owing to the notion that the phenomenal world is illusion or mere 'appearance', Christian philosophy favoured in a sense the investigation of nature, or at least set no theoretical bar to it, because it regarded the material world not only as real but also as the creation of God, and so as worthy of study. At the same time the emphasis laid by a Christian theologian, philosopher and saint like Bonaventure on the religious orientation of man led to a natural concentration on those aspects of the material world which could be most easily looked on not only as manifestations of God but also as means to elevate the mind from the material to the spiritual. The saint was not particularly interested in studying the world for its own sake: he was much more interested in detecting in it the mirror of the divine. Nevertheless, Christian philosophy, apart from this natural concentration of interest, was not radically hostile to the study of the world; and in the case of thirteenth-century philosophers like St. Albert the Great and Roger Bacon we find a combination of the spiritual outlook with an interest in the empirical study of nature. In the fourteenth century we find this interest in scientific studies growing, in association with the Ockhamist movement and favoured by the rift which was introduced into the thirteenth-century synthesis of theology and philosophy. The way was being prepared for a philosophy of nature which, while not necessarily anti-Christian, emphasized nature as an intelligible totality governed by its own immanent laws. It might perhaps be better to say that the way was being gradually prepared for the scientific study of nature, which was in the course of time, though only at a later period, to shed the name of 'natural philosophy' or 'experimental philosophy' and to become conscious of itself as a separate discipline, or set of disciplines, with its own method or methods. But at the time of the Renaissance we find a number of philosophies of nature arising which stand apart from the development of physical science as such, in that they are characterized by a marked speculative trait which sometimes manifested itself in fanciful and bizarre ideas. These philosophies varied from the Christian and strongly Platonic or neo-Platonic philosophy of a Nicholas of Cusa to the pantheistic philosophy of a Giordano Bruno. But they were marked by common characteristics, by a belief, for example, in nature as a developing system which was infinite, or potentially infinite, and which was regarded either as the created infinite, mirroring the uncreated and divine infinite, or as itself in some sense divine. God was certainly not denied; but the emphasis was placed, in varying degrees with different philosophers, on nature itself. Nature tended to be looked on as the macrocosm and man as the microcosm. This was, indeed, an old idea, going back to Greek times; but it represented a change of emphasis from that characteristic of the mediaeval outlook. In other words, there was a tendency to regard nature as an autonomous system, even though nature's dependence on God was not denied. The bizarre and fantastic aspects of some of these philosophies may tend to make one impatient of them and their authors; but they are of importance in that they marked the rise of a new direction of interest and because of the fact that they formed a kind of mental background against which the purely scientific study of nature could go forward. Indeed, it was against the background of these philosophies, which were the ancestors of philosophies like those of Spinoza and Leibniz, rather than against the background of fourteenth-century Ockhamism, that the great advances of the scientific phase of the Renaissance were achieved. Not infrequently the philosophers anticipated speculatively hypotheses which the physicists were to verify or confirm. Even Newton, it may be remembered, looked upon himself as a philosopher.

When we turn to the Renaissance scientists, we find them interested primarily in knowledge for its own sake. But at the same time it was a characteristic of some Renaissance thinkers to emphasize the practical fruits of knowledge. The new scientific discoveries and the opening up of the new world naturally suggested a contrast between a knowledge of nature, gained by study of her laws and making possible a use of nature for man's benefit, and the older abstract discipline which seemed devoid of practical utility. Study of final causes gets one nowhere; study of efficient causes enables one to control nature and to extend man's dominion over nature. The best-known expression of this outlook is to be found in the writings of Francis Bacon (d. 1626), who, though often assigned to 'modern philosophy', may reasonably be assigned to the Renaissance period. (Distinctions of this sort are to a certain extent a matter of personal choice, of course.) It would be a mistake to father this sort of attitude on the great scientific figures; but it is an attitude which has come to dominate a great part of the modern mentality. One can detect it even in some of the political thinkers of the Renaissance. Machiavelli (d. 1527), for example, neglecting theoretical problems of sovereignty and of the nature of the state in favour of 'realism' wrote his *Prince* as a text for princes who wanted to know how to conserve and augment their power.

Finally, one has to consider the great scientific figures, like Kepler and Galileo, who laid the foundations of the classical science of the modern era, the Newtonian science, as it is often known. If the first phase of the Renaissance was that of Italian humanism, the last was that of the growth of modern science. This development came to exercise a profound influence not only on philosophy but also on the modern mentality in general. But of this influence it will be more proper to speak in other volumes.

4. Martin Luther was very strongly anti-Aristotelian and anti-Scholastic; but Melanchthon, his most eminent disciple and associate, was a humanist who introduced into Lutheran Protestantism a humanistic Aristotelianism set to the service of religion. The Reformers were naturally much more concerned with religion and theology than with philosophy; and men like Luther and Calvin could hardly be expected to have very much sympathy with the predominantly aesthetic attitude of the humanists, even though Protestantism stressed the need for education and had to come to terms with humanism in the educational field.

However, though humanism, a movement which was unsympathetic to Scholasticism, began in Catholic Italy, and though the greatest figures of humanism in northern Europe, Erasmus above all, but also men like Thomas More in England, were Catholics, the late Renaissance witnessed a revival of Scholasticism, a brief treatment of which I have included in the present volume. The centre of this revival was, significantly, Spain, a country which was not much affected either by the religious upheavals and divisions which afflicted so much of Europe or, indeed, by Renaissance philosophy. The revival came at the end of the fifteenth century, with Thomas de Vio (d. 1534), known as Cajetan, De Sylvestris (d. 1520) and others; and in the sixteenth century we find two principal groups, the Dominican group, represented by writers like Francis of Vitoria (d. 1546), Dominic Soto (d. 1560), Melchior Cano (d. 1566), and Dominic Báñez (d. 1640), and the Jesuit group, represented, for example, by Toletus (d. 1596), Molina (d. 1600), Bellarmine (d. 1621), and Suárez (d. 1617). The most important of these late Scholastics is probably Suárez, of whose philosophy I shall give a more extended treatment than in the case of any of the others.

The themes treated by the Renaissance Scholastics were for the most part those themes and problems already set by preceding mediaeval Scholasticism; and if one looks at the extensive works of Suárez, one finds abundant evidence of the author's very wide knowledge of preceding philosophies. The rise of Protestantism naturally led the Scholastic theologians to discuss relevant theological problems which had their repercussions in the field of philosophy; but the Scholastics were not much affected by the characteristically Renaissance philosophies. A thinker like Suárez bears more resemblance to the theologian-philosophers of the thirteenth century than to the intellectual free-lances of the Renaissance. Yet, as we shall see later, contemporary movements influenced Suárez in two ways at least. First, the old philosophical method of commenting on a text was abandoned by him in his *Metaphysical Disputations* for a continuous discussion in a more modern, even if, it must be confessed, somewhat prolix style. Philosophy came to be treated, not in predominantly or largely theological works, but in separate treatises. Secondly, the rise of national states was reflected in a fresh development of political theory and of the philosophy of law, of a much more thorough character than anything produced by mediaeval Scholasticism. In this connection one thinks naturally of the study of international law by the Dominican Francis of Vitoria and of Suárez' treatise on law.

Part One

THE FOURTEENTH CENTURY

Chapter Two

DURANDUS AND PETRUS AUREOLI

James of Metz – Durandus – Petrus Aureoli – Henry of Harclay – The relation of these thinkers to Ockhamism.

1. One is naturally inclined to think that all the theologians and philosophers of the Dominican Order in the late Middle Ages followed the teaching of St. Thomas Aquinas. In 1279 those who did not embrace Thomism were forbidden by the Chapter of Paris to condemn it, and in 1286 the same Chapter enacted that non-Thomists should be removed from their chairs. In the following century the Chapters of Saragossa (1309) and of Metz (1313) made it obligatory to accept the teaching of St. Thomas (who was not canonized until 1323). But these enactments did not succeed in making all Dominicans conform. Leaving out of account Meister Eckhart, whose philosophy will be discussed in the chapter on speculative mysticism, one may mention among the dissentients James of Metz, though his two commentaries on the *Sentences* of Peter Lombard, which seem to have been composed the one before 1295 and the other in 1302, antedated the official imposition of Thomism on members of the Order.

James of Metz was not an anti-Thomist in the sense of being an opponent of St. Thomas's teaching in general; nor was he a philosophic revolutionary; but he did not hesitate to depart from the teaching of St. Thomas and to question that teaching when he saw fit. For example, he did not accept the Thomist view of matter as the principle of individuation. It is form which gives unity to the substance and so constitutes it; and we must accordingly recognize form as the principle of individuation, since individuality presupposes substantiality. James of Metz appears to have been influenced by thinkers like Henry of Ghent and Peter of

Auvergne. Thus he developed Henry's idea of the 'modes of being' (*modi essendi*). There are three modes of being, that of sustance, that of real accident (quantity and quality) and that of relation. The modes are distinct from one another; but they are not things which together with their foundations make up composite beings. Thus relation is a mode of being which relates a substance or an absolute accident to the term of the relation: it is not itself a thing. Most relations, like similarity, for example, or equality, are mental: the causal relation is the only 'real' relation, independent of our thought. James was something of an eclectic; and his divagations from the teaching of St. Thomas called forth criticism and reproof from the pen of Hervé Nédellec,[1] a Dominican who published a *Correctorium fratris Jacobi Metensis*.

2. Durandus (Durand de Saint-Pourçain) was much more of an *enfant terrible* than was James of Metz. Born between 1270 and 1275, he entered the Dominican Order and did his studies at Paris, where he is supposed to have followed the lectures of James of Metz. At the beginning of the first edition of his commentary on the *Sentences* he laid down the principle that the proper procedure in speaking and writing of things which do not touch the Faith is to rely on reason rather than on the authority of any Doctor however famous or grave. Armed with this principle Durandus proceeded on his way, to the displeasure of his Dominican colleagues. He then published a second edition of his commentary, omitting the offending propositions; but nothing was gained thereby, for the first edition continued in circulation. The Dominican Chapter of Metz condemned his peculiar opinions in 1313, and in 1314 a commission presided over by Hervé Nédellec censured 91 propositions taken from the first edition of Durandus's commentary. The latter, who was at this time a lecturer at the papal court of Avignon, defended himself in his *Excusationes*; but Hervé Nédellec pursued the attack in his *Reprobationes excusationum Durandi* and followed it up by attacking Durandus's teaching at Avignon. In 1316 the Dominican General Chapter at Montpellier, considering that a 'remedy' should be provided for this shocking state of affairs, drew up a list of 235 points on which Durandus had differed from the teaching of St. Thomas. In 1317 Durandus became Bishop of Limoux, being translated to Puy in 1318 and finally to Meaux in 1326. Strengthened by his episcopal position, he published, sometime after 1317, a third edition of

his commentary on the *Sentences*, in which he returned, in part, to the positions he had once retracted. One can safely assume that he had always continued to hold the theories in question. As a matter of fact, though possessed of an independent spirit in regard to St. Thomas's teaching, Durandus was not a revolutionary. He was influenced by the doctrine of Henry of Ghent, for example, while on some points he spoke like an Augustinian. In 1326, when Bishop of Meaux, he was a member of the commission which censured 51 propositions taken from William of Ockham's commentary on the *Sentences*. He died in 1332.

One of Durandus's opinions which offended his critics concerned relations. For Durandus, as for James of Metz, relation is a *modus essendi*, a mode of being. Henry of Ghent, as we have seen, had distinguished three modes of being, that of a substance, that of an absolute accident (quantity and quality) which inheres in a substance, and that of a relation. A relation was regarded by Henry as being a kind of internal tendency of a being towards another being. As far as the real being of a relation is concerned, then, it is reducible to the being of a substance or of a real accident; and the Aristotelian categories are to be regarded as comprising substance, quantity, quality, relation, and the six subdivisions of relation. This doctrine of the three basic modes of being was adopted by James of Metz and Durandus. As the modes of being are really distinct, it follows that the relation is really distinct from its foundation. On the other hand, as the relation is simply the foundation or subject in its relatedness to something else,[2] it cannot properly be a 'thing' or 'creature'; at least, it cannot enter into composition with its foundation.[3] There is a real relation only when a being related to another possesses an objective, internal exigency for this relatedness. This means that there is a real relation, so far as creatures are concerned, only when there is real dependence; and it follows therefore that the causal relation is the only real relation in creatures.[4] Similarity, equality and all relations other than the causal relation are purely conceptual; they are not real relations.

Durandus applied this doctrine to knowledge. The act of knowing is not an absolute accident which inheres in the soul, as St. Thomas thought; it is a *modus essendi* which does not add anything to the intellect or make it more perfect. 'It must be said that sensation and understanding do not imply the addition to the sense and the intellect of anything real which enters into composition with them.'[5] Sensation and understanding are immanent acts which are really identical with the sense and the intellect. Why did Durandus hold this? Because he considered that to maintain that the soul, when it enters into cognitive relation with an object, receives accidents by way of addition is to imply that an external object can act on a spiritual principle or a non-living object on a living subject, a view which he calls 'ridiculous'. Durandus's thought on this matter is clearly of Augustinian inspiration. For example, one of the reasons why St. Augustine maintained that sensation is an act of the soul alone was the impossibility of a material thing acting on the soul. The object is a *conditio sine qua non*, but not a cause, of knowledge; the intellect itself is the cause.

From this theory of knowledge as a relation Durandus drew the conclusion that the whole apparatus of cognitive *species*, in the sense of accidental forms, can be dispensed with. It follows also that it is unnecessary to postulate an active intellect which is supposed to abstract these *species*. Similarly, Durandus got rid of 'habits' in the intellect and will, and he followed the Augustinian tradition in denying any real distinction between intellect and will.

The principal reason why Durandus got into trouble over his doctrine of relations was its application to the doctrine of the Trinity. In the first edition of his commentary on the *Sentences*[6] he asserted that there is a real distinction between the divine essence or nature and the divine relations or Persons, though in the second passage referred to he speaks with some hesitation. This opinion was condemned by the commission of 1314 as 'entirely heretical'. Durandus tried to explain away his assertions, but Hervé Nédellec drew attention to his actual words. In the Avignon *Quodlibet* he admitted that one could not properly speak of a real distinction between the divine nature and the divine internal relations; the latter are *modi essendi vel habendi essentiam divinam* and the distinction is only *secundum quid*. A renewed attack by Hervé Nédellec followed this change, and in the final edition of the commentary Durandus proposed another view.[7] There are, he says, three possible theories. First, essence and relation, though not two things, differ in that they are not the same 'adequately and convertibly'. Secondly, essence and relation differ as thing and 'mode of possessing the thing'. This was the view of Henry of Ghent, James of Metz and, formerly, of Durandus himself. Thirdly, essence and relation differ *formaliter ex natura rei*, although they are identically the same thing. Durandus adopts this third view, that of Scotus, though he adds that he does not understand what *formaliter* means unless this view contains the other two. The first view is included, in that essence and relation, while they are the same thing, are not the same thing 'adequately and convertibly'. The second view is also included, namely that essence and relation differ as *res et modus habendi rem*. In other words, Durandus's opinion did not undergo any very startling change.

It used to be said that Durandus was a pure conceptualist in regard to universals and that he thus helped to prepare the way for Ockhamism. But it is now clear that he did not deny that there was some real foundation in things for the universal concept. He held, indeed, that it is 'frivolous to say that there is universality in things, for universality cannot be in things, but only singularity';[8] but the unity of nature which is thought by the intellect as being common to a multiplicity of objects exists really in things, though not as an objective universal. Universality belongs to concepts, but the nature which is conceived by the intellect as a universal exists really in individual things.

Durandus certainly rejected a considerable number of theories which had been maintained by St. Thomas. We have seen that he denied the doctrines of *species* and of habits or dispositions, and the real distinction between intellect and will. Moreover, in regard to the immortality of the soul he followed Scotus in saying that it is not demonstrable; or, at least, that it is difficult to demonstrate in a rigorous manner. But, as already mentioned, he was not a revolutionary even if he was an independent and critical thinker. His psychology was largely Augustinian in character and inspiration, while even his doctrine of relations was founded on that of Henry of Ghent. And in regard to universals he did not reject the position maintained by the mediaeval Aristotelians. In other words, the former picture of Durandus as a closely-related predecessor of William of Ockham has had to be abandoned, though it is true, of course, that he employed the principle of economy, known as 'Ockham's razor'.

3. Petrus Aureoli (Pierre d'Auriole) entered the Order of Friars Minor and studied at Paris. After having lectured at Bologna (1312) and Toulouse (1314) he returned to Paris where he received the doctorate of theology in 1318. In 1321 he became Archbishop of Aix-en-Provence. He died shortly

afterwards, in January 1322. His first philosophical work was the uncompleted *Tractatus de principiis naturae*, which dealt with questions of natural philosophy. His main work, a commentary on the *Sentences* of Peter Lombard, was published in two successive editions. We have also his *Quodlibeta*.

Petrus Aureoli takes his stand firmly on the statement that everything which exists is, by the very fact that it exists, an individual thing. Speaking of the dispute concerning the principle of individuation, he asserts that in reality there is no question at all to discuss, 'since every thing, by the very fact that it exists, exists as an individual thing' (*singulariter est*).[9] Conversely, if anything is common or universal or can be predicated of a plurality of objects, it is shown by that very fact to be a concept. 'Therefore to seek for something whereby an extramental object is rendered individual is to seek for nothing.'[10] For this is tantamount to asking in what way an extramental universal is individualized, when in point of fact there is no such thing as an extramental universal which could be individualized. The metaphysical problem of individuation is thus no problem at all. There is no universal outside the mind. But this does not mean that God cannot create a number of individuals of the same species; and we know, in fact, that He has done so. Material things have forms, and certain of these forms possess a quality which we call 'likeness' (*similitudo*). If it is asked what sort of a thing (*quale quid*) Socrates is, the answer is that he is a man: there is a quality of likeness in Socrates and Plato of such a kind that though there is nothing in Socrates which is in Plato, there is not in Plato anything to which there cannot be a likeness in Socrates. 'I and you are not the same; but I can be such as you are. So the Philosopher says that Callias, by generating Socrates, generates a similar being.'[11] The extramental foundation of the universal concept is this quality of likeness. Petrus Aureoli does not deny, then, that there is an objective foundation for the universal concept: what he does deny is that there is any common reality which exists extramentally. As to immaterial forms, these can also be alike. Hence there is no reason why several angels should not belong to the same species.

The intellect, as active, assimilates to itself this likeness and, as passive, is assimilated to it, thus conceiving the thing, that is, producing an 'objective concept' (*conceptus obiectivus*). This concept is intramental, of course, and, as such, it is distinct from the thing; but on the other hand it is the thing as known. Thus Petrus Aureoli says that when the intellectual assimilation takes place 'the thing immediately receives *esse apparens*'. If the assimilation is clear, the thing will have a clear *esse apparens* or phenomenal existence; if the assimilation is obscure, the *esse apparens* will be obscure. This 'appearance' is in the intellect alone.[12] 'From the fact that a thing produces an imperfect impression of itself in the intellect, there arises the generic concept, by which the thing is conceived imperfectly and indistinctly, while from the fact that the same thing produces a perfect impression of itself in the intellect there arises the concept of (specific) difference, by which the thing is conceived in its specific and distinct existence.'[13] The 'objective' diversity of concepts is the result of the formal diversity of the impression made by one and the same object on one and the same mind. 'Therefore if you ask in what the specific unity of humanity consists, I say that it consists in humanity, not in animality, but in humanity as conceived. And in this way it is the same as the objective concept of man. But this unity exists in potency and inchoately in the extramental thing, inasmuch as the latter is capable of causing in the intellect a perfect impression like to the impression caused by another thing.'[14]

Every extramentally existing thing is individual; and it is 'nobler' to know it directly in its unique individuality than to know it by means of a universal concept. The human intellect, however, cannot grasp, directly and primarily, the thing in its incommunicable individuality, though it can know it secondarily, by means of the imagination: primarily and immediately it apprehends the form of the material thing by means of a universal concept.[15] But to say that the intellect knows the thing 'by means of a universal concept' does not mean that there is a *species intelligibilis* in the Thomist sense which acts as a *medium quo* of knowledge. 'No real form is to be postulated as existing subjectively in the intellect, or in the imagination . . . but that form which we are conscious of beholding when we know the rose as such or the flower as such is not something real impressed subjectively on the intellect, or on the imagination; nor is it a real subsistent thing; it is the thing itself as possessing *esse intentionale*. . . .'[16] Petrus Aureoli thus dispenses with the *species intelligibilis* as *medium quo* of knowledge and insists that the intellect knows the thing itself directly. This is one reason why Étienne Gilson can say that Petrus Aureoli 'admits no other reality than that of the knowable object' and that his solution does not consist of eliminating the *species intelligibilis* in favour of the concept, but in suppressing even the concept.[17] On the other hand, the thing which is known, that is, the object of knowledge, is the extramental thing as possessing *esse intentionale* or *esse apparens*; and it acquires this *esse intentionale* through 'conception' (*conceptio*). The thing as possessing *esse intentionale* is thus the concept (that is to say, the 'objective concept' as distinguished from the 'subjective concept' or psychological act as such); and it follows that the concept is the object of knowledge. 'All understanding demands the placing of a thing in *esse intentionali*', and this is the *forma specularis*.[18] 'The thing posited in *esse apparenti* is said to be conceived by the act of the intellect, indeed, it is the intellectual concept; but a concept remains within the conceiver, and is (owes its being to) the conceiver. Therefore the thing as appearing depends effectively on the act of the intellect, both in regard to production and in regard to content.'[19] Dr. B. Geyer can say, then, that 'the *species*, the *forma specularis*, is thus, according to Aureoli, no longer the *medium quo* of knowledge, as with Thomas Aquinas, but its immediate object'.[20] But, even if Petrus Aureoli may speak on occasion as though he wished to maintain a form of subjective idealism, he insists, for example, that 'health as conceived by the intellect and health as it is present extramentally are one and the same thing in reality (*realiter*), although they differ in their mode of being, since in the mind health has *esse apparens et intentionale*, while extramentally, in the body, it has *esse existens et reale*. . . . They differ in mode of being (*in modo essendi*), although they are one and the same thing.'[21] 'Hence it is clear that things themselves are conceived by the mind, and that that which we intuit is not another *forma specularis*, but the thing itself as having *esse apparens*; and this is the mental concept or objective idea (*notitia obiectiva*).'[22]

Knowledge, for Petrus Aureoli, is rooted in the perception of the concrete, of actually existing things. But a thing as known *is* the thing as having *esse apparens et intentionale*; it *is* the concept. According to the degree of clarity in the knowledge of the thing there arises a generic or specific concept. Genera and species, considered as universals, do not, however, exist extramentally, and are to be regarded as 'fabricated' by the mind. Petrus Aureoli may thus be called a 'conceptualist' inasmuch as he rejects any extramental existence on the part of universals; but he cannot rightly be called a 'nominalist', if 'nominalism' is taken to involve a denial of the objective similarity of natures. This is not to say, however, that he does not speak, more or less frequently, in an ambiguous and even inconsistent fashion. His idea of logic may be said to favour nominalism in that the logician is said to deal with words (*voces*). 'Therefore the logician considers them ("second intentions"), not as *entia rationis*, for it belongs to the metaphysician to decide about real being and conceptual being, but in so far as they are reduced to speech. . . .'[23] But, though the doctrine that logic is concerned with words (*voces*) may seem, if taken by itself, to favour nominalism, Petrus Aureoli adds that the logician is concerned with words as expressing concepts. 'The word, as well as the concept (*ut expressiva conceptus*), is the subject-matter of logic.'[24] In his logic, says Petrus Aureoli, Aristotle always implies that he is considering words as expressing concepts.[25] Moreover, speech, which expresses concepts, is the subject of truth and falsity: it is the sign of truth and falsity (*voces enim significant verum vel falsum in ordine ad conceptum*).[26] The theory of the *suppositio*, as formed in the terministic logic, may be implied in Petrus Aureoli's idea of logic; but he was not a 'nominalist' in metaphysics. It is true that he emphasized the qualitative similarity of things rather than the similarity of nature or essence; but he does not seem to have denied essential similarity as the foundation of the specific concept: rather did he presuppose it.

We have seen that for Petrus Aureoli conceptual knowledge is of the extramental thing in its likeness to other things rather than of the thing precisely as individual. But it is better, he insists, to know the individual thing in its individuality than to know it by means of a universal concept. If the human intellect in its present state knows things rather *per modum abstractum et universalem* than precisely in their individuality, this is an imperfection. The individual thing can make an impression on the senses in such a way that there is sense-knowledge or intuition of the individual thing as individual; but the material thing cannot make an impression of this sort on the immaterial intellect; its form is known abstractly by the intellect, which cannot directly and immediately attain the individual thing as individual. But this does not alter the fact that an intellectual intuition or knowledge of the individual thing as individual would be more perfect than abstract and universal knowledge. 'For the knowledge which attains to the thing precisely as the thing exists is more perfect than knowledge which attains to the thing in a manner in which the thing does not exist. But it is clear that a universal thing does not exist, except in individual things and through individual things, as the Philosopher says against Plato, in the seventh book of the *Metaphysics*. . . . It is quite clear that science, which apprehends essences (*quidditates*), does not apprehend things precisely as they exist . . . but knowledge of this precise individual is knowledge of the thing as it exists. Therefore, it is nobler to know the individual thing as such (*rem individuatam et demonstratam*) than to know it in an abstract and universal way.'[27] It follows that even if the human intellect cannot have that perfect knowledge of individual things which must be attributed to God, it should approach as near thereto as possible by keeping in close contact with experience. We should adhere to 'the way of experience rather than to any logical reasonings, since science arises from experience'.[28] Petrus Aureoli also stressed inner experience of our psychic acts, and he frequently appeals to inner experience or introspection to support his statements about knowledge, volition and psychic activity in general. He shows a strong 'empiricist' bent in his treatment of universals, in his insistence on keeping close to experience, and in his interest in natural science, which is shown by the examples he takes from Aristotle and his Islamic commentators; but Dreiling's investigation led him to conclude that 'the empiricist tendency of Aureoli has a centripetal rather than a centrifugal direction and is turned towards the psychic life more than towards external nature'.[29]

Mention of Petrus Aureoli's appeals to introspection or inner experience leads one on to discuss his idea of the soul. First of all, it can be proved that the soul is the form of the body, in the sense that the soul is an essential part of man which together with the body makes up man. Indeed, 'no philosopher ever denied this proposition'.[30] But it cannot be proved that the soul is the form of the body in the sense that it is simply the forming and termination of matter (*formatio et terminatio materiae*) or that it makes the body to be a body. 'This has not yet been demonstrated, either by Aristotle or by the Commentator or by any other Peripatetic.'[31] In other words, it can be proved, according to Petrus Aureoli, that the soul is an essential part of man and that it is the principal part (*pars principalior*) of man; but it cannot be proved that it is simply that which makes matter to be a human body or that its relation to the body is analogous to the shape of a piece of copper. If a piece of copper is shaped into a statue, its figure may be called a form; but it is no more than the termination (*terminatio*) or figure of the copper; it is not a distinct nature. The human soul, however, is a distinct nature.

Now, Petrus Aureoli declared that a substantial form is simply the actuation of matter (*pura actuatio materiae*) and that, together with matter, it composes one simple nature.[32] It follows that if the human soul is a distinct nature and is not simply the actuation of matter, it is not a form in the same way and in the same sense that other forms are forms. 'I say, therefore, in answer to the question that it can be demonstrated that the soul is the form of the body and an essential part of us, though it is not the actuation and perfection of the body in the way that other souls are.'[33] The spiritual soul of man and the soul or vital principle of a plant, for example, are not forms in a univocal sense.

On the other hand, the Council of Vienne (1311–12) had just laid down that the intellectual or rational soul of man is 'truly, *per se* and essentially the form of the body'. So, after asserting that the human soul is not the form of the body in the same sense in which other forms which inform matter are forms, Petrus Aureoli goes on to say that 'the ninth decree of the sacred Council of Vienne' has asserted the opposite, namely that 'the soul is the form of the body, just like other forms or souls'.[34] In face of this embarrassing situation Petrus Aureoli, while adhering to his position that it cannot be proved that the human soul is the form of the body in the same way that other souls are forms, declares that though this cannot be proved, it is nevertheless known by faith. He makes a comparison with the doctrine of the Trinity. This doctrine cannot be philosophically proved, but it has been revealed and we accept it on faith.[35] He allows that it cannot be demonstrated that the human soul is *not* the form of the body in the same sense that other souls are the forms of their respective matters; but he refuses to allow that it can be demonstrated that the soul *is* the form of the body in this sense. He obviously thought that reason inclines one to think that the human soul and the souls of brutes or plants are forms in an equivocal sense; and he remarks that the teaching of the Saints and Doctors of the Church would not lead one to expect the doctrine laid down by the Council; but, none the less, he accepts the Council's doctrine, as he understands it, and draws a strange conclusion. 'Although it cannot be demonstrated that the soul is the form of the body in the way that other forms (are forms of their respective matters), yet it must be held, as it seems to me, that, just as the shape of wax is the form and perfection of wax, so the soul is simply the actuation and forming of the body in the same way as other forms. And just as no cause is to be sought why from the wax and its shape there results one thing, so no cause is to be sought why from the soul and body there results one thing. Thus the soul is simply the act and perfection of matter, like the shape of the wax . . . I hold this conclusion precisely on account of the decision of the Council, which, according to the apparent sense of the words, seems to mean this.'[36]

The Fathers of the Council would have been startled to hear this interpretation put on their words; but, as he interpreted the Council's decision in this way and accepted it in this sense, Petrus Aureoli obviously found himself in considerable difficulty on the subject of the human soul's immortality. 'Faith holds that the soul is separated (i.e. outlives the body); but it is difficult to see how this can be done if the soul is assumed to be like other forms, simply the actuation of matter. I say, however, that just as God can separate accidents from the subject (i.e. substance), although they are no more than actuations of the subject, so He can miraculously separate the soul, although it is simply the actuation of matter.'[37] It is, indeed, necessary to say that in forms or 'pure perfections' there are degrees. If the form is extended, it can be affected (and so corrupted) by a natural extended agent; but if the form is unextended, then it cannot be affected (and so corrupted) by a natural extended agent. Now the human soul, although it is *pura perfectio materiae*, cannot be affected (i.e. corrupted) by a natural extended agent; it can be 'corrupted' only by God. This is not, however, a very satisfactory answer to the difficulty which Petrus Aureoli created for himself by his interpretation of the Council of Vienne; and he declares that our minds are not capable of understanding how the soul is naturally incorruptible if it is what the Council stated it to be.[38]

Petrus Aureoli obviously did not think that the natural immortality of the human soul can be philosophically demonstrated; and he seems to have been influenced by the attitude adopted by Duns Scotus in this matter. Various arguments have been produced to prove that the human soul 's naturally immortal; but they are scarcely conclusive.[39] Thus ome people have argued 'from the proportion of the object to he power' or faculty. The intellect can know an incorruptible bject. Therefore the intellect is incorruptible. Therefore he substance of the soul is incorruptible. But the reply night be made that in this case the eye would be incorruptible (presumably because it sees the incorruptible heavenly odies) or that our intellect must be infinite and uncreated ecause it can know God, who is infinite and uncreated. Again, thers argue that there is a 'natural desire' to exist for ever nd that a natural desire cannot be frustrated. Petrus Aureoli nswers, like Scotus though more summarily, that the brutes oo desire to continue in existence inasmuch as they shun leath. The argument, if valid, would thus prove too much. Others, again, argue that justice requires the rewarding of he good and the punishment of the wicked in another life. This argument is moral and theological, and moreover, it s not conclusive.' For it might be answered that sin is its wn punishment and virtue its own reward.

Petrus Aureoli proceeds to give some arguments of his own; ut he is not very confident as to their probative force. 'Now give my arguments, but I do not know if they are conclusive.'[40] First of all, man can choose freely, and his free hoices are not affected by the heavenly bodies nor by any naterial agent. Therefore the principle of this operation of ree choice also is unaffected by any material agent. Secondly, ve experience in ourselves immanent, and therefore spiritual perations. Therefore the substance of the soul is spiritual. But the material cannot act on the spiritual or destroy it. Therefore the soul cannot be corrupted by any material gent.

If man is truly free, it follows, according to Petrus Aureoli, hat a judgment concerning a future free act is neither true or false. 'The opinion of the Philosopher is a conclusion which has been thoroughly demonstrated, namely that no ingular proposition can be formed concerning a future contingent event, concerning which proposition it can be conceded that it is true and that its opposite is false, or conversely. No proposition of the kind is either true or false.'[41] To deny his is to deny an obvious fact, to destroy the foundation of noral philosophy and to contradict human experience. If t is now true that a certain man will perform a certain free ct at a certain future time, the act will necessarily be perormed and it will not be a free act, since the man will not be free to act otherwise. If it is to be a free act, then it cannot now be either true or false that it will be performed.

To say this may appear to involve a denial of the 'law' that a proposition must be either true or false. If we are going to say of a proposition that it is not true, are we not compelled to say that it is false? Petrus Aureoli answers that a proposition receives its determination (that is, becomes true or false) from the being of that to which it refers. In the case of a contingent proposition relating to the future that to which the proposition refers has as yet no being: it cannot, therefore, determine the proposition to be either true or false. We can say of a given man, for example, that on Christmas day he will either drink wine or not drink wine, but we cannot affirm separately either that he will drink wine or that he will not drink wine. If we do, then the statement is neither true nor false: it cannot become true or false until the man actually drinks wine on Christmas day or fails to do so. And Petrus Aureoli appeals to Aristotle in the *De Interpretatione* (9) in support of his view.

As to God's knowledge of future free acts, Petrus Aureoli insists that God's knowledge does not make a proposition concerning the future performance or non-performance of such acts either true or false. For example, God's foreknowledge of Peter's denial of his Master did not mean that the proposition 'Peter will deny his Master' was either true or false. Apropos of Christ's prophecy concerning Peter's threefold denial Petrus Aureoli observes: 'therefore Christ would not have spoken falsely, even had Peter not denied Him thrice'.[42] Why not? Because the proposition, 'you will deny Me thrice', could not be either true or false. Aureoli does not deny that God knows future free acts; but he insists that, although we cannot help employing the word 'foreknowledge' (*praescientia*), there is no foreknowledge, properly speaking, in God.[43] On the other hand, he rejects the view that God knows future free acts as present. According to him, God knows such acts in a manner which abstracts from past, present and future; but we cannot express the mode of God's knowledge in human language. If the problem of the relation of future free acts to God's knowledge or 'foreknowledge' of them is raised, the problem 'cannot be solved otherwise than by saying that foreknowledge does not make a proposition concerning a future contingent event a true proposition';[44] but this does not tell us what God's 'foreknowledge' is positively. 'We must bear in mind that the difficulty of this problem arises either from the poverty of human language, which cannot express statements save by propositions referring to present, past and future time, or from the condition of our mind, which is always involved in time (*qui semper est cum continuo et tempore*).'[45] Again, 'it is very difficult to find the right way of expressing the knowledge which God has of the future. . . . No proposition in which a reference is made to the future expresses the divine foreknowledge properly: indeed, such a proposition is, strictly speaking, false. . . . But we can say that it (a contingent event) was eternally known to God by a knowledge which neither was distant from that event nor preceded it', although our understanding is unable to grasp what this knowledge is in itself.[46]

It should be noted that Petrus Aureoli is not embracing the opinion of St. Thomas Aquinas, for whom God, in virtue of His eternity, knows all things as present. He admits that God knows all events eternally; but he will not allow that God knows them as present; he objects to any introduction of words like 'present', 'past' and 'future' into statements concerning God's knowledge, if these statements are meant to express the actual mode of God's knowledge. What it comes to, then, is that Petrus Aureoli affirms God's knowledge of future free acts and at the same time insists that no proposition relating to such future acts is either true or false. Exactly how God knows such acts we cannot say. It is perhaps needless to add that Petrus Aureoli rejects decisively any theory according to which God knows future free acts through the determination or decision of His divine will. In his view a theory of this kind is incompatible with human freedom. Thomas Bradwardine, whose theory was directly opposed to that of Petrus Aureoli, attacked him on this point.

Petrus Aureoli's discussion of statements concerning God's knowledge which involve a reference, explicit or implicit, to time serves as an illustration of the fact that mediaeval philosophers were not so entirely blind to problems of language and meaning as might perhaps be supposed. The language used about God in the Bible forced upon Christian thinkers at a very early date a consideration of the meaning of the terms used; and we find the mediaeval theories of analogical prediction worked out as a response to this problem. The precise point which I have mentioned in connection with Petrus Aureoli should not be taken as an indication that this thinker was conscious of a problem to which other mediaeval philosophers were blind. Whether one is satisfied or not with mediaeval discussions and solutions of the problem, one could not justifiably claim that the mediaevals did not even suspect the existence of the problem.

4. Henry of Harclay, who was born about 1270, studied and taught in the university of Oxford, where he became Chancellor in 1312. He died at Avignon in 1317. He has sometimes been spoken of as a precursor of Ockhamism, that is to say of 'nominalism'; but in reality the type of theory concerning universals which he defended was rejected by Ockham as unduly realist in character. It is quite true that Henry of Harclay refused to allow that there is any common nature existing, as common, in members of the same species, and he certainly held that the universal concept as such is a production of the mind; but his polemics were directed against Scotist realism, and it was the Scotist doctrine of the *natura communis* which he rejected. The nature of any given man is his individual nature, and it is in no way 'common'. However, existent things can be similar to one another, and it is this similarity which is the objective foundation of the universal concept. One can speak of abstracting something 'common' from things, if one means that one can consider things according to their likeness to one another. But the universality of the concept, its predicability of many individuals, is superimposed by the mind: there is nothing objectively existing in a thing which can be predicated of any other thing.

On the other hand, Henry evidently thought of the universal concept as a confused concept of the individual. An individual man, for example, can be conceived distinctly as Socrates or Plato, or he may be conceived 'confusedly' not as this or that individual, but simply as 'man'. The similarity which makes this possible is, of course, objective; but the genesis of the universal concept is due to this confused impression of individuals, while the universality, formally considered, of the concept is due to the work of the mind.

5. It is clear enough that the three thinkers, some of whose philosophical ideas we have considered in this chapter, were not revolutionaries in the sense that they set themselves against the traditional philosophical currents in general. For example, they did not manifest any marked preoccupation with purely logical questions and they did not show that mistrust of metaphysics which was characteristic of Ockhamism. They were, indeed, in varying degrees critical of the doctrine

of St. Thomas. But Henry of Harclay was a secular priest, not a Dominican; and in any case he showed no particular hostility towards Thomism, though he rejected St. Thomas's doctrine concerning the principle of individuation, affirmed the older theory of a plurality of formal principles in man and protested against the attempt to make a Catholic of the 'heretical' Aristotle. Again, Petrus Aureoli was a Franciscan, not a Dominican, and he was not under any obligation to accept the teaching of St. Thomas. Of these three philosophers, then, it is only Durandus whose departures from Thomism might be called 'revolutionary'; and, even in his case, his opinions can be called 'revolutionary' only in regard to his position as a Dominican and to the obligation on the members of his Order of following the teaching of St. Thomas, the Dominican Doctor. In this restricted sense he might be called a revolutionary: he was certainly independent. Hervé Nédellec, the Dominican theologian who wrote against Henry of Ghent and James of Metz, conducted a prolonged warfare against Durandus, while John of Naples and Peter Marsh (Petrus de Palude), both Dominicans, drew up a long list of points on which Durandus had offended against the teaching of Aquinas.[47] Bernard of Lombardy, another Dominican, also attacked Durandus; but his attack was not sustained like that of Hervé Nédellec; he admired and was partly influenced by Durandus. A sharp polemic (the *Evidentiae Durandelli contra Durandum*) came from the pen of Durandellus who was identified for a time with Durandus of Aurillac but who may have been, according to J. Koch, another Dominican, Nicholas of St. Victor.[48] But, as we have seen, Durandus did not turn against or reject the thirteenth-century tradition as such: on the contrary, his interests were in metaphysics and in psychology much more than in logic, and he was influenced by speculative philosophers like Henry of Ghent.

But, though one can hardly call Durandus or Petrus Aureoli a precursor of Ockhamism, if by this one means that the shift of emphasis from metaphysics to logic, coupled with a critical attitude towards metaphysical speculation as such, is a feature of their respective philosophies, yet it is probably true that in a broad sense they helped to prepare the way for nominalism and that they can be called, as they often have been called, transition-thinkers. It is perfectly true that Durandus, as has already been mentioned, was a member of the commission which censured a number of propositions taken from Ockham's commentary on the *Sentences*; but though this fact obviously manifests his personal disapproval of Ockham's teaching it does not prove that his own philosophy had no influence at all in favouring the spread of Ockhamism. Durandus, Petrus Aureoli and Henry of Harclay all insist that only individual things exist. It is true that St. Thomas Aquinas held precisely the same; but Petrus Aureoli drew from it the conclusion that the problem of a multiplicity of individuals within the same species is no problem at all. Quite apart from the question whether there is or is not such a problem, the resolute denial that there is a problem facilitates, I think, the taking of further steps on the road to nominalism which Petrus Aureoli himself did not take. After all, Ockham regarded his theory of universals as simply the logical conclusion of the truth that only individuals exist. Again, though it can be said with truth that Durandus's assertion that universality belongs only to the concept and Petrus Aureoli's and Henry of Harclay's assertions that the universal concept is a fabrication of the mind and that universality has *esse obiectivum* only in the concept do not constitute a rejection of moderate realism, yet the tendency shown by Petrus Aureoli and Henry of Harclay to explain the genesis of the universal concept by reference to a confused or less clear impression of the individual does facilitate a breakaway from the theory of universals maintained by Thomas Aquinas. Further, cannot one see in these thinkers a tendency to wield what is known as 'Ockham's razor'? Durandus sacrificed the Thomist cognitive *species* (that is 'species' in its psychological sense) while Petrus Aureoli often made use of the principle *pluralitas non est ponenda sine necessitate* in order to get rid of what he regarded as superfluous entities. And Ockhamism belonged, in a sense, to this general movement of simplification. In addition, it carried further that spirit of criticism which one can observe in James of Metz, Durandus and Petrus Aureoli. Thus I think that while historical research has shown that thinkers like Durandus, Petrus Aureoli and Henry of Harclay cannot be called 'nominalists', there are aspects of their thought which enable one to link them in some degree to the general movement of thought which facilitated the spread of Ockhamism. Indeed, if one accepted Ockham's estimation of himself as a true Aristotelian and if one looked on Ockhamism as the final overthrow of all vestiges of non-Aristotelian realism, one could reasonably regard the philosophers whom we have been considering as carrying a step further the general anti-realist movement which culminated in Ockhamism.

But it would be necessary to add that they were still more or less moderate realists and that in the eyes of the Ockhamists they did not proceed far enough along the anti-realist path. Ockham certainly did not regard these thinkers as 'Ockhamists' before their time.

Chapter Three

OCKHAM (1)

Life – Works – Unity of thought.

1. William of Ockham was probably born at Ockham in Surrey, though it is possible that he was simply William Ockham and that his name had nothing to do with the village. The date of his birth is uncertain. Though usually placed between 1290 and 1300, it is possible that it took place somewhat earlier.[1] He entered the Franciscan Order and did his studies at Oxford, where he began the study of theology in 1310. If this is correct, he would have lectured on the Bible from 1315 to 1317 and on the *Sentences* from 1317 to 1319. The following years, 1319–24, were spent in study, writing and Scholastic disputation. Ockham had thus completed the studies required for the *magisterium* or doctorate; but he never actually taught as *magister regens*, doubtless because early in 1324 he was cited to appear before the pope at Avignon. His title of *inceptor* (beginner) is due to this fact that he never actually taught as doctor and professor; it has nothing at all to do with the founding of a School.[2]

In 1323 John Lutterell, former Chancellor of Oxford, arrived at Avignon where he brought to the attention of the Holy See a list of 56 propositions taken from a version of Ockham's commentary on the *Sentences*. It appears that Ockham himself, who appeared at Avignon in 1324, presented another version of the commentary, in which he had made some emendations. In any case the commission appointed to deal with the matter did not accept for condemnation all the propositions complained of by Lutterell: in its list of 51 propositions it confined itself more or less to theological points, accepting 33 of Lutterell's propositions and adding others of its own. Some propositions were condemned as heretical, others, less important, as erroneous but not heretical; but the process was not brought to a final conclusion, perhaps because Ockham had in the meantime fled from Avignon. It has also been conjectured that the influence of Durandus, who was a member of the commission, may have been exerted in Ockham's favour, on one or two points at least.

At the beginning of December 1327 Michael of Cesena, the Franciscan General, arrived at Avignon, whither Pope John XXII had summoned him, to answer for his attacks on the papal Constitutions concerning evangelical poverty. At the instance of the General Ockham interested himself in the poverty dispute, and in May 1328 Michael of Cesena, who had just been re-elected General of the Franciscans, fled from Avignon, taking with him Bonagratia of Bergamo, Francis of Ascoli and William of Ockham. In June the pope excommunicated the four fugitives, who joined the Emperor Ludwig of Bavaria at Pisa and went with him to Munich. Thus there began Ockham's participation in the struggle between emperor and pope, a struggle in which the emperor was also assisted by Marsilius of Padua. While some of Ockham's polemics against John XXII and his successors, Benedict XII and Clement VI, concerned theological matters, the chief point of the whole dispute was, of course, the right relation of the secular to the ecclesiastical power, and to this point we shall return.

On October 11th, 1347, Ludwig of Bavaria, Ockham's protector, suddenly died, and Ockham took steps to reconcile himself with the Church. It is not necessary to suppose that his motives were merely prudential. A formula of submission was prepared but it is not known if Ockham actually signed it or whether the reconciliation was ever formally effected. Ockham died at Munich in 1349, apparently of the Black Death.

2. The commentary on the first book of the *Sentences* was written by Ockham himself, and the first edition of this *Ordinatio*[3] seems to have been composed between 1318 and 1323. The commentaries on the other three books of the *Sentences* are *reportationes*, though they also belong to an early period. Boehner thinks that they were composed before the *Ordinatio*. The *Expositio in librum Porphyrii*, the *Expositio in librum Praedicamentorum*, the *Expositio in duos libros Elenchorum* and the *Expositio in duos libros Perihermenias* appear to have been composed while Ockham was working on his commentary on the *Sentences* and to have antedated the

first *Ordinatio* though not the *Reportatio*. The text of these logical works, minus the *In libros Elenchorum*, in the 1496 Bologna edition is entitled *Expositio aurea super artem veterem*. The *Expositio super octo libros Physicorum* was composed after the commentary on the *Sentences* and before the *Summa totius logicae*, which was itself composed before 1329. As to the *Compendium logicae*, its authenticity has been questioned.

Ockham also composed *Summulae in libros Physicorum* (or *Philosophia naturalis*) and *Quaestiones in libros Physicorum*. As to the *Tractatus de successivis*, this is a compilation made by another hand from an authentic work of Ockham, namely the *Expositio super libros Physicorum*. Boehner makes it clear that it can be used as a source for Ockham's doctrine. 'Almost every line was written by Ockham, and in this sense the *Tractatus de successivis* is authentic.'[4] The authenticity of the *Quaestiones diversae: De relatione, de puncto, de negatione*, is also doubtful.

Theological works by Ockham include the *Quodlibeta* VII, the *Tractatus de Sacramento Altaris* or *De Corpore Christi* (which seems to contain two distinct treatises) and the *Tractatus de praedestinatione et de praescientia Dei et de futuris contingentibus*. The authenticity of the *Centiloquium theologicum* or *summa de conclusionibus theologicis* has not been proved. On the other hand, the arguments adduced to prove that the work is unauthentic do not appear to be conclusive.[5] To Ockham's Munich period belong among other works the *Opus nonaginta dierum*, the *Compendium errorum Ioannis papae* XXII, the *Octo quaestiones de potestate papae*, the *An princeps pro suo succursu, scilicet guerrae, possit recipere bona ecclesiarum, etiam invito papa*, the *Consultatio de causa matrimoniali* and the *Dialogus inter magistrum et discipulum de imperatorum et pontificum potestate*. The last-named work is Ockham's chief political publication. It consists of three parts, composed at different times. But it has to be used with care, as many opinions for which Ockham does not make himself responsible are canvassed in it.

3. Ockham possessed an extensive knowledge of the work of the great Scholastics who had preceded him and a remarkable acquaintance with Aristotle. But even though we can discern anticipations in other philosophers of certain theses of Ockham, it would appear that his originality is incontestable. Though the philosophy of Scotus gave rise to certain of Ockham's problems and though certain of Scotus's views and

tendencies were developed by Ockham, the latter constantly attacked the system of Scotus, particularly his realism; so that Ockhamism was a strong reaction to, rather than a development of, Scotism. No doubt Ockham was influenced by certain theories of Durandus (those on relations, for example) and Petrus Aureoli; but the extent of such influence, such as it was, does little to impair Ockham's fundamental originality. There is no adequate reason for challenging his reputation as the fountainhead of the terminist or nominalist movement. Nor is there, I think, any cogent reason for representing Ockham as a mere Aristotelian (or, if preferred, as a mere would-be Aristotelian). He certainly tried to overthrow Scotist realism with the help of the Aristotelian logic and theory of knowledge, and further he regarded all realism as a perversion of true Aristotelianism; but he also endeavoured to rectify the theories of Aristotle which excluded any admission of the liberty and omnipotence of God. Ockham was not an 'original' thinker in the sense of one who invented novelties for the sake of novelty, though his reputation as a destructive critic might lead one to suppose that he was; but he was an original thinker in the sense that he thought out his problems for himself and developed his solutions thoroughly and systematically.

The question has been raised and discussed[6] whether or not Ockham's literary career must be regarded as falling into two more or less unconnected parts and, if so, whether this indicates a dichotomy in his character and interests. For it might seem that there is little connection between Ockham's purely logical and philosophical activities at Oxford and his polemical activities at Munich. It might appear that there is a radical discrepancy between Ockham the cold logician and academic philosopher and Ockham the impassioned political and ecclesiastical controversialist. But such a supposition is unnecessary. Ockham was an independent, bold and vigorous thinker, who showed a marked ability for criticism; he held certain clear convictions and principles which he was ready to apply courageously, systematically and logically; and the difference in tone between his philosophical and polemical works is due rather to a difference in the field of application of his principles than to any unreconciled contradiction in the character of the man. No doubt his personal history and circumstances had emotional repercussions which manifested themselves in his polemical writings; but the emotional overtones of these writings cannot conceal the fact that they are the work of the same vigorous, critical and logical mind which composed the commentary on the *Sentences*. His career falls into two phases, and in the second phase a side of Ockham manifests itself which had no occasion to show itself in the same way during the first phase; but it seems to me an exaggeration to imply that Ockham the logician and Ockham the politician were almost different personalities. It is rather that the same personality and the same original mind manifested itself in different ways according to the different circumstances of Ockham's life and the different problems with which he was faced. One would not expect the exile of Munich, his Oxford career cut short and the ban of excommunication on his head, to have treated the problems of Church and State in exactly the same way that he treated the problem of universals at Oxford; but on the other hand one would not expect the exiled philosopher to lose sight of logic and principle and to become simply a polemical journalist. If one knew sufficient of Ockham's character and temperament, the apparent discrepancies between his activities in the two phases would, I think, seem quite natural. The trouble is that we really know very little of Ockham the man. This fact prevents one from making any categorical assertion that he was not a kind of split or double personality; but it seems more sensible to attempt to explain the different aspects of his literary activity on the supposition that he was not a split personality. If this can be done, then we can apply Ockham's own razor to the contrary hypothesis.

As we shall see, there are various elements or strands in Ockham's thought. There are the 'empiricist' element, the rationalist and logical elements, and the theological element. It does not seem to me very easy to synthesize all the elements of his thought; but perhaps it might be as well to remark immediately that one of Ockham's main preoccupations as a philosopher was to purge Christian theology and philosophy of all traces of Greek necessitarianism, particularly of the theory of essences, which in his opinion endangered the Christian doctrines of the divine liberty and omnipotence. His activity as a logician and his attack on all forms of realism in regard to universals can thus be looked on as subordinate in a sense to his preoccupations as a Christian theologian. This is a point to bear in mind. Ockham was a Franciscan and a theologian: he should not be interpreted as though he were a modern radical empiricist.

Chapter Four

OCKHAM (2)

Ockham and the metaphysic of essences – Peter of Spain and the terminist logic – Ockham's logic and theory of universals – Real and rational science – Necessary truths and demonstration.

1. At the end of the last chapter I mentioned Ockham's preoccupation as a theologian with the Christian doctrines of the divine omnipotence and liberty. He thought that these doctrines could not be safeguarded without eliminating the metaphysic of essences which had been introduced into Christian theology and philosophy from Greek sources. In the philosophy of St. Augustine and in the philosophies of the leading thirteenth-century thinkers the theory of divine ideas had played an important part. Plato had postulated eternal forms or 'ideas', which he most probably regarded as distinct from God but which served as models or patterns according to which God formed the world in its intelligible structure; and later Greek philosophers of the Platonic tradition located these exemplary forms in the divine mind. Christian philosophers proceeded to utilize and adapt this theory in their explanation of the free creation of the world by God. Creation considered as a free and intelligent act on God's part, postulates in God an intellectual pattern or model, as it were, of creation. The theory was, of course, constantly refined; and St. Thomas took pains to show that the ideas in God are not really distinct from the divine essence. We cannot help using language which implies that they are distinct; but actually they are ontologically identical with the divine essence, being simply the divine essence known by God as imitable externally (that is, by creatures) in different ways. This doctrine was the common doctrine in the Middle Ages up to and

including the thirteenth century, being considered necessary in order to explain creation and to distinguish it from a purely spontaneous production. Plato had simply postulated universal subsistent forms; but though the Christian thinkers, with their belief in divine providence extending to individuals, admitted ideas of individuals in God, they retained the originally Platonic notion of universal ideas. God creates man, for example, according to His universal idea of human nature. From this it follows that the natural moral law is not something purely arbitrary, capriciously determined by the divine will: given the idea of human nature, the idea of the natural moral law follows.

Correlative to the theory of universal ideas in God is the acceptance of some form of realism in the explanation of our own universal ideas. Indeed, the former would never have been asserted without the latter; for if a class-word like 'man' were devoid of any objective reference and if there were no such thing as human nature, there would be no reason for ascribing to God a universal idea of man, that is, an idea of human nature. In the second volume of this work an account has been given of the course of the controversy concerning universals in the Middle Ages up to the time of Aquinas; and there it was shown how the early mediaeval form of ultra-realism was finally refuted by Abelard. That only individuals exist came to be the accepted belief. At the same time the moderate realists, like Aquinas, certainly believed in the objectivity of real species and natures. If X and Y are two men, for example, they do not possess the same individual nature; but none the less each possesses his own human nature or essence, and the two natures are similar, each nature being, as it were, a finite imitation of the divine idea of human nature. Duns Scotus proceeded further in the realist direction by finding a formal objective distinction between the human nature of X and the X-ness of X and between the human nature of Y and the Y-ness of Y. Yet, though he spoke of a 'common nature', he did not mean that the actual nature of X is individually the same as the actual nature of Y.

William of Ockham attacked the first part of the metaphysic of essences. He was, indeed, willing to retain something of the language of the theory of divine ideas, doubtless largely out of respect for St. Augustine and tradition; but he emptied the theory of its former content. He thought of the theory as implying a limitation of the divine freedom and omnipotence, as though God would be governed, as it were, and limited in His creative act by the eternal ideas or essences. Moreover, as we shall see later, he thought that the traditional connection of the moral law with the theory of divine ideas constituted an affront to the divine liberty: the moral law depends ultimately, according to Ockham, on the divine will and choice. In other words, for Ockham there is on the one hand God, free and omnipotent, and on the other hand creatures, utterly contingent and dependent. True, all orthodox Christian thinkers of the Middle Ages held the same; but the point is that according to Ockham the metaphysic of essences was a non-Christian invention which had no place in Christian theology and philosophy. As to the other part of the metaphysic of essences Ockham resolutely attacked all forms of 'realism', especially that of Scotus, and he employed the terminist logic in his attack; but, as we shall see, his view of universals was not quite so revolutionary as is sometimes supposed.

Mention will be made later of Ockham's answer to the question, in what sense is it legitimate to speak of ideas in God; at present I propose to outline his logical theory and his discussion of the problem of universals. It must be remembered, however, that Ockham was a gifted and acute logician with a love for simplicity and clarity. What I have been saying about his theological preoccupations should not be taken to mean that his logical inquiries were simply 'apologetic': I was not trying to suggest that Ockham's logic can be waved aside as informed by interested and extrinsic motives. It is rather that in view of some of the pictures which have been given of Ockham it is as well to bear in mind the fact that he *was* a theologian and that he did have theological preoccupations: remembrance of this fact enables one to form a more unified view of his intellectual activity than is otherwise possible.

2. I have said that Ockham 'employed the terminist logic'. This was not a tendentious statement, but it was meant to indicate that Ockham was not the original inventor of the terminist logic. And I wish to make some brief remarks about its development before going on to outline Ockham's own logical theories.

In the thirteenth century there naturally appeared a variety of commentaries on the Aristotelian logic and of logical handbooks and treatises. Among English authors may be mentioned William of Shyreswood (d. 1249), who composed *Introductiones ad logicam*, and among French authors Lambert of Auxerre and Nicholas of Paris. But the most popular and influential work on logic was the *Summulae logicales* of Peter of Spain, a native of Lisbon, who taught at Paris and later became Pope John XXI. He died in 1277. At the beginning of this work we read that 'dialectic is the art of arts and the science of sciences' which opens the way to the knowledge of the principles of all methods.[1] A similar statement of the fundamental importance of dialectic was made by Lambert of Auxerre. Peter of Spain goes on to say that dialectic is carried on only by means of language, and that language involves the use of words. One must begin, then, by considering the word, first as a physical entity, secondly as a significant term. This emphasis on language was characteristic of the logicians and grammarians of the faculty of arts.

When Peter of Spain emphasized the importance of dialectic, he meant by 'dialectic' the art of probable reasoning; and in view of the fact that some other thirteenth-century logicians shared this tendency to concentrate on probable reasoning as distinct from demonstrative science on the one hand and sophistical reasoning on the other, it is tempting to see in their works the source of the fourteenth-century emphasis on probable arguments. No doubt there may have been a connection; but one must remember that a thinker like Peter of Spain did not abandon the idea that metaphysical arguments can give certainty. In other words, Ockham was doubtless influenced by the emphasis placed by the preceding logicians on dialectic or syllogistic reasoning leading to probable conclusions; but that does not mean that one can father on his predecessors his own tendency to look on arguments in philosophy, as distinct from logic, as probable rather than demonstrative arguments.

A number of the treatises in Peter of Spain's *Summulae logicales* deal with the Aristotelian logic; but others deal with the 'modern logic' or logic of terms. Thus in the treatise headed *De suppositionibus* he distinguishes the *significatio* from the *suppositio* of terms. The former function of a term consists in the relation of a sign to the thing signified. Thus in the English language the term 'man' is a sign, while in the French language the term 'homme' has the same sign-function. But in the sentence 'the man is running' the term 'man', which already possesses its *significatio*, acquires the function of standing for (*supponere pro*) a definite man, whereas in the sentence 'man dies' it stands for all men. One must thus, says Peter, distinguish between *significatio* and *suppositio*, inasmuch as the latter presupposes the former.

Now, this logic of terms, with its doctrine of signs and of 'standing-for', undoubtedly influenced William of Ockham, who took from his predecessors much of what one might call his technical equipment. But it does not follow, of course, that Ockham did not develop the terminist logic very considerably. Nor does it follow that Ockham's philosophical views and the use to which he put the terminist logic were borrowed from a thinker like Peter of Spain. On the contrary, Peter was a conservative in philosophy and was very far from showing any tendency to anticipate Ockham's 'nominalism'. To find the antecedents of the terminist logic in the thirteenth century is not the same thing as attempting to push back the whole Ockhamist philosophy into that century: such an attempt would be futile.

The theory of supposition was, however, only one of the features of fourteenth-century logic. I have given it special mention here because of the use made of it by Ockham in his discussion of the problem of universals. But in any history of mediaeval logic prominence would have to be given to the theory of consequences or of the inferential operations between propositions. In his *Summa Logicae*[2] Ockham deals with this subject after treating in turn of terms, propositions and syllogisms. But in the *De puritate artis logicae*[3] of Walter Burleigh the theory of consequences is given great prominence, and the author's remarks on syllogistics form a kind of appendix to it. Again, Albert of Saxony in his *Perutilis Logica* treats syllogistics as part of the general theory of consequences, though he follows Ockham in starting his treatise with a consideration of terms. The importance of this development of the theory of consequences in the fourteenth century is the witness it bears to the growing conception of logic as formalistic in character. For this feature of the later mediaeval logic reveals an affinity, which was for long disregarded or even unsuspected, between mediaeval and modern logic. Research into the history of mediaeval logic has not indeed yet reached the point at which an adequate account of the subject becomes possible. But further lines for reflection and research are indicated in Father Boehner's little work, *Mediaeval Logic*, which is mentioned in the Bibliography. And the reader is referred to this work for further information.

3. I turn now to Ockham's logic, with special attention to his attack on all realist theories of universals. What has been

said in the preceding section will suffice to show that the ascription to Ockham of various logical words and notions should not necessarily be taken to imply that he invented them.

(i) There are various kinds of terms, traditionally distinguished from one another. For example, some terms refer directly to a reality and have a meaning even when they stand by themselves. These terms ('butter', for instance) are called categorematic terms. Other terms, however, like 'no' and 'every' acquire a definite reference only when standing in relation to categorematic terms, as in the phrases 'no man' and 'every house'. These are called syncategorematic terms. Again, some terms are absolute, in the sense that they signify a thing without reference to any other thing, while other terms are called connotative terms, because, like 'son' or 'father', they signify an object considered only in relation to some other thing.

(ii) If we consider the word 'man', we shall recognize that it is a conventional sign: it signifies something or has a meaning, but that this particular word has that particular meaning or exercises that particular sign-function is a matter of convention. This is easily seen to be the case if we bear in mind the fact that in other languages 'homme' and 'homo' are used with the same meaning. Now, the grammarian can reason about words as words, of course; but the real material of our reasoning is not the conventional but the natural sign. The natural sign is the concept. Whether we are English and use the word 'man' or whether we are French and use the word 'homme', the concept or logical significance of the term is the same. The words are different, but their meaning is the same. Ockham distinguished, therefore, both the spoken word (*terminus prolatus*) and the written word (*terminus scriptus*) from the concept (*terminus conceptus* or *intentio animae*), that is, the term considered according to its meaning or logical significance.

Ockham called the concept or *terminus conceptus* a 'natural sign' because he thought that the direct apprehension of anything causes naturally in the human mind a concept of that thing. Both brutes and men utter some sounds as a natural reaction to a stimulus; and these sounds are natural signs. But 'brutes and men utter sounds of this kind only to signify some feelings or some accidents present in themselves', whereas the intellect 'can elicit qualities to signify any sort of thing naturally'.[4] Perceiving a cow results in the formation of the same idea or 'natural sign' (*terminus conceptus*) in the mind of the Englishman and of the Frenchman though the former will express this concept in word or writing by means of one conventional sign, 'cow', while the latter will express it by means of another conventional sign, 'vache'. This treatment of signs was an improvement on that given by Peter of Spain, who does not seem to give sufficient explicit recognition to the identity of logical significance which may attach to corresponding words in different languages.

To anticipate for a moment, one may point out that when Ockham is called a 'nominalist', it is not meant, or should not be meant, that he ascribed universality to words considered precisely as *termini prolati* or *scripti*, that is, to terms considered as conventional signs: it was the natural sign, the *terminus conceptus*, of which he was thinking.

(iii) Terms are elements of propositions, the term standing to the proposition as *incomplexum* to *complexum*; and it is only in the proposition that a term acquires the function of 'standing for' (*suppositio*). For example, in the statement 'the man is running' the term 'man' stands for a precise individual. This is an instance of *suppositio personalis*. But in the statement 'man is a species' the term 'man' stands for all men. This is *suppositio simplex*. Finally, in the statement '*Man* is a noun' one is speaking of the word itself. This is *suppositio materialis*. Taken in itself the term 'man' is capable of exercising any of these functions; but it is only in a proposition that it actually acquires a determinate type of the functions in question. *Suppositio*, then, is 'a property belonging to a term, but only in a proposition'.[5]

(iv) In the statement 'man is mortal' the term 'man', which is, as we have seen, a sign, stands for things, that is, men, which are not themselves signs. It is, therefore, a term of 'first intention' (*primae intentionis*). But in the statement 'species are subdivisions of genera' the term 'species' does not stand immediately for things which are not themselves signs: it stands for class-names, like 'man', 'horse', 'dog', which are themselves signs. The term 'species' is thus a term of second intention (*secundae intentionis*). In other words, terms of second intention stand for terms of first intention and are predicated of them, as when it is said that 'man' and 'horse' are species.

In a broad sense of 'first intention' syncategorematic terms may be called first intentions. Taken in themselves, they do not signify things; but when conjoined with other terms they make those other terms stand for things in a determinate manner. For example, the term 'every' cannot by itself stand for definite things; but as qualifying the term 'man' in the sentence 'every man is mortal' it makes the term 'man' stand for a definite set of things. In the strict sense of 'first intention', however, a term of first intention is an 'extreme term' in a proposition, one, that is, which stands for a thing which is not a sign or for things which are not signs. In the sentence 'arsenic is poisonous', the term 'arsenic' is both an 'extreme term' and one which stands in the proposition for something which is not itself a sign. A term of second intention, strictly understood, will thus be a term which naturally signifies first intentions and which can stand for them in a proposition. 'Genus', 'species' and 'difference' are examples of terms of second intention.[6]

(v) Ockham's answer to the problem of universals has been already indicated in effect: universals are terms (*termini concepti*) which signify individual things and which stand for them in propositions. Only individual things exist; and by the very fact that a thing exists it is individual. There are not and cannot be existent universals. To assert the extramental existence of universals is to commit the folly of asserting a contradiction; for if the universal exists, it must be individual. And that there is no common reality existing at the same time in two members of a species can be shown in several ways. For example, if God were to create a man out of nothing, this would not affect any other man, as far as his essence is concerned. Again, one individual thing can be annihilated without the annihilation or destruction of another individual thing. 'One man can be annihilated by God without any other man being annihilated or destroyed. Therefore there is not anything common to both, because (if there were) it would be annihilated, and consequently no other man would retain his essential nature.'[7] As to the opinion of Scotus that there is a formal distinction between the common nature and the individuality, it is true that he 'excelled others in subtlety of judgment';[8] but if the alleged distinction is an objective and not purely mental distinction, it must be real. The opinion of Scotus is thus subject to the same difficulties which were encountered by older theories of realism.

Whether the universal concept is a quality distinct from the act of the intellect or whether it is that act itself is a question of but secondary importance: the important point is that 'no universal is anything existing in any way outside the soul; but everything which is predicable of many things is of its nature in the mind, whether subjectively or objectively; and no universal belongs to the essence or quiddity of any substance whatever'.[9] Ockham does not appear to have attached very great weight to the question whether the universal concept is an accident distinct from the intellect as such or whether it is simply the intellect itself in its activity: he was more concerned with the analysis of the meaning of terms and propositions than with psychological questions. But it is fairly clear that he did not think that the universal has any existence in the soul except as an act of the understanding. The existence of the universal consists in an act of the understanding and it exists only as such. It owes its existence simply to the intellect: there is no universal reality corresponding to the concept. It is not, however, a fiction in the sense that it does not stand for anything real: it stands for individual real things, though it does not stand for any universal thing. It is, in short, a way of conceiving or knowing individual things.

(vi) Ockham may sometimes imply that the universal is a confused or indistinct image of distinct individual things; but he was not concerned to identify the universal concept with the image or phantasm. His main point was always that there is no need to postulate any factors other than the mind and individual things in order to explain the universal. The universal concept arises simply because there are varying degrees of similarity between individual things. Socrates and Plato are more similar to one another than either is to an ass; and this fact of experience is reflected in the formation of the specific concept of man. But we have to be careful of our way of speaking. We ought not to say that 'Plato and Socrates agree (share) in something or in some things, but that they agree (are alike) by some things, that is, by themselves and that Socrates agrees with (*convenit cum*) Plato, not in something, but by something, namely himself'.[10] In other words, there is no nature common to Socrates and Plato, *in* which they come together or share or agree; but the nature which is Socrates and the nature which is Plato are alike. The foundation of generic concepts can be explained in a similar manner.

(vii) The question might well be raised how this conceptualism differs from the position of St. Thomas. After all, when Ockham says that the notion that there are universal things corresponding to universal terms is absurd and destructive of the whole philosophy of Aristotle and of all science,[11] St. Thomas would agree. And it was certainly St. Thomas's opinion that while the natures of men, for example, are alike there is no common nature considered as a thing in which all individual men have a share. But it must be remembered that St. Thomas gave a metaphysical explanation of the similarity of natures; for he held that God creates things belonging to the same species, things, that is, with similar natures, according to an idea of human nature in the divine mind. Ockham, however, discarded this theory of divine ideas. The consequence was that for him the similarities which give rise to universal concepts are simply similarities, so to speak, of fact: there is no metaphysical reason for these similarities except the divine choice, which is not dependent on any divine ideas. In other words, although St. Thomas and William of Ockham were fundamentally at one in denying that there is any *universale in re*, the former combined his rejection of ultra-realism with the Augustinian doctrine of the *universale ante rem*, whereas the latter did not.[12]

Another, though less important, difference concerns the way of speaking about universal concepts. Ockham, as we have seen, held that the universal concept is an act of the understanding. 'I say that the first intention as well as the second intention is truly an act of the understanding, for whatever is saved by the fiction can be saved by the act.'[13] Ockham appears to be referring to the theory of Petrus Aureoli, according to which the concept, which is the object appearing to the mind, is a 'fiction'. Ockham prefers to say that the concept is simply the act of the understanding. 'The first intention is an act of the understanding signifying things which are not signs. The second intention is the act signifying first intentions.'[14] And Ockham proceeds to say that both first and second intentions are truly real entities, and that they are truly qualities subjectively existent in the soul. That they are real entities, if they are acts of the understanding, is clear; but it seems rather odd perhaps to find Ockham calling them qualities. However, if his various utterances are to be interpreted as consistent with one another, he cannot be supposed to mean that universal concepts are qualities really distinct from the acts of understanding. 'Everything which is explained through positing something distinct from the act of understanding can be explained without positing such a distinct thing.'[15] In other words, Ockham is content to talk simply about the act of the understanding; and he applies the principle of economy to get rid of the apparatus of abstracting *species intelligibiles*. But though there is certainly a difference between the theory of Aquinas and that of Ockham in this respect, it must be remembered that Aquinas insisted strongly that the *species intelligibiles* is not the object of knowledge: it is *id quo intelligitur* and not *id quod intelligitur*.[16]

4. We are now in a position to consider briefly Ockham's theory of science. He divides science into two main types, real science and rational science. The former (*scientia realis*) is concerned with real things, in a sense to be discussed presently, while the latter (*scientia rationalis*) is concerned with terms which do not stand immediately for real things. Thus logic, which deals with terms of second intention, like 'species' and 'genus', is a rational science. It is important to maintain the distinction between these two types of science: otherwise concepts or terms will be confused with things. For example, if one does not realize that Aristotle's intention in the *Categories* was to treat of words and concepts and not of things, one will interpret him in a sense quite foreign to his thought. Logic is concerned with terms of second intention, which cannot exist *sine ratione*, that is, without the mind's activity; it deals, therefore, with mental 'fabrications'. I said earlier that Ockham did not much like speaking of universal concepts as fictions or fictive entities; but the point I then had in mind was that Ockham objected to the implication that what we know by means of a universal concept is a fiction and not a real thing. He was quite ready to speak of terms of second intention, which enter into the propositions of logic, as 'fabrications', because these terms do not refer directly to real things. But logic, which is rational science, presupposes real science; for terms of second intention presuppose terms of first intention.

Real science is concerned with things, that is, with individual things. But Ockham also says that 'real science is not always of things as the objects which are immediately known'.[17] This might seem to be a contradiction; but Ockham proceeds to explain that any science, whether real or rational, is only of propositions.[18] In other words, when he says that real science is concerned with things, Ockham does not mean to deny the Aristotelian doctrine that science is of the universal; but he is determined to hold to the other

Aristotelian doctrine that it is only individuals which exist. Real science, then, is concerned with universal propositions; and he gives as examples of such propositions 'man is capable of laughter' and 'every man is capable of training'; but the universal terms stand for individual things, and not for universal realities existing extramentally. If Ockham says, then, that real science is concerned with individual things by means of terms (*mediantibus terminis*), he does not mean that real science is unconnected with actual existents which are individual things. Science is concerned with the truth or falsity of propositions; but to say that a proposition of real science is true is to say that it is verified in all those individual things of which the terms of the proposition are the natural signs. The difference between real and rational science consists in this, that 'the parts, that is, the terms of the propositions known by real science stand for things, which is not the case with the terms of propositions known by rational science, for these terms stand for other terms'.[19]

5. Ockham's insistence on individual things as the sole existents does not mean, therefore, that he rejects science considered as a knowledge of universal propositions. Nor does he reject the Aristotelian ideas of indemonstrable principles and of demonstration. As regards the former, a principle may be indemonstrable in the sense that the mind cannot but assent to the proposition once it grasps the meaning of the terms, or it may be indemonstrable in the sense that it is known evidently only by experience. 'Certain first principles are not known through themselves (*per se nota* or analytic) but are known only through experience as in the case of the proposition "all heat is calefactive".'[20] As to demonstration, Ockham accepts the Aristotelian definition of demonstration as a syllogism which produces knowledge; but he proceeds to analyse the various meanings of 'know' (*scire*). It may mean the evident understanding of truth; and in this sense even contingent facts, such as the fact that I am now sitting, can be known. Or it may mean the evident understanding of necessary, as distinct from contingent, truths. Or, thirdly, it may mean 'the understanding of one necessary truth through the evident understanding of two necessary truths; . . . and it is in this sense that "knowing" is understood in the aforementioned definition'.[21]

This insistence on necessary truths must not be taken to mean that for Ockham there can be no scientific knowledge of contingent things. He did not think, indeed, that an affirmative and assertoric proposition concerning contingent things and referring to present time (that is, in relation to the speaker) can be a necessary truth; but he held that affirmative and assertoric propositions which include terms standing for contingent things can be necessary, if they are, or can be considered as equivalent to, negative or hypothetical propositions concerning possibility.[22] In other words, Ockham regarded necessary propositions including terms standing for contingent things as equivalent to hypothetical propositions, in the sense that they are true of each thing for which the subject-terms stand *at the time of the existence of that thing*. Thus the proposition, 'every X is Y' where X stands for contingent things and Y for possessing a property) is necessary if considered as equivalent to 'if there is an X, it is Y' or 'if it is true to say of anything that it is an X, it is also true to say of it that it is Y'.

Demonstration for Ockham is demonstration of the attributes of a subject, not of the existence of the subject. We cannot demonstrate, for example, that a certain kind of herb exists; but we may be able to demonstrate the proposition that it has a certain property. True, we can know by experience that it has this property, but if we merely know the fact because we have experienced it, we do not know the 'reason' of the fact. If, however, we can show from the nature of the herb (knowledge of which presupposes experience, of course) that it necessarily possesses this property, we have demonstrative knowledge. To this sort of knowledge Ockham attached considerable importance: he was very far from being a despiser of the syllogism. 'The syllogistic form holds equally in every field.'[23] Ockham did not mean by this, of course, that all true propositions can be proved syllogistically; but he considered that in all matters where scientific knowledge is obtainable syllogistic reasoning holds good. In other words, he adhered to the Aristotelian idea of demonstrative 'science'. In view of the fact that Ockham is not infrequently called an 'empiricist' it is as well to bear in mind the 'rationalist' side of his philosophy. When he said that science is concerned with propositions he did not mean that science is entirely divorced from reality or that demonstration is incapable of telling us anything about things.

Chapter Five

OCKHAM (3)

Intuitive knowledge – God's power to cause intuitive 'knowledge' of a non-existent object – Contingency of the world-order – Relations – Causality – Motion and time – Conclusion.

1. Science, according to Ockham, is concerned with universal propositions, and syllogistic demonstration is the mode of reasoning proper to science in the strict sense: an assent in science is an assent to the truth of a proposition. But this does not mean that for Ockham scientific knowledge is *a priori* in the sense of being a development of innate principles or ideas. On the contrary, intuitive knowledge is primary and fundamental. If we consider, for example, the proposition that the whole is greater than the part, we shall recognize that the mind assents to the truth of the proposition as soon as it apprehends the meaning of the terms; but this does not mean that the principle is innate. Without experience the proposition would not be enunciated; nor should we apprehend the meaning of the terms. Again, in a case where it is possible to demonstrate that an attribute belongs to a subject it is by experience or intuitive knowledge that we know that there is such a subject. Demonstration of a property of man, for example, presupposes an intuitive knowledge of men. 'Nothing can be known naturally in itself unless it is known intuitively.'[1] Ockham is here arguing that we cannot have a natural knowledge of the divine essence as it is in itself, because we have no natural intuition of God; but the principle is a general one. All knowledge is based on experience.

What is meant by intuitive knowledge? 'Intuitive knowledge (*notitia intuitiva*) of a thing is knowledge of such a kind that one can know by means of it whether a thing is or not; and if it is, the intellect immediately judges that the thing exists and concludes evidently that it exists, unless perchance it is hindered on account of some imperfection in that knowledge.'[2] Intuitive knowledge is thus the immediate apprehension of a thing as existent, enabling the mind to form a contingent proposition concerning the existence of that thing. But intuitive knowledge is also knowledge of such a kind that 'when some things are known, of which the one inheres in the other or is locally distant from the other or is related in some other way to the other, the mind straightway knows, by virtue of that simple apprehension of those things, whether the thing inheres or does not inhere, whether it is distant or not, and so with other contingent truths. . . . For example, if Socrates is really white, that apprehension of Socrates and whiteness by means of which it can be known evidently that Socrates is white is intuitive knowledge. And, in general, every simple apprehension of a term or of terms, that is, of a thing or things, by means of which some contingent truths, especially concerning the present, can be known, is intuitive knowledge.'[3] Intuitive knowledge is thus caused by the immediate apprehension of existent things. The concept of an individual thing is the natural expression in the mind of the apprehension of that thing, provided that one does not interpret the concept as a *medium quo* of knowledge. 'I say that in no intuitive apprehension, whether sensitive or intellectual, is the thing placed in any state of being which is a medium beween the thing and the act of knowing. That is, I say that the thing itself is known immediately without any medium between itself and the act by which it is seen or apprehended.'[4] In other words, intuition is immediate apprehension of a thing or of things leading naturally to the judgment that the thing exists or to some other contingent proposition about it, such as 'it is white'. The guarantee of such judgments is simply evidence, the evident character of the intuition, together with the natural character of the process leading to the judgment. 'I say, therefore, that intuitive knowledge is proper individual knowledge . . . because it is naturally caused by one thing and not by another, not can it be caused by another thing.'[5]

It is clear that Ockham is not speaking simply of sensation: he is speaking of an intellectual intuition of an individual thing, which is caused by that thing and not by anything else. Moreover, intuition for him is not confined to intuition of sensible or material things. He expressly says that we know our own acts intuitively, this intuition leading to the formation of propositions like 'there is an understanding' and 'there is a will'.[6] 'Aristotle says that nothing of those things which are external is understood, unless first it falls under sense; and those things are only sensibles according to him. And this authority is true in regard to those things; but in regard to spirits it is not.'[7] As intuitive knowledge precedes abstractive knowledge, according to Ockham, we can say, using a later language, that for him sense-perception and introspection are the two sources of all our natural knowledge concerning existent reality. In this sense one can call him an 'empiricist'; but on this point he is no more of an 'empiricist' than any other mediaeval philosopher who disbelieved in innate ideas and in purely *a priori* knowledge of existent reality.

2. We have seen that for Ockham intuitive knowledge of a thing is caused by that thing and not by any other thing. In other words, intuition, as immediate apprehension of the individual existent, carries its own guarantee. But, as is well known, he maintained that God could cause in us the intuition of a thing which was not really there. 'Intuitive knowledge cannot be caused naturally unless the object is present at the right distance; but it could be caused supernaturally.'[8] 'If you say that it (intuition) can be caused by God alone, that is true.'[9] 'There can be by the power of God intuitive knowledge (*cognitio intuitiva*) concerning a non-existent object.'[10] Hence among the censured propositions of Ockham's we find one to the effect that 'intuitive knowledge in itself and necessarily is not more concerned with an existent than with a non-existent thing, nor does it regard existence more than non-existence'. This is doubtless an interpretative summary of Ockham's position; and since it appears to contradict his account of the nature of intuitive knowledge as distinct from abstractive knowledge (in the sense of knowledge which abstracts from the existence or non-existence of the things for which the terms in the proposition stand), the following remarks may help to make his position clearer.

(i) When Ockham says that God could produce in us intuition of a non-existent object, he is relying on the truth of the proposition that God can produce and conserve immediately whatever He normally produces through the mediation of secondary causes. For example, the intuition of the stars is normally and naturally produced in us by the actual presence of the stars. To say this is to say that God produces in us intuitive knowledge of the stars by means of a secondary cause, namely the stars themselves. On Ockham's principle, then, God could produce this intuition directly, without the secondary cause. He could not do this if it would involve a contradiction; but it would not involve a contradiction. 'Every effect which God causes through the mediation of a secondary cause He can produce immediately by Himself.'[11]

(ii) But God could not produce in us evident knowledge of the proposition that the stars are present when they are not present; for the inclusion of the word 'evident' implies that the stars really are present. 'God cannot cause in us knowledge such that by it a thing is seen evidently to be present although it is absent, for that involves a contradiction, because such evident knowledge means that it is thus in fact as is stated by the proposition to which assent is given.'[12]

(iii) Ockham's point seems to be, then, that God could cause in us the act of intuiting an object which was not really present, in the sense that He could cause in us the physiological and psychological conditions which would normally lead us to assent to the proposition that the thing is present. For example, God could produce immediately in the organs of vision all those effects which are naturally produced by the light of the stars. Or one can put the matter this way. God could not produce in me the actual vision of a present white patch, when the white patch was not present; for this would involve a contradiction. But He could produce in me all the psycho-physical conditions involved in seeing a white patch, even if the white patch was not really there.

(iv) To his critics, Ockham's choice of terms seemed to be confusing and unfortunate. On the one hand, after saying that God cannot cause evident knowledge that a thing is present when it is not present, he adds that 'God can cause a "creditive" act by which I believe that an absent is present', and he explains that 'that "creditive" idea will be abstractive, not intuitive'.[13] This seems to be fairly plain sailing, if it can be taken as meaning that God could produce in us, in the absence of the stars, all the psycho-physical conditions which we would naturally have in the presence of the stars, and that we would thereby have a knowledge of what the stars are (so far as this can be obtained by sight), though the knowledge could not properly be called 'intuition'. On the other hand, Ockham seems to speak of God as being able to produce in us 'intuitive knowledge' of a non-existent object, though this knowledge is not 'evident'. Moreover, he does not seem to mean simply that God could produce in us intuitive knowledge of the nature of the object; for he allows that 'God can produce an assent which belongs to the same species as that evident assent to the contingent proposition, "this whiteness exists", when it does not exist'.[14] If God can properly be said to be capable of producing in us assent to a proposition affirming the existence of a non-existent object, and if this assent can properly be called not only a 'creditive act' but also 'intuitive knowledge', then one can only suppose that it is proper to speak of God as capable of producing in us intuitive knowledge which is not in fact intuitive knowledge at all. And to say this would seem to involve a contradiction. To qualify 'intuitive knowledge' by the words 'not evident' would appear to amount to a cancellation of the former by the latter.

Possibly these difficulties are capable of being cleared up satisfactorily, from Ockham's point of view, I mean. For example, he says that 'it is a contradiction that a chimera be seen intuitively'; but 'it is not a contradiction that that which is seen is nothing in actuality outside the soul, so long as it can be an effect or was at some time an actual reality'.[15] If God had annihilated the stars, He could still cause in us the act of seeing what had once been, so far as the act is considered subjectively, just as He could give us a vision of what will be in the future. Either act would be an immediate apprehension, in the first case of what has been and in the second case of what will be. But, even then, it would be peculiar to imply that if we assented to the proposition, 'these things exist *now*', the assent could be produced by God, unless one were willing to say that God could deceive us. Presumably this was the point to which exception was taken by Ockham's theological opponents, and not the mere assertion that God could act directly on our sense organs. However, it must be remembered that Ockham distinguished evidence, which is objective, from certitude as a psychological state. Possession of the latter is not an infallible guarantee of possession of the former.

(v) In any case one must remember that Ockham is not speaking of the natural course of events. He does not say that God acts in this way as a matter of fact: he simply says that God could act in this way in virtue of His omnipotence. That God is omnipotent was not, however, for Ockham a truth which can be philosophically proved: it is known only by faith. If we look at the matter from the purely philosophical point of view, therefore, the question of God's producing in us intuitions of non-existent objects simply does not come up. On the other hand, what Ockham has to say on the matter admirably illustrates his tendency, as a thinker with marked theological preoccupations, to break through, as it were, the purely philosophic and natural order and to subordinate it to the divine liberty and omnipotence. It illustrates, too, one of his main principles, that when two things are distinct there is no absolutely necessary connection between them. Our act of seeing the stars, considered as an act, is distinct from the stars themselves: it can therefore be separated from them, in the sense that divine omnipotence could annihilate the latter and conserve the former. Ockham's tendency was always to break through supposedly necessary connections which might seem to limit in some way the divine omnipotence, provided that it could not be shown to his satisfaction that denial of the proposition affirming such a necessary connection involved the denial of the principle of contradiction.

3. Ockham's insistence on intuitive knowledge as the basis and source of all our knowledge of existents represents, as we have seen, the 'empiricist' side of his philosophy. This aspect of his thought may also be said to be reflected in his insistence that the order of the world follows the divine choice. Scotus had made a distinction between God's choice of the end and His choice of the means, as though one could speak significantly of God 'first' willing the end and 'then' choosing the means. Ockham, however, rejected this way of speaking. 'It does not seem to be well said that God wills the end before that which is (ordered) to the end, because there is not there (in God) such a priority of acts, nor are there (in God) such instants as he postulates.'[16] Apart from the anthropomorphisms of such language it seems to impair the utter contingency of the order of the world. The choice of the end and the choice of the means are both utterly contingent. This does not mean, of course, that we have to picture God as a sort of capricious superman, liable to alter the world-order from day to day or from moment to moment. On the supposition that God has chosen a world-order, that order remains stable. But the choice of the order is in no way necessary: it is the effect of the divine choice and of the divine choice alone.

This position is intimately associated, of course, with Ockham's concern for the divine omnipotence and liberty; and it may appear out of place to speak of it as in any way reflecting the 'empiricist' aspect of his philosophy, since it is the position of a theologian. But what I meant was this. If the order of the world is entirely contingent on the divine choice, it is obviously impossible to deduce it *a priori*. If we want to know what it is, one must examine what it is in fact. Ockham's position may have been primarily that of a theologian; but its natural effect would be to concentrate attention on the actual facts and to discourage any notion that one could reconstruct the order of the world by purely *a priori* reasoning. If a notion of this kind makes its appearance in the pre-Kantian continental rationalism of the classical period of 'modern' philosophy, its origin is certainly not to be looked for in fourteenth-century Ockhamism: it is to be associated, of course, with the influence of mathematics and of mathematical physics.

4. Ockham's tendency, then, was to split up the world, as it were, into 'absolutes'. That is to say, his tendency was to split up the world into distinct entities, each of which depends on God but between which there is no necessary connection: the order of the world is not logically prior to the divine choice, but it is logically posterior to the divine choice of individual contingent entities. And the same tendency is reflected in his treatment of relations. Once granted that there exists only individual distinct entities and that the only kind of distinction which is independent of the mind is a real distinction in the sense of a distinction between separate or separable entities, it follows that if a relation is a distinct entity, distinct, that is, from the terms of the relation, it must be really distinct from the terms in the sense of being separate or separable. 'If I held that a relation were a thing, I should say with John (Scotus) that it is a thing distinct from its foundation, but I should differ (from him) in saying that every relation differs really from its foundation . . . because I do not admit a formal distinction in creatures.'[17] But it would be absurd to hold that a relation is really distinct from its foundation. If it were, God could produce the relation of paternity and confer it on someone who had never generated. The fact is that a man is called a 'father' when he has generated a child; and there is no need to postulate the existence of a third entity, a relation of paternity, linking father to child. Similarly Smith is said to be like Brown because, for example, Smith is a man and Brown is a man or because Smith is white and Brown is white: it is unnecessary to postulate a third entity, a relation of similarity, in addition

to the 'absolute' substances and qualities; and if one does postulate a third entity, absurd conclusions result.[18] Relations are names or terms signifying absolutes; and a relation as such has no reality outside the mind. For example, there is no order of the universe which is actually or really distinct from the existent parts of the universe.[19] Ockham does not say that a relation is identical with its foundation. 'I do not say that a relation is really the same as its foundation; but I say that a relation is not the foundation but only an "intention" or concept in the soul, signifying several absolute things.'[20] The principle on which Ockham goes is, of course, the principle of economy: the way in which we speak about relations can be analysed or explained satisfactorily without postulating relations as real entities. This was, in Ockham's view, the opinion of Aristotle. The latter would not allow, for example, that every mover is necessarily itself moved. But this implies that relations are not entities distinct from absolute things; for, if they were, the mover would receive a relation and would thus be itself moved.[21] Relations are thus 'intentions' or terms signifying absolutes; though one must add that Ockham restricts the application of this doctrine to the created world: in the Trinity there are real relations.

This theory naturally affected Ockham's view of the relation between creatures and God. It was a common doctrine in the Middle Ages among Ockham's predecessors that the creature has a real relation to God, although God's relation to the creature is only a mental relation. On Ockham's view of relations, however, this distinction becomes in effect null and void. Relations can be analysed into two existent 'absolutes'; and in this case to say that between creatures and God there are different kinds of relation is simply to say, so far as this way of speaking is admissible, that God and creatures are different kinds of beings. It is perfectly true that God produced and conserves creatures and that the latter could not exist apart from God; but this does not mean that the creatures are affected by a mysterious entity called an essential relation of dependence. We conceive and speak about creatures as essentially related to God; but what actually exists is God on the one hand and creatures on the other, and there is no need to postulate any other entity. Ockham distinguishes various senses in which 'real relation' and 'mental relation' can be understood;[22] and he is willing to say that the relation of creatures to God is a 'real' and not a 'mental' relation, if the statement is taken to mean, for example, that a stone's production and conservation by God is real and does not depend on the human mind. But he excludes any idea of there being any additional entity in the stone, in addition, that is, to the stone itself, which could be called a 'real relation'.

One particular way in which Ockham tries to show that the idea of real relations distinct from their foundations is absurd deserves special mention. If I move my finger, its position is changed in regard to all the parts of the universe. And, if there are real relations distinct from their foundation, 'it would follow that at the movement of my finger the whole universe, that is, heaven and earth, would be at once filled with accidents'.[23] Moreover, if, as Ockham says, the parts of the universe are infinite in number, it would follow that the universe is peopled with an infinite number of fresh accidents whenever I move my finger. This conclusion he considered absurd.

For Ockham, then, the universe consists of 'absolutes', substances and absolute accidents, which can be brought into a greater or lesser local approximation to one another, but which are not affected by any relative entities called 'real relations'. From this it would seem to follow that it is futile to think that one could read off, as it were, a mirror of the whole universe. If one wants to know anything about the universe, one must study it empirically. Very possibly this point of view should be regarded as favouring an 'empiricist' approach to knowledge of the world; but it does not follow, of course, that modern science actually developed against a mental background of this sort. Nevertheless, Ockham's insistence on 'absolutes' and his view of relations may reasonably be said to have favoured the growth of empirical science in the following way. If the creature is regarded as having a real essential relation to God, and if it cannot be properly understood without this relation being understood, it is reasonable to conclude that the study of the way in which creatures mirror God is the most important and valuable study of the world, and that a study of creatures in and for themselves alone, without any reference to God, is a rather inferior kind of study, which yields only an inferior knowledge of the world. But if creatures are 'absolutes', they can perfectly well be studied without any reference to God. Of course, as we have seen, when Ockham spoke of created things as 'absolutes' he had no intention of questioning their utter dependence on

God; his point of view was very much that of a theologian; but none the less, if we can know the natures of created things without any advertence to God, it follows that empirical science is an autonomous discipline. The world can be studied in itself in abstraction from God, especially if, as Ockham held, it cannot be strictly proved that God, in the full sense of the term 'God', exists. In this sense it is legitimate to speak of Ockhamism as a factor and stage in the birth of the 'lay spirit', as M. de Lagarde does. At the same time one must remember that Ockham himself was very far from being a secularist or modern 'rationalist'.

5. When one turns to Ockham's account of causality one finds him expounding the four causes of Aristotle. As to the exemplary cause, which, he says, Seneca added as a fifth type of cause, 'I say that strictly speaking nothing is a cause unless it is a cause in one of the four ways laid down by Aristotle. So the idea or exemplar is not strictly a cause; though, if one extends the name "cause" to (cover) everything the knowledge of which is presupposed by the production of something, the idea or exemplar is a cause in this sense; and Seneca speaks in this extended sense.'[24] Ockham accepts, then, the traditional Aristotelian division of causes into the formal, material, final and efficient causes; and he affirms that 'to any type of cause there corresponds its own (type of) causation'.[25]

Moreover, Ockham did not deny that it is possible to conclude from the characteristics of a given thing that it has or had a cause; and he himself used causal arguments. He did, however, deny that the simple knowledge (*notitia incomplexa*) of one thing can provide us with the simple knowledge of another thing. We may be able to establish that a given thing has a cause; but it does not follow that we thereby gain a simple and proper knowledge of the thing which is its cause. The reason of this is that the knowledge in question comes from intuition; and the intuition of one thing is not the intuition of another thing. This principle has, of course, its ramifications in natural theology; but what I want to emphasize at the moment is that Ockham did not deny that a causal argument can have any validity. It is true that for him two things are always really distinct when the concepts of the two things are distinct, and that when two things are distinct God could create the one without the other; but, given empirical reality as it is, one can discern causal connections.

But, though Ockham enumerates four causes in the traditional manner and though he does not reject the validity of causal argument, his analysis of efficient causality has a marked 'empiricist' colouring. In the first place he insists that, though one may know that a given thing has *a* cause, the only way in which we can ascertain that this definite thing is the cause of that definite thing is by experience: we cannot prove by abstract reasoning that X is the cause of Y, where X is one created thing and Y is another created thing. In the second place the experiential test of a causal relation is the employment of the presence and absence methods or the method of exclusion. We are not entitled to assert that X is the cause of Y, unless we can show that when X is present Y follows and that when X is absent, whatever other factors may be present, Y does not follow. For example, 'it is proved that fire is the cause of heat, since, when fire is there and all other things (that is, all other possible causal factors) have been removed, heat follows in a heatable object which has been brought near (the fire) . . . (Similarly) it is proved that the object is the cause of intuitive knowledge, for when all other factors except the object have been removed intuitive knowledge follows'.[26]

That it is by experience we come to know that one thing is the cause of another is, of course, a common-sense position. So, for the matter of that, is Ockham's idea of the test which should be applied in order to ascertain whether *A*, *B* or *C* is the cause of *D* or whether we have to accept a plurality of causes. If we find that when *A* is present *D* always follows, even when *B* and *C* are absent, and that when *B* and *C* are present but *A* is absent *D* never follows, we must take it that *A* is the cause of *D*. If, however, we find that when *A* alone is present *D* never follows, but that when *A* and *B* are both present *D* always follows, even though *C* is absent, we must conclude that both *A* and *B* are causal factors in the production of *D*. In calling these positions common-sense positions I mean that they are positions which would naturally commend themselves to ordinary common sense and that there is nothing revolutionary about either position in itself: I do not mean to suggest that from the scientific point of view the matter was adequately stated by Ockham. It does not need very much reflection to see that there are cases in which the supposed cause of an event cannot be 'removed', in order to see what happens in its absence. We cannot, for example, remove the moon and see what happens to the movement of the tides in the absence of the moon, in order to ascertain whether the moon exercises any causal influence on the tides. However, that is not the point to which I really want to draw attention. For it would be absurd to expect an adequate treatment of scientific induction from a thinker who was not really concerned with the matter and who showed comparatively little interest in matters of pure physical science; especially at a time when science had not attained that degree of development which would appear to be required before reflection on scientific method can really be valuable. The point to which I draw attention is rather this, that in his analysis of efficient causality Ockham shows a tendency to interpret the causal relation as invariable or regular sequence. In one place he distinguishes two senses of cause. In the second sense of the word an antecedent proposition may be called a 'cause' in relation to the consequent. This sense does not concern us, as Ockham expressly says that the antecedent is not the cause of the consequent in any proper sense of the term. It is the first sense which is of interest. 'In one sense it (cause) means something which has another thing as its effect; and in this sense that can be called a cause on the positing of which another thing is posited and on the non-positing of which that other thing is not posited.'[27] In a passage like this Ockham seems to imply that causality means regular sequence and does not seem to be talking simply of an empirical test which should be applied to ascertain whether one thing is actually the cause of another thing. To state without more ado that Ockham reduced causality to regular succession would be incorrect; but he does seem to show a tendency to reduce efficient causality to regular succession. And, after all, to do so would be very much in harmony with his theological view of the universe. God has created distinct things; and the order which prevails between them is purely contingent. There are regular sequences as a matter of fact; but no connection between two distinct things can be said to be necessary, unless one means by necessary simply that the connection, which depends on God's choice, is always observable in fact. In this sense one can probably say that Ockham's theological outlook and his tendency to give an empiricist account of efficient causality went hand in hand. However, as God has created things in such a way that a certain order results, we can predict that the causal relations we have experienced in the past will be experienced in the future, even though God by the use of His absolute power *could* interfere with the order. This theological background is, of course, generally absent from modern empiricism.

6. It is clear that Ockham utilized his razor in his discussion of causality, just as in that of relations in general. He utilized it too in his treatment of the problem of motion. Indeed, his use of the razor or principle of economy was often connected with the 'empiricist' side of his philosophy, inasmuch as he wielded the weapon in an effort to get rid of unobservable entities the existence of which was not, in his opinion, demanded by the data of experience (or taught by revelation). His tendency was always towards the simplification of our view of the universe. To say this is not to say, of course, that Ockham made any attempt to reduce things to sense-data or to logical constructions out of sense-data. Such a reduction he would doubtless have regarded as an oversimplification. But, once granted the existence of substance and absolute accidents, he made an extensive use of the principle of economy.

Employing the traditional Aristotelian division of types of movement, Ockham asserts that neither qualitative alteration nor quantitative change nor local motion is anything positive in addition to permanent things.[28] In the case of qualitative alteration a body acquires a form gradually or successively, part after part, as Ockham puts it; and there is no need to postulate anything else but the thing which acquires the quality and the quality which is acquired. It is true that the negation of the simultaneous acquisition of all the parts of the form is involved; but this negation is not a thing; and to imagine that it is is to be misled by the false supposition that to every distinct term or name there corresponds a distinct thing. Indeed, if it were not for the use of abstract words like 'motion', 'simultaneity', 'succession', etc., the problems connected with the nature of motion would not create such difficulty for people.[29] In the case of quantitative change it is obvious, says Ockham, that nothing is involved save 'permanent things'. As to local motion, nothing need be postulated except a body and its place, that is, its local situation. To be moved locally 'is first to have one place, and afterwards, without any other thing being postulated, to have another place, without any intervening state of rest, . . . and to proceed thus continuously. . . . And consequently the whole nature of motion can be saved (explained) by this without anything else but the fact that a body is successively in distinct places and is not at rest in any of them.'[30] In the whole of his treatment of motion, both in the *Tractatus de successivis*[31] and in the commentary on the *Sentences*[32] Ockham makes frequent appeal to the principle of economy. He does the same when dealing with sudden change (*mutatio subita*, that is, substantial change), which is nothing in addition to 'absolute' things. Of course, if we say that 'a form is acquired by change' or 'change belongs to the category of relation', we shall be tempted to think that the word 'change' stands for an entity. But a proposition like 'a form is lost and a form is gained through sudden change' can be translated into a proposition like 'the thing which changes loses a form and acquires a form together (at the same moment) and not part after part'.[33]

The principle of economy was invoked too in Ockham's treatment of place and time. Expounding the Aristotelian definitions,[34] he insists that place is not a thing distinct from the surface or surfaces of the body or bodies in regard to which a certain thing is said to be in a place; and he insists that time is not a thing distinct from motion. 'I say that neither time nor any *successivum* denotes a thing, either absolute or relative, distinct from permanent things; and this is what the Philosopher means.'[35] In whichever of the possible senses one understands 'time', it is not a thing in addition to motion. 'Primarily and principally "time" signifies the same as "motion", although it connotes both the soul and an act of the soul, by which it (the soul or mind) knows the before and after of that motion. And so, presupposing what has been said about motion, and (presupposing) that the statements are understood . . . , it can be said that "time" signifies motion directly and the soul or an act of the soul directly; and on this account it signifies directly the before and after in motion.'[36] As Ockham expressly says that the meaning of Aristotle in the whole of this chapter about time is, in brief, this, that 'time' does not denote any distinct thing outside the soul beyond what 'motion' signifies,[37] and as this is what he himself held, it follows that in so far as one can distinguish time from motion it is mental, or, as Ockham would say, a 'term' or 'name'.

7. As a conclusion to this chapter one can remind oneself of three features of Ockham's 'empiricism'. First, he bases all knowledge of the existent world on experience. We cannot, for example, discover that A is the cause of *B*, or that *D* is the effect of *C*, by *a priori* reasoning. Secondly, in his analysis

of existent reality, or of the statements which we make about things, he uses the principle of economy. If two factors will suffice to explain motion, for example, one should not add a third. Lastly, when people do postulate unnecessary and unobservable entities, it is not infrequently because they have been misled by language. There is a striking passage on this matter in the *Tractatus de successivis*.[38] 'Nouns which are derived from verbs and also nouns which derive from adverbs, conjunctions, prepositions, and in general from syncategorematic terms . . . have been introduced only for the sake of brevity in speaking or as ornaments of speech; and many of them are equivalent in signification to propositions, when they do not stand for the terms from which they derive; and so they do not signify any things in addition to those from which they derive. . . . Of this kind are all nouns of the following kind: negation, privation, condition, perseity, contingency, universality, action, passion, . . . change, motion, and in general all verbal nouns deriving from verbs which belong to the categories of *agere* and *pati*, and many others, which cannot be treated now.'

Chapter Six

OCKHAM (4)

The subject-matter of metaphysics – The univocal concept of being – The existence of God – Our knowledge of God's nature – The divine ideas – God's knowledge of future contingent events – The divine will and omnipotence.

1. Ockham accepts the statement of Aristotle that being is the subject of metaphysics; but he insists that this statement must not be understood as implying that metaphysics, considered in a wide sense, possesses a strict unity based on its having one subject-matter. If Aristotle and Averroes say that being is the subject of metaphysics, the statement is false if it is interpreted as meaning that all the parts of metaphysics have being as their subject-matter. The statement is true, however, if it is understood as meaning that 'among all the subjects of the different parts of metaphysics being is first with a priority of predication (*primum primitate praedicationis*). And there is a similarity between the question, what is the subject of metaphysics or of the book of categories and the question who is the king of the world or who is the king of all Christendom. For just as different kingdoms have different kings, and there is no king of the whole (world), though sometimes these kings may stand in a certain relation, as when one is more powerful or richer than another, so nothing is the subject of the whole of metaphysics, but here the different parts have different subjects, though these subjects may have a relation to one another.'[1] If some people say that being is the subject of metaphysics, while others say that God is the subject of metaphysics, a distinction must be made, if both statements are to be justified. Among all the subjects of metaphysics God is the primary subject as far

as primacy of perfection is concerned; but being is the primary subject as far as primacy of predication is concerned.[2] For the metaphysician, when treating of God, considers truths like 'God is good', predicating of God an attribute which is primarily predicated of being.[3] There are, then, different branches of metaphysics, or different metaphysical sciences with different subjects. They have a certain relationship to one another, it is true; and this relationship justifies one in speaking of 'metaphysics' and in saying, for example, that being is the subject-matter of metaphysics in the sense mentioned, though it would not justify one's thinking that metaphysics is a unitary science, that is, that it is numerically one science.

2. In so far as metaphysics is the science of being as being it is concerned not with a thing but with a concept.[4] This abstract concept of being does not stand for a mysterious something which has to be known before we can know particular beings: it signifies all beings, not something in which beings participate. It is formed subsequently to the direct apprehension of existing things. 'I say that a particular being can be known, although those general concepts of being and unity are not known.'[5] For Ockham being and existing are synonymous: essence and existence signify the same, though the two words may signify the same thing in different ways. If 'existence' is used as a noun, then 'essence' and 'existence' signify the same thing grammatically and logically; but if the verb 'to be' is used instead of the noun 'existence', one cannot simply substitute 'essence', which is a noun, for the verb 'to be', for obvious grammatical reasons.[6] But this grammatical distinction cannot properly be taken as a basis for distinguishing essence and existence as distinct things: they are the same thing. It is clear, then, that the general concept of being is the result of the apprehension of concrete existing things; it is only because we have had direct apprehension of actual existents that we can form the general concept of being as such.

The general concept of being is univocal. On this point Ockham agrees with Scotus, so far as the use of the word 'univocal' is concerned. 'There is one concept common to God and creatures and predicable of them':[7] 'being' is a concept predicable in a univocal sense of all existent things.[8] Without a univocal concept we could not conceive God. We cannot in this life attain an intuition of the divine essence; nor can we have a simple 'proper' concept of God; but we can conceive

God in a common concept predicable of Him and of other beings.[9] This statement must, however, be properly understood. It does not mean that the univocal concept of being acts as a bridge between a direct apprehension of creatures and a direct apprehension of God. Nor does it mean that one can form the abstract concept of being and deduce therefrom the existence of God. The existence of God is known in other ways, and not by an *a priori* deduction. But without a univocal concept of being one would be unable to conceive the existence of God. 'I admit that the simple knowledge of one creature in itself leads to the knowledge of another thing in a common concept. For example, by the simple knowledge of a whiteness which I have seen I am led to the knowledge of another whiteness which I have never seen, inasmuch as from the first whiteness I abstract a concept of whiteness which refers indifferently to them both. In the same way from some accident which I have seen I abstract a concept of being which does not refer more to that accident than to substance, nor to the creature more than to God.'[10] Obviously, my seeing a white patch does not assure me of the existence of any other white patch; nor did Ockham ever imagine that it could do so. To say that it could would be in flagrant contradiction with his philosophical principles. But, according to him, my seeing a white patch leads to an idea of whiteness which is applicable to other white patches when I see them. Similarly, my abstraction of the concept of being from apprehended existent beings does not assure me of the existence of any other beings. Yet unless I had a common concept of being I could not conceive of the existence of a being, God, which, unlike white patches, cannot be directly apprehended in this life. If, for example, I have no knowledge of God already and then I am told that God exists, I am able to conceive His existence in virtue of the common concept of being, though this does not mean, of course, that I have a 'proper' concept of the divine being.

Ockham was very careful to state his theory of the univocal concept of being in a way which would exclude any pantheistic implication. We must distinguish three types of univocity. In the first place a univocal concept may be a concept which is common to a number of things which are perfectly alike. In the second place a univocal concept may be a concept common to a number of things which are like in some points and unlike in other points. Thus man and ass are alike in being animals; and their matters are similar, though their forms are different. Thirdly, a univocal concept may mean a concept which is common to a plurality of things which are neither accidentally nor substantially alike; and it is in this way that a concept common to God and the creature is univocal, since they are alike neither substantially nor accidentally.[11] In regard to the contention that the concept of being is analogous and not univocal, Ockham observes that analogy can be understood in different ways. If by analogy is meant univocity in the third sense mentioned above, then the univocal concept of being may, of course, be called 'analogous';[12] but, since being as such is a concept and not a thing, there is no need to have recourse to the doctrine of analogy in order to avoid pantheism. If by saying that there can be a univocal concept of being predicable of God as well as of creatures, one meant to imply either that creatures are modes, as it were, of a being identified with God, or that God and creatures share in being, as something real in which they participate, then one would be forced either into accepting pantheism or into reducing God and creatures to the same level; but the doctrine of univocity does not imply anything of the kind, since there is no reality corresponding to the term 'being' when it is predicated univocally. Or, rather, the corresponding reality is simply different beings which are simply conceived as existing. If one considered these beings separately, one would have a plurality of concepts, for the concept of God is not the same as the concept of the creature. And in this case the term 'being' would be predicated equivocally, not univocally. Equivocation does not belong to concepts but to words, that is, to spoken or written terms. As far as the concept is concerned, when we conceive a plurality of beings we either have one concept or a number of concepts. If a word corresponds to one concept, it is used univocally; if it corresponds to several concepts, it is used equivocally. There is, then, no room for analogy, either in the case of concepts or in that of spoken or written words. 'There is no analogical predication, as contradistinguished from univocal, equivocal and denominative predication.'[13] In fact, as denominative (that is, connotative) predication is reducible to univocal or to equivocal predication, one must say that predication must be either univocal or equivocal.[14]

3. But, though God can be conceived in some way, can it be philosophically shown that God exists? God is indeed the most perfect object of the human intellect, the supreme intelligible reality; but He is certainly not the first object of the

human intellect in the sense of being the object which is first known.[15] The primary object of the human mind is the material thing or embodied nature.[16] We possess no natural intuition of the divine essence; and the proposition that God exists is not a self-evident proposition as far as we are concerned. If we imagine someone enjoying the vision of God and making the statement 'God exists', the statement may seem to be the same as the statement 'God exists' made by someone in this life who does not enjoy the vision of God. But though the two statements are verbally the same, the terms or concepts are really different; and in the second case it is not a self-evident proposition.[17] Any natural knowledge of God must, therefore, be derived from reflection on creatures. But can we come to know God from creatures? And, if so, is this knowledge certain knowledge?

Given Ockham's general position in regard to the subject of causality, one could hardly expect him to say that God's existence can be proved with certainty. For if we can only know of a thing that it has *a* cause, and if we cannot establish with certainty by any other way than by actual experience that *A* is the cause of *B*, we could not establish with certainty that the world is caused by God, if the term 'God' is understood in a recognized theistic sense. It is not very surprising, then, to find Ockham criticizing the traditional proofs of God's existence. He did not do so in the interests of scepticism, of course, but rather because he thought that the proofs were not logically conclusive. It does not follow, however, that once given his attitude scepticism, agnosticism or fideism, as the case might be, would not naturally follow.

As the authenticity of the *Centiloquium theologicum* is doubtful, it would scarcely be appropriate to discuss the treatment of the 'first mover' argument which is given by the author of that work. It is sufficient to say that the author refuses to allow that the basic principle of this Aristotelian-Thomist argument is either self-evident or demonstrable.[18] In fact, there are exceptions to the principle, inasmuch as an angel, and the human soul too, moves itself; and such exceptions show that the alleged principle cannot be a necessary principle and that it cannot form a basis for any strict proof of God's existence, especially as it cannot be proved that an infinite regress in the series of movers is impossible. The argument may be a probable argument in the sense that it is more probable that there is a first unmoved mover than that there is no such first unmoved mover; but it is not a certain argument. This criticism follows the line already suggested by Scotus; and even if the work in which it occurs is not a work of Ockham, the criticism would seem to be in harmony with Ockham's ideas. Moreover, there can be no question of his having accepted St. Thomas's *manifestior via* as a certain argument for God's existence, as distinct from the existence of a first mover in a general sense. The first mover might be an angel or some being less than God, if we mean by 'God' an infinite, unique and absolutely supreme being.[19]

The proof from finality also goes by the board. Not only is it impossible to prove that the universe is ordered to one end, God,[20] but it cannot even be proved that individual things act for ends in a way which would justify any certain argument to God's existence. In the case of things which act without knowledge and will, all that we are warranted in saying is that they act because of a natural necessity: it makes no sense to say that they act 'for' an end.[21] Of course, if one presupposes God's existence, one can then speak of inanimate things as acting for ends, that is, for ends determined by God, who created their natures;[22] but if a statement is based on the presupposition of God's existence, it cannot itself be used to prove God's existence. As to agents endowed with intelligence and will, the reason for their voluntary actions is to be found in their own wills; and it cannot be shown that all wills are moved by the perfect good, God.[23] In fine, it is impossible to prove that there is in the universe an immanent teleological order, the existence of which makes it necessary to assert God's existence. There is no order distinct from 'absolute' natures themselves; and the only way in which one could prove God's existence would be as efficient cause of the existence of finite things. Is it, however, possible to do so?

In the *Quodlibet* Ockham states that one must stop at a first efficient cause and not proceed to infinity: but he adds immediately that this efficient cause might be a heavenly body, since 'we know by experience that it is the cause of other things'.[24] He says expressly not only that 'it cannot be proved by the natural reason that God is the immediate efficient cause of all things', but also that it cannot be proved that God is the mediate efficient cause of any effect. He gives as one reason of this the impossibility of proving that there exist any things other than corruptible things. It cannot be proved, for instance, that there is a spiritual and immortal soul in man. And the heavenly bodies can cause corruptible things, without its being possible to prove that the heavenly bodies themselves are caused by God.

However, in the commentary on the *Sentences*, Ockham gives his own version of the proof from efficient causality. It is better, he says, to argue from conservation to conserver rather than from product to producer. The reason for this is that 'it is difficult or impossible to prove against the philosophers that there cannot be an infinite regress in causes of the same kind, of which one can exist without the other'.[25] For example, Ockham does not think that it can be strictly proved that a man does not owe his total being to his parents, and they to their parents, and so on indefinitely. If it is objected that even in the case of an infinite series of this kind the infinite series would itself depend for its production on a being intrinsic to the series, Ockham answers that 'it would be difficult to prove that the series would not be possible unless there were one permanent being, on which the whole infinite series depended'.[26] He therefore prefers to argue that a thing which comes into being (that is, a contingent thing) is conserved in being as long as it exists. It can then be asked whether the conserver is itself dependent for its conservation or not. But in this case we cannot proceed to infinity, because an infinite number of *actual* conservers is, says Ockham, impossible. It may be possible to admit an infinite regress in the case of beings which exist one after the other, since in this case there would not be an actually existent infinity; but in the case of actual conservers of the world here and now, an infinite regress would imply an actual infinity. That an actual infinity of this sort is impossible is shown by the arguments of philosophers and others, which are 'reasonable enough' (*satis rationabiles*).

But even though reasonable arguments can be adduced for the existence of God as first conserver of the world, the unicity of God cannot be demonstrated.[27] It can be shown that there is some ultimate conserving being in *this* world; but we cannot exclude the possibility of there being another world or other worlds, with its or their own relatively first beings. To prove that there is a first efficient cause which is more perfect than *its* effects is not the same thing as proving the existence of a being which is superior to every other being, unless you can first prove that every other being is the effect of one single cause.[28] The unicity of God is known with certainty only by faith.

In answer, therefore, to the question whether Ockham admitted any philosophical proof of God's existence one must first make a distinction. If by 'God' one means the absolutely supreme, perfect, unique and infinite being, Ockham did not think that the existence of such a being can be strictly proved by the philosopher. If, on the other hand, one means by 'God' the first conserving cause of this world, without any certain knowledge about the nature of that cause, Ockham did think that the existence of such a being can be philosophically proved. But, as this second understanding of the term 'God' is not all that is usually understood by the term, one might just as well say, without further ado, that Ockham did not admit the demonstrability of God's existence. Only by faith do we know, as far at least as certain knowledge is concerned, that the supreme and unique being in the fullest sense exists. From this it would seem to follow, as historians have argued, that theology and philosophy fall apart, since it is not possible to prove the existence of the God whose revelation is accepted on faith. But it does not follow, of course, that Ockham himself was concerned to separate theology from philosophy. If he criticized the traditional proofs of God's existence, he criticized them from the point of view of a logician, and not in order to break apart the traditional synthesis. Moreover, though it may be tempting to a modern philosopher to depict Ockham as assigning to theological propositions a purely 'emotional' significance by relegating a large number of the propositions of traditional metaphysics to dogmatic theology, this would be an inaccurate interpretation of his position. When he said, for example, that theology is not a science, he did not mean that theological propositions are not informative propositions or that no theological syllogism can be a correct piece of reasoning: what he meant was that since the premisses of theological arguments are known by faith the conclusions too fall within the same sphere, and that since the premisses are not self-evident the arguments are not scientific demonstrations in the strict sense of 'scientific demonstration'. Ockham did not deny that a probable argument can be given for God's existence. What he denied was that the existence of God as the unique absolutely supreme being can be philosophically 'demonstrated'.

4. If the existence of God as the absolutely supreme being cannot be strictly proved by the natural reason, it is obvious that it cannot be proved that there is an infinite and omnipotent being, creator of all things. But the question may be

raised whether, given the concept of God as the absolutely supreme being, it can then be demonstrated that God is infinite and omnipotent. Ockham's answer to this question is that attributes like omnipotence, infinity, eternity or the power to create out of nothing cannot be demonstrated to belong to the divine essence. His reason for saying this is a technical one. A *priori* demonstration involves the use of a middle term to which the predicate in question belongs in a prior manner. But in the case of an attribute like infinity there can be no middle term to which infinity belongs; and so there can be no demonstration that God is infinite. It may be said that concepts like infinity or the power of creating out of nothing can be demonstrated to belong to the divine essence by using their definitions as middle terms. For example, one can argue in this way. Anything which can produce something from nothing is capable of creating. But God can produce something from nothing. Therefore God can create. A syllogism of this kind, says Ockham, is not what is meant by a demonstration. A demonstration in the proper sense increases knowledge; but the syllogism just mentioned does not increase knowledge, since the statement that God produces or can produce something from nothing is precisely the same as the statement that God creates or can create. The syllogism is useless unless one knows the meaning of the term 'create'; but if we know the meaning of the term 'create' we know that the statement that God can produce something from nothing is the statement that God can create. Thus the conclusion which is professedly demonstrated is already assumed: the argument contains the fallacy of begging the question.[29]

On the other hand, there are some attributes which can be demonstrated. We can argue, for example, as follows. Every being is good: but God is a being: therefore God is good. In a syllogism of this sort there is a middle term, a concept common to God and creatures. But the term 'good' must here be understood as a connotative term, as connoting a relation to the will, if the argument is to be a demonstration. For if the term 'good' is not taken as a connotative term, it is simply synonymous with the term 'being'; and in this case we learn nothing at all from the argument. No attribute can be demonstrated to belong to a subject, unless the conclusion of the demonstration is *dubitabilis*, that is, unless one can significantly raise the question whether the attribute is to be predicated of the subject or not. But if the term 'good' is taken not as a connotative term but as synonymous with 'being', we could not know that God is a being and significantly raise the question whether God is good. It is not required, of course, that the attribute predicated of a subject should be really distinct from a subject. Ockham rejected the Scotist doctrine of a formal distinction between the divine attributes, and maintained that there is no distinction. But we do not possess an intuition of the divine essence; and though the realities represented by our concepts of the divine essence and attributes are not distinct we can argue from one concept to another provided that there is a middle term. In the case of concepts common to God and creatures there is a middle term.

But in our knowledge of God's nature what is it precisely that constitutes the term of our cognition? We do not enjoy intuitive knowledge of God, which it is beyond the scope of the human intellect to attain by its own efforts. Nor can there be any natural 'abstractive' knowledge of God as He is in Himself, since it is impossible for us by our natural powers to have an abstractive knowledge of something in itself without an intuitive knowledge of that thing. It follows, therefore, that in our natural state it is impossible for us to know God in such a way that the divine essence is the immediate and sole term of the act of knowing.[30] Secondly, we cannot in our natural state conceive God in a simple concept, proper to Him alone. For 'no thing can be known by us through our natural powers in a simple concept proper to itself, unless the thing is known in itself. For otherwise we could say that colour can be known in a concept proper to colours by a man born blind.'[31] But, thirdly, God can be conceived by us in connotative concepts and in concepts which are common to God and creatures, like being. As God is a simple being, without any internal distinction save that between the three divine Persons, proper quidditative concepts (*conceptus quidditativi*) would be convertible; and so they would not be distinct concepts. If we can have distinct concepts of God, this is due to the fact that our concepts are not proper quidditative concepts of God. They are not convertible because they are either connotative concepts, like the concept of infinity which connotes the finite negatively, or concepts common to God and creatures, like the concept of wisdom. It is only a proper quidditative concept which corresponds to a single reality. A connotative concept connotes a reality other than the subject of which it is predicated; and a common concept is predicable of other realities than the one of which it is in fact predicated. Moreover, the common concepts which we predicate of God are due to a reflection on other realities than God and presuppose them.

An important consequence follows. If we have, as we do have, distinct concepts of God, a simple being, our conceptual knowledge of the divine nature is a knowledge of concepts rather than a knowledge of God as He is. What we attain is not the divine essence but a mental representation of the divine essence. We can form, it is true, a composite concept which is predicable of God alone; but this concept is a mental construction; we cannot have a simple concept proper to God which would adequately mirror the divine essence. 'Neither the divine essence . . . nor anything intrinsic to God nor anything which is really God can be known by us without something other than God being involved as object.'[32] 'We cannot know in themselves either the unity of God . . . or His infinite power or the divine goodness or perfection; but what we know immediately are concepts, which are not really God but which we use in propositions to stand for God.'[33] We know the divine nature, then, only through the medium of concepts; and these concepts, not being proper quidditative concepts, cannot take the place of an immediate apprehension of the essence of God. We do not attain a reality (*quid rei*), but a nominal representation (*quid nominis*). This is not to say that theology is not true or that its propositions have no meaning; but it is to say that the theologian is confined to the sphere of concepts and mental representation and that his analyses are analyses of concepts, not of God Himself. To imagine, for example, as Scotus did, that because we conceive divine attributes in distinct concepts these attributes are formally distinct in God is to misunderstand the nature of theological reasoning.

The foregoing inadequate account of what Ockham has to say on the subject of our knowledge of the divine nature really belongs to an account of his theological rather than of his philosophical ideas. For if the existence of God as the absolutely supreme being cannot be firmly established by the philosopher, it is obvious that the philosopher cannot give us any certain knowledge of God's nature. Nor can the theologian's reasoning, according to Ockham, give us certain knowledge of God's nature. As far as the analysis of concepts goes, an unbeliever could perform the same analysis as is performed by the believing theologian. What gives us certain knowledge of the truth of theological propositions is not the theologian's reasoning as such, nor his demonstrations, so far as demonstration is possible for him, but God's revelation accepted on faith. The theologian can reason correctly from certain premisses; but so can the unbeliever. The former, however, accepts the premisses and the conclusions on faith; and he knows that the propositions are true, that is, that they correspond to reality. But he knows this by faith; and his knowledge is not, in the strict sense, 'science'. For there is no intuitive knowledge lying at the basis of his reasoning. Ockham did not intend to question the truth of theological dogmas: he set out to examine the nature of theological reasoning and theological concepts, and he treated his problems from the point of view of a logician. His theological nominalism was not, in his own mind, equivalent to agnosticism or scepticism: it was rather, in intention at any rate, a logical analysis of a theology which he accepted.

But though Ockham's discussion of our knowledge of God's nature belongs more properly to the theological than to the philosophical sphere, it has its place in a discussion of his philosophy, if only for the reason that in it he deals with matters which preceding mediaeval philosophers had considered to fall within the metaphysician's competence. Similarly, though the philosopher as such could scarcely, in Ockham's eyes, establish anything with certainty about the divine 'ideas', this topic had been a salient feature of the traditional mediaeval metaphysics, and Ockham's treatment of it is closely linked wih his general philosophic principles. It is desirable, therefore, to say something about it here.

5. In the first place there cannot be any plurality in the divine intellect. The divine intellect is identical with the divine will and the divine essence. We may speak about 'the divine will', 'the divine intellect' and 'the divine essence'; but the reality referred to is one single and simple being. Hence, talk about the 'divine ideas' cannot be taken to refer to realties in God which are in any way distinct either from the divine essence or from one another. If there were a distinction at all, it would be a real distinction; and a real distinction cannot be admitted. In the second place, it is quite unnecessary, and also misleading, to postulate divine ideas as a kind of intermediary factor in creation. Apart from the fact that if the divine ideas are in no way distinct from the divine intellect, which is itself identical with the divine essence, they cannot be an intermediary factor in creation, God

can know creatures and create them without the intervention of any 'ideas'.[34] Ockham makes it clear that in his opinion the theory of ideas in God is simply a piece of anthropomorphism. It also involves a confusion between *quid rei* and *quid nominis*.[35] The upholders of the theory would certainly admit that there is not a real distinction either between the divine essence and the divine ideas or between the ideas themselves but that the distinction is a mental distinction; yet they talk as though the distinction of ideas in God were prior to the production of creatures. Moreover, they postulate in God ideas of universals, which as a matter of fact do not correspond to any reality. In fine, Ockham applies the principle of economy to the theory of divine ideas in so far as this theory implies that there are ideas in God which are distinct from creatures themselves, whether the ideas are interpreted as real or as mental relations. It is unnecessary to postulate such ideas in God to explain either His production of or His knowledge of creatures.

In one sense, therefore, Ockham may be said to have rejected the theory of divine ideas. But this does not mean that he was prepared to declare that St. Augustine was in error or that there was no acceptable interpretation of the theory. On the contrary, as far as verbal acceptance was concerned, he must be said to have accepted the theory. But the meaning which he attaches to the statements he makes has to be clearly understood, if he is not to be judged guilty of flagrant self-contradiction. He asserts, for instance, that there is an infinite number of distinct ideas; and this assertion appears at first hearing to be in obvious contradiction with his condemnation of any ascription of distinct ideas to God.

In the first place, the term 'idea' is a connotative term. It denotes directly the creature itself; but it connotes indirectly the divine knowledge or knower. 'And so it can be predicated of the creature itself that it is an idea but not of the knowing agent nor of the knowledge, since neither the knowledge nor the knower is an idea or pattern.'[36] We can say, then, that the creature itself is the idea. 'The ideas are not in God subjectively and really; but they are in Him only objectively, that is, as certain things which are known by Him, for the ideas are the things themselves which are producible by God.'[37] In other words, it is quite sufficient to postulate God on the one hand and creatures on the other hand: the creatures as known by God are the 'ideas', and there are no other ideas. The creature as known from eternity by God can be considered as the pattern or exemplar of the creature as actually existent. 'The ideas are certain known patterns (*exempla*); and it is by reference to them that the knower can produce something in real existence. . . . This description does not fit the divine essence itself, nor any mental relation, but the creature itself. . . . The divine essence is not an idea . . . (Nor is the idea either a real or a mental relation) . . . Not a real relation, since there is no real relation on God's part to the creature; and not a mental relation, both because there is no mental relation of God to the creature to which the name "idea" could be given and because a mental relation cannot be the exemplar of the creature, just as an *ens rationis* cannot be the exemplar of a real being.'[38] But if creatures themselves are the ideas, it follows that 'there are distinct ideas of all makable things, as the things themselves are distinct from one another'.[39] And thus there are distinct ideas of all the essential and integral parts of producible things, like matter and form.[40]

On the other hand, if the ideas are the creatures themselves, it follows that the ideas are of individual things, 'since individual things alone are producible outside (the mind) and no others'.[41] There are, for example, no divine ideas of genera; for the divine ideas are creatures makable by God, and genera cannot be produced as real existents. It follows, too, that there are no ideas of negations, privations, evil, guilt and the like, since these are not and cannot be distinct things.[42] But, as God can produce an infinity of creatures, we must say that there is an infinite number of ideas.[43]

Ockham's discussion of the theory of divine ideas illuminates both the general mediaeval outlook and his own mentality. The respect for St. Augustine in the Middle Ages was too great for it to be possible for a theologian simply to reject one of his main theories. We find, then, the language of the theory being retained and used by Ockham. He was willing to speak of distinct ideas and of these ideas as patterns or exemplars of creation. On the other hand, using the principle of economy and determined to get rid of anything which might seem to come between the omnipotent Creator and the creature so as to govern the divine will, he pruned the theory of all Platonism and identified the ideas with creatures themselves as producible by God and as known by God from eternity as producible. From the philosophical point of view he fitted the theory to his general philosophy by eliminating universal ideas, while from the theological point of view he safeguarded, as he thought, the divine omnipotence and eliminated what he considered to be the contamination of Greek metaphysics. (Having identified the ideas with creatures he was able, however, to observe that Plato acted rightly in neither identifying the ideas with God nor placing them in the divine mind.) This is not to say, of course, that Ockham's use of the language of the Aristotelian theory was insincere. He postulated the theory, in so far as it could be taken to mean simply that creatures are known by God, for one of the main traditional reasons, namely that God creates rationally and not irrationally.[44] But at the same time it is clear that in Ockham's hands the theory was so purged of Platonism that to all intents and purposes it was rejected in its original form. Abelard, while rejecting ultra-realism, had retained the theory of universal ideas in God, largely out of respect for St. Augustine; but Ockham eliminated these universal divine ideas. His version of the theory of ideas is thus consistent with his general principle that there are only individual existents and with his constant attempt to get rid of any other factors which could be got rid of. It might be said, of course, that to speak of producible creatures as known by God from all eternity ('things were ideas from eternity; but they were not actually existent from eternity')[45] is to admit the essence of the theory of ideas; and this is, in fact, what Ockham thought and what justified him, in his opinion, in appealing to St. Augustine. But it is perhaps questionable if Ockham's theory is altogether consistent. As he would not confine God's creative power in any way, he had to extend the range of 'ideas' beyond the things actually produced by God; but to do this is, of course, to admit that the 'ideas' cannot be identified with creatures that have existed, do exist and will exist; and to admit this is to come very close to the Thomist theory, except that no ideas of universals are admitted. The conclusion that should probably be drawn is not that Ockham made an insincere use of the language of a theory which he had really discarded, but rather that he sincerely accepted the theory, though he interpreted it in such a way as to fit in with his conviction that only individuals exist or can exist and that universal concepts belong to the level of human thought and are not to be attributed to God.

6. When it comes to discussing the divine knowledge Ockham shows a marked and, indeed, very understandable re-

luctance to make assertions concerning a level of cognition which lies entirely outside our experience.

That God knows, besides Himself, all other things cannot be proved philosophically. Any proof would rest principally on God's universal causality; but, apart from the fact that it cannot be proved by means of the principle of causality that a cause knows its immediate effect, it cannot be proved philosophically that God is the immediate cause of all things.[46] Probable arguments can be given for saying that God knows some things other than Himself; but the arguments are not conclusive. On the other hand, it cannot be proved that God knows nothing other than Himself; for it cannot be proved that every act of cognition depends on its object.[47] Nevertheless, though it cannot be philosophically proved that God is omniscient, that is, that He knows not only Himself but also all other things as well, we know by faith that He is.

But, if God knows all things, does this mean that He knows future contingent events, in the sense of events which depend on free wills for their actuality? 'I say to this question that it must be held without any doubt that God knows all future contingent events with certainty and evidence. But it is impossible for any intellect in our present state to make evident either this fact or the manner in which God knows all future contingent events.'[48] Aristotle, says Ockham, would have said that God has no certain knowledge of any future contingent events for the following reasons. No statement that a future contingent event depending on free choice will happen or will not happen is true. The proposition that it either will or will not happen is true; but neither the statement that it will happen nor the statement that it will not happen is true. And if neither statement is true, neither statement can be known. 'In spite of this reason, however, we must hold that God evidently knows all future contingents. But the way (in which God knows them) I cannot explain.'[49] But Ockham goes on to say that God does not know future contingent events as present to Him,[50] or by means of ideas as media of knowledge, but by the divine essence itself, although this cannot be proved philosophically. Similarly in the *Tractatus de praedestinatione et de praescientia Dei et de futuris contingentibus*[51] Ockham states: 'So I say that it is impossible to express clearly the way in which God knows future contingent events. However, it must be held that He does (know them), though contingently.' By saying that God knows future contingent facts 'contingently' Ockham means that God knows them as contingent and that His knowledge does not make them necessary. He goes on to suggest that 'the divine essence is intuitive knowledge which is so perfect and so clear that it is itself evident knowledge of all past and future events, so that it knows which part of a contradiction will be true and which part false'.[52]

Thus Ockham affirms that God does not merely know that, for example, I shall choose tomorrow either to go for a walk or to stop at home and read; He knows which alternative is true and which false. This affirmation is not one that can be proved philosophically: it is a theological matter. As to the mode of God's knowledge, Ockham does not offer any suggestion beyond saying that the divine essence is such that God does know future contingent facts. He does not have recourse to the expedient of saying that God knows which part of a disjunctive proposition concerning a future contingent event is true because He determines it to be true: he very sensibly admits that he cannot explain how God knows future contingent events. It is to be noted, however, that Ockham is convinced that one part of a disjunctive proposition concerning such an event is true, and that God knows it as true. This is the important fact from the purely philosophical point of view: the relation of God's knowledge of future free events to the theme of predestination does not concern us here. It is an important fact because it shows that Ockham did not admit an exception to the principle of excluded middle. Some fourteenth-century philosophers did admit an exception. For Petrus Aureoli, as we have seen, propositions which either affirm or deny that a definite contingent event will happen in the future are neither true nor false. Petrus Aureoli did not deny that God knows future contingent events; but he maintained that as God's knowledge does not look forward, as it were, to the future, it does not make an affirmative or a negative statement which concerns a definite free act in the future either true or false. One can say, then, that he admitted an instance of a 'three-valued' logic, though it would, of course, be an anachronism to depict him as elaborating such a logic. This is not the case, however, with William of Ockham, who does not admit any propositions to be neither true nor false. He rejected Aristotle's arguments designed to show that there are such propositions, though there are one or two passages which seem at first sight to support Aristotle's point of view. Moreover, in the

Summa totius logicae[53] Ockham expressly states, in opposition to Aristotle, that propositions about future contingent events are true or false. Again, in the *Quodlibet*[54] he maintains that God can reveal knowledge of affirmative propositions concerning future contingent events, because such propositions are true. God made revelations of this sort to the prophets; though precisely how it was done 'I do not know, because it has not been revealed to me.' One cannot say, then, that Ockham admitted an exception to the principle of excluded middle. And because he did not admit an exception he was not faced with the problems of reconciling the admission with the divine omniscience.

7. If the terms 'will', 'intellect' and 'essence' are understood in an absolute sense, they are synonymous. 'If some name were used to signify precisely the divine essence and nothing else, without any connotation of anything else whatever, and similarly if some name were used to signify the divine will in the same manner, those names would be simply synonymous names; and whatever was predicated of the one could be predicated of the other.'[55] Accordingly, if the terms 'essence' and 'will' are taken absolutely, there is no more reason to say that the divine will is the cause of all things than that the divine essence is the cause of all things: it comes to the same thing. However, whether we speak of the 'divine essence' or of the 'divine will', God is the immediate cause of all things, though this cannot be demonstrated philosophically.[56] The divine will (or the divine essence) is the immediate cause of all things in the sense that without the divine causality no effect would follow, even though all other conditions and dispositions were present. Moreover, the power of God is unlimited, in the sense that He can do all that is possible. But to say that God cannot do what is intrinsically impossible is not to limit God's power; for it makes no sense to speak of doing or making what is intrinsically impossible. However, God can produce every possible effect, even without a secondary cause; He could, for instance, produce in the human being an act of hatred of Himself, and if He were to do so He would not sin.[57] That God can produce every possible effect, even without the concurrence of a secondary cause, cannot be proved by the philosopher; but it is none the less to be believed.

The divine omnipotence cannot, then, be philosophically proved. But once it is assumed as an article of faith the world appears in a special light. All empirical causal relations, that is, all regular sequences, are seen as contingent, not only in the sense that causal relations are matters for experiential verification and not for *a priori* deduction, but also in the sense that an external agent, namely God, can always produce *B* without employing A as secondary cause. Of course, in all mediaeval systems of thought the uniformity and regularity of natural processes were regarded as contingent, inasmuch as the possibility of God's miraculous intervention was admitted by all Christian thinkers. But the metaphysic of essences had conferred on Nature a comparative stability of which Ockham deprived it. With him relations and connections in nature were really reduced to the co-existence or successive existence of 'absolutes'. And in the light of the divine omnipotence, believed on faith, the contingency of relations and of order in nature was seen as the expression of the all-powerful will of God. Ockham's view of nature, taken in isolation from its theological background, might reasonably be regarded as a stage on the path to a scientific view of nature through the elimination of the metaphysical; but the theological background was not for Ockham himself an irrelevant excrescence. On the contrary, the thought of the divine omnipotence and liberty pervaded, explicitly or implicitly, his whole system; and in the next chapter we shall see how his convictions on this matter influenced his moral theory.

Chapter Seven

OCKHAM (5)

That an immaterial and incorruptible soul is the form of the body cannot be philosophically proved – The plurality of really distinct forms in man – The rational soul possesses no really distinct faculties – The human person – Freedom – Ockham's ethical theory.

1. Just as Ockham criticized the traditional proofs of God's existence, so also did he criticize a number of the proofs advanced by his predecessors in psychology. We experience acts of understanding and willing; but there is no compelling reason to attribute these acts to an immaterial form or soul. We experience these acts as acts of the form of the body; and, as far as experience takes us, we might reasonably conclude that they are the acts of an extended and corporeal form.[1] 'Understanding by intellectual soul an immaterial and incorruptible form which is wholly in the whole and wholly in every part (of the body), it cannot be known evidently either by arguments or by experience that there is such a form in us or that the activity of understanding belongs to a substance of this kind in us, or that a soul of this kind is the form of the body. I do not care what Aristotle thought about this, for he seems to speak always in an ambiguous manner. But these three things we hold only by faith.'[2] According to Ockham, then, we do not experience the presence of an immaterial and incorruptible form in ourselves; nor can it be proved that the acts of understanding which we do experience are the acts of such a form. And even if we could prove that the acts of understanding which we experience are the acts of an immaterial substance, it would not follow that this substance is the form of the body. And if it cannot be shown by philosophic reasoning or by experience that we possess immaterial and incorruptible souls, it obviously can-

not be shown that these souls are created directly by God.[3] Ockham does not say, of course, that we do not possess immortal souls: what he says is that we cannot prove that we possess them. That we do possess them is a revealed truth, known by faith.

2. But though Ockham accepted on faith the existence of an immaterial and incorruptible form in man, he was not prepared to say that this form informs matter directly. The function of matter is to support a form; and it is clear that the matter of the human body has a form. But the corruptibility of the human body shows that it is not an incorruptible form which informs matter immediately. 'I say that one must postulate in man another form in addition to the intellectual soul, namely a sensitive form, on which a natural agent can act by way of corruption and production.'[4] This sensitive form or soul is distinct from man's intellectual soul and, unless God wills otherwise, it perishes with the body.[5] There is only one sensitive form in an animal or in a man; but it is extended in such a way that 'one part of the sensitive soul perfects one part of matter, while another part of the same soul perfects another part of matter'.[6] Thus the part of the sensitive soul which perfects the organ of sight is the power of seeing, while the part which perfects the organ of hearing is the power of hearing.[7] In this sense, then, we can speak of sensitive powers which are really distinct from one another; for 'the accidental dispositions which are of necessity required for the act of seeing are really distinct from the dispositions which are of necessity required for the act of hearing'.[8] This is clear from the fact that one can lose the power of sight, for example, without losing the power of hearing. But if we mean by 'powers' forms which are the eliciting principles of the various acts of sensation, there is no need to postulate really distinct powers corresponding to the various organs of sense: the principle of economy can be applied. The one eliciting principle is the sensitive form or soul itself, which is extended throughout the body and works through the different sense-organs.

In one place Ockham speaks as follows. 'According to the opinion which I consider the true one there are in man several substantial forms, at least a form of corporeity and the intellectual soul.'[9] In another place he says that though it is difficult to prove that there are or are not several substantial forms in man, 'it is proved (that there are) in the following way, at least in regard to the intellectual soul and the sensitive soul, which are distinct in man'.[10] His remark about the difficulty of proof is explained in the *Quodlibet*,[11] where he says that it is difficult to prove that the sensitive and intellectual souls are distinct in man 'because it cannot be proved from self-evident propositions'. But this does not prevent his going on to offer arguments based on experience, such as the argument that we can desire a thing with the sensitive appetite, while at the same time we turn away from it with the rational will. As to the fact that in one place he seems to insist on the intellectual soul and the form of corporeity, whereas in another place he seems to insist on the presence in man of intellectual and sensitive souls, the apparent inconsistency seems to be explicable in terms of the two contexts. In any case Ockham clearly maintained the existence in man of three distinct forms. He argues not only that the intellectual soul and the sensitive soul are distinct in man,[12] but also that the sensitive soul and the form of corporeity are really distinct both in men and brutes.[13] In maintaining the existence of a form of corporeity in man Ockham was, of course, continuing the Franciscan tradition; and he gives the traditional theological argument, that the form of corporeity must be postulated in order to explain the numerical identity of Christ's dead body with His living body, though he gives other arguments as well.

In saying that there is in man a form of corporeity and in maintaining that the intellectual soul does not inform prime matter directly Ockham was continuing, then, a traditional position, in favour of which he rejected that of St. Thomas. Moreover, though he maintained the doctrine of the plurality of substantial forms, he did not deny that man, taken in his totality, is a unity. 'There is only one total being of man, but several partial beings.'[14] Nor did he deny that the intellectual soul is the form of the body, though he did not think that this can be proved philosophically. Hence it can hardly be said that Ockham contradicted the teaching of the Council of Vienne (1311), since the Council did not assert that the rational or intellectual soul informs prime matter directly. The majority of the members of the Council themselves held the doctrine of the form of corporeity; and when they declared that the rational soul informs the body directly they left the question entirely open whether or not the body which is informed by the rational soul is constituted as a body by its own form of corporeity or not. On the other hand, the Council had clearly intended to defend the unity of the human being against the implications of Olivi's psychological theories;[15] and it is at least questionable whether Ockham's teaching satisfied this demand. It must be remembered that for Ockham a real distinction meant a distinction between things which can be separated, at least by the divine power: he rejected the Scotist doctrine of formal objective distinctions, that is, of objective distinctions between different 'formalities' of one and the same thing, which cannot be separated from one another. When discussing the question whether the sensitive soul and the intellectual soul are really distinct in man, he remarks that the sensitive soul of Christ, though always united to the Deity, remained where God pleased during the time between Christ's death and the resurrection. 'But whether it remained with the body or with the intellectual soul God alone knows; yet both can well be said.'[16] If, however, the sensitive form is really separable from man's rational form and from his body, it is difficult to see how the unity of man can be preserved. It is true, of course, that all the mediaeval Christian thinkers would have admitted that the rational soul is separable from the body: they obviously could not do otherwise. And it might be argued that to assert the separability of the sensitive from the rational soul does not impair man's unity any more than does the assertion that man's rational soul is separable from his body. However, one is entitled to say at least that Ockham's doctrine of the real distinction between the sensitive and rational souls in man makes it harder to safeguard the unity of man than does Scotus's doctrine of the formal distinction. Ockham, of course, disposed of Scotus's formal distinction by means of the principle of economy, and he supported his theory of the real distinction between the sensitive and rational souls by an appeal to experience. It was, indeed, for similar reasons that Scotus maintained the formal distinction; but he seems to have realized better than Ockham the fundamental unity of man's intellectual and sensitive life. In certain respects he appears to have been less influenced by Aristotle than was Ockham, who envisaged the possibility at any rate of the rational soul's being united to the body more as a mover than as a form, though, as we have seen, he accepted on faith the doctrine that the intellectual soul is the form of the body.

3. Though Ockham asserted the existence in man of a plurality of forms, really distinct from one another, he would not admit a real distinction between the faculties of a given

form. We have already seen that he refused to allow that the sensitive soul or form possesses powers which are really distinct from the sensitive soul itself and from one another, unless by 'powers' one means simply accidental dispositions in the various sense-organs. He also refused to allow that the rational soul or form possesses faculties which are really distinct from the rational soul itself and from one another. The rational soul is unextended and spiritual; and it cannot have parts or ontologically distinct faculties. What is called the intellect is simply the rational soul understanding, and what we call the will is simply the soul willing. The rational soul produces acts; and the intellectual power or faculty 'does not signify only the essence of the soul, but it connotes the act of understanding. And similarly in the case of the will.'[17] In one sense, then, intellect and will are really distinct, that is, if we are taking them as connotative terms; for an act of understanding is really distinct from an act of willing. But if we are referring to that which produces the acts, intellect and will are not really distinct. The principle of economy can be applied in the elimination of really distinct faculties or principles.[18] There is one rational soul, which can elicit different acts. As to the existence of an active intellect distinct from the passive intellect there is no compelling reason for accepting it. The formation of universal concepts, for example, can be explained without postulating any activity of the intellect.[19] Nevertheless, Ockham is prepared to accept the active intellect on account of the authority 'of the saints and philosophers',[20] in spite of the fact that the arguments for its existence can be answered and that in any case no more than probable arguments can be given.

4. In asserting a plurality of substantial forms in man and in denying at the same time that intellect and will are really distinct faculties Ockham remained faithful to two features of the Franciscan tradition. But the doctrine of the plurality of forms in man traditionally meant an acceptance of the form of corporeity in addition to the one human soul, not a breaking-up, as it were, of the soul into distinct forms in Ockham's sense of distinction. His substitution of the real distinction, involving separability, for Scotus's formal objective distinction was scarcely compatible with the assertion of the unity of the human being. Yet in discussing human personality Ockham insisted on this unity. The person is a *suppositum intellectuale*, a definition which holds good for both created and uncreated persons.[21] A *suppositum* is 'a com-

plete being, incommunicable by identity, incapable of inhering in anything, and not supported (*sustentatum*) by anything'.[22] The words 'a complete being' exclude from the class of *supposita* all parts, whether essential or integral, while the words 'incommunicable by identity' exclude the divine essence, which, though a complete being, is 'communicated' identically to the divine Persons. The phrase 'incapable of inhering in anything' excludes accidents, while 'not supported (Ockham means "taken up" or "assumed") by anything' excludes the human nature of Christ, which was assumed by the second Person and is consequently not a person. In the commentary on the *Sentences* Ockham defines 'person' as 'an intellectual and complete nature, which is neither supported (*nec sustentatur*, is not assumed) by anything else nor is able, as a part, to form with another thing one being'.[23] In the case of the three divine Persons each *suppositum intellectuale* or Person is constituted by the divine essence and a relation.[24]

The human person, then, is the total being of man, not the rational form or soul alone. It is in virtue of the rational form that a human being is a *suppositum intellectuale* as distinct from any other kind of *suppositum;* but it is the whole man, not the rational form alone, which constitutes the human person. Ockham, therefore, maintains with St. Thomas that the human soul in the state of separation from the body after death is not a person.[25]

5. One of the principal characteristics of a rational creature is freedom.[26] Freedom is the power 'by which I can indifferently and contingently produce an effect in such a way that I can cause or not cause that effect, without any difference in that power having been made'.[27] That one possesses this power cannot be proved by *a priori* reasoning, but 'it can, however, be known evidently through experience, that is, through the fact that every man experiences that however much his reason dictates something his will can will it or not will it'.[28] Moreover, the fact that we blame and praise people, that is, that we impute to them the responsibility for their actions, or for some of their actions, shows that we accept freedom as a reality. 'No act is blameworthy unless it is in our power. For no one blames a man born blind, for he is blind by sense (*caecus sensu*). But if he is blind by his own act, then he is blameworthy.'[29]

According to Ockham, the will is free to will or not to will happiness, the last end; it does not will it necessarily.

This is clear in regard to the last end considered in the concrete, that is to say, God. 'No object other than God can satisfy the will, because no act which is directed to something other than God excludes all anxiety and sadness. For, whatever created object may be possessed, the will can desire something else with anxiety and sadness.'[30] But that the enjoyment of the divine essence is possible to us cannot be proved philosophically; it is an article of faith.[31] If then we do not know that the enjoyment of God is possible, we cannot will it. And even if we know by faith that it is possible, we can still will it or not will it, as is clear from experience. What is more, we do not will necessarily even perfect happiness in general. For the intellect may believe that perfect happiness is not possible for man and that the only condition possible for us is the one in which we actually find ourselves. But if the intellect can believe that perfect happiness is impossible, it can dictate to the will that it should not will something which is impossible and incompatible with the reality of human life. And in this case the will is able not to will what the intellect says that it should not will. The judgment of the intellect is, indeed, erroneous; but though 'the will does not necessarily conform to the judgment of the reason, it can conform with the judgment of the reason, whether that judgment be right or erroneous'.[32]

In emphasizing the freedom of the will in the face of the judgment of the intellect Ockham was following in the common tradition of the Franciscan philosophers. But it may be remarked that his view on the will's freedom even in regard to the willing of happiness in general (*beatitudo in communi*) fitted in very much with his ethical theory. If the will is free to will or not to will happiness, it would scarcely be possible to analyse the goodness of human acts in terms of a relation to an end which is necessarily desired. And in point of fact Ockham's ethical theory was, as we shall see presently, markedly authoritarian in character.

It is only to be expected that Ockham would insist that the will is free to elicit an act contrary to that to which the sensitive appetite is strongly inclined.[33] But he admitted, of course, the existence of habits and inclinations in the sensitive appetite and in the will.[34] There is some difficulty, he says, in explaining how it is that habits are formed in a free power like the will as a result of repeated acts of the sensitive appetite; but that they are formed is a matter of experience. 'It is difficult to give the cause why the will is more inclined not to will an object which causes pain in the sensitive appetite.' The cause cannot be found in a command of the intellect, because the intellect can equally well say that the will should will that object as that it should not will it. But 'it is obvious through experience that even if the intellect says that death should be undergone for the sake of the State, the will is naturally, so to speak, inclined to the contrary'. On the other hand, we cannot simply say that the cause of the will's inclination is pleasure in the sensitive appetite. For, 'however intense may be the pleasure in the sensitive appetite, the will can, in virtue of its freedom, will the opposite'. 'And so I say that there does not seem to be any other cause for the will's natural inclination except that such is the nature of the matter; and this fact becomes known to us through experience.'[35] In other words, it is an undoubted fact of experience that the will is inclined to follow the sensitive appetite; but it is difficult to give a satisfactory theoretical explanation of the fact, though this does not alter the nature of the fact. If we indulge the sensitive appetite in a certain direction, a habit is formed, and this habit is reflected in what we can call a habit in the will, and this habit grows in strength if the will does not react sufficiently against the sensitive appetite. On the other hand, it remains in the will's power to act against habit and inclination, even if with difficulty, because the will is essentially free. A human act can never be attributed simply to habit and inclination; for it is possible for the will to choose in a manner contrary to the habit and inclination.

6. A created free will is subject to moral obligation. God is not, and cannot be, under any obligation; but man is entirely dependent upon God, and in his free acts his dependence expresses itself as moral obligation. He is morally obliged to will what God orders him to will and not to will what God orders him not to will. The ontological foundation of the moral order is thus man's dependence on God, as creature on Creator; and the content of the moral law is supplied by the divine precept. 'Evil is nothing else than to do something when one is under an obligation to do the opposite. Obligation does not fall on God, since He is not under any obligation to do anything.'[36]

This personal conception of the moral law was closely connected with Ockham's insistence on the divine omnipotence and liberty. Once these truths are accepted as revealed truths, the whole created order, including the moral law, is viewed by Ockham as wholly contingent, in the sense that not only its existence but also its essence and character depend on the divine creative and omnipotent will. Having got rid of any universal idea of man in the divine mind, Ockham was able to eliminate the idea of a natural law which is in essence immutable. For St. Thomas man was contingent, of course, in the sense that his existence depends on God's free choice; but God could not create the particular kind of being which we call man and impose on him precepts irrespective of their content. And, though he considered, for exegetic reasons connected with the Scriptures, that God can dispense in the case of certain precepts of the natural law, Scotus was fundamentally of the same mind as St. Thomas.[37] There are acts which are intrinsically evil and which are forbidden because they are evil: they are not evil simply because they are forbidden. For Ockham, however, the divine will is the ultimate norm of morality: the moral law is founded on the free divine choice rather than ultimately on the divine essence. Moreover, he did not hesitate to draw the logical consequences from this position. God concurs, as universal creator and conserver, in any act, even in an act of hatred of God. But He could also cause, as total cause, the same act with which He concurs as partial cause. 'Thus He can be the total cause of an act of hatred of God, and that without any moral malice.'[38] God is under no obligation; and therefore He could cause an act in the human will which would be a morally evil act if the man were responsible for it. If the man were responsible for it, he would commit sin, since he is obliged to love God and not hate Him; but obligation, being the result of divine imposition, cannot affect God Himself. 'By the very fact that God wills something, it is right for it to be done. . . . Hence if God were to cause hatred of Himself in anyone's will, that is, if He were to be the total cause of the act (He is, as it is, its partial cause), neither would that man sin nor would God; for God is not under any obligation, while the man is not (in the case) obliged, because the act would not be in his own power.'[39] God can do anything or order anything which does not involve logical contradiction. Therefore, because, according to Ockham, there is no natural or formal repugnance between loving God and loving a creature in a way which has been forbidden by God, God could order fornication. Between loving God and loving a creature in a manner which is illicit there is only an extrinsic repugnance, namely the repugnance which arises from the fact that God has actually forbidden that way of loving a creature. Hence, if God were to order fornication, the latter would be not only licit but meritorious.[40] Hatred of God, stealing, committing adultery, are forbidden by God. But they could be ordered by God; and, if they were, they would be meritorious acts.[41] No one can say that Ockham lacked the courage to draw the logical conclusions from his personal theory of ethics.

Needless to say, Ockham did not mean to suggest that adultery, fornication, theft and hatred of God are legitimate acts in the present moral order; still less did he mean to encourage the commission of such acts. His thesis was that such acts are wrong because God has forbidden them; and his intention was to emphasize the divine omnipotence and liberty, not to encourage immorality. He made use of the distinction between the absolute power (*potentia absoluta*) of God, by which God could order the opposite of the acts which He has, as a matter of fact, forbidden, and the *potentia ordinata* of God, whereby God has actually established a definite moral code. But he explained the distinction in such a way as to make it clear not only that God could have established another moral order but that He could at any time order what He has actually forbidden.[42] There is no sense, then, in seeking for any more ultimate reason of the moral law than the divine *fiat*. Obligation arises through the encounter of a created free will with an external precept. In God's case there can be no question of an external precept. Therefore God is not obliged to order any kind of act rather than its opposite. That He has ordered this and forbidden that is explicable in terms of the divine free choice; and this is a sufficient reason.

The authoritarian element in Ockham's moral theory is, very naturally, the element which has attracted the most attention. But there is another element, which must also be mentioned. Apart from the fact that Ockham analyses the moral virtues in dependence on the Aristotelian analysis, he makes frequent use of the Scholastic concept of 'right reason' (*recta ratio*). Right reason is depicted as the norm, at least the proximate norm, of morality. 'It can be said that every right will is in conformity with right reason.'[43] Again, 'no moral virtue, nor any virtuous act, is possible unless it is in conformity with right reason; for right reason is included in the definition of virtue in the second book of the *Ethics*'.[44]

Moreover, for an act to be virtuous, not only must it be in accordance with right reason but it must also be done because it is in accordance with right reason. 'No act is perfectly virtuous unless in that act the will wills that which is prescribed by right reason because it is prescribed by right reason.'[45] For if one willed that which is prescribed by right reason simply because it is pleasant or for some other motive, without regard to its being prescribed by right reason, one's act 'would not be virtuous, since it would not be elicited in conformity with right reason. For to elicit an act in conformity with right reason is to will what is prescribed by right reason on account of its being so prescribed.'[46] This insistence on motive was not, of course, a sudden outbreak of 'puritanism' on Ockham's part: Aristotle had insisted that for an act to be perfectly virtuous it must be done for its own sake, that is, because it is the right thing to do. We call an act just, he says, if it is what the just man would do; but it does not follow that a man is just, that is, that he has the virtue of justice, simply because he does the act which the just man would do in the circumstances. He has to do it as the just man would do it; and this includes doing it because it is the just thing to do.[47]

Right reason, then, is the norm of morality. A man may be mistaken in what he thinks is the dictate of right reason; but, even if he is mistaken, he is obliged to conform his will to what he believes to be prescribed by right reason. In other words, conscience is always to be followed, even if it is an erroneous conscience. A man may, of course, be responsible for his having an erroneous conscience; but it is also possible for him to be in 'invincible ignorance', and in this case he is not responsible for his error. In any case, however, he is bound to follow what happens to be the judgment of his conscience. 'A created will which follows an invincibly erroneous conscience is a right will; for the divine will wills that it should follow its reason when this reason is not blameworthy. If it acts against that reason (that is, against an invincibly erroneous conscience), it sins. . . .'[48] A man is morally obliged to do what he in good faith believes to be right. This doctrine, that one is morally obliged to follow one's conscience, and that to follow an invincibly erroneous conscience, so far from being a sin, is a duty, was not a new doctrine in the Middle Ages; but Ockham expressed it in a clear and unequivocal manner.

It would seem, then, at least at first sight, that we are faced with what amounts to two moral theories in Ockham's philosophy. On the one hand there is his authoritarian conception of the moral law. It would appear to follow from this conception that there can be only a revealed moral code. For how otherwise than through revelation could man know a moral code which depends entirely on God's free choice? Rational deduction could not give us knowledge of it. On the other hand there is Ockham's insistence on right reason, which would seem to imply that reason can discern what is right and what is wrong. The authoritarian conception of morality expresses Ockham's conviction of the freedom and omnipotence of God as they are revealed in Christianity, while the insistence on right reason would seem to represent the influence on his thought of Aristotle's ethical teaching and of the moral theories of his mediaeval predecessors. It might seem, then, that Ockham presents one type of ethical theory in his capacity as theologian and another type in his capacity as philosopher. It has thus been maintained that in spite of his authoritarian conception of the moral law Ockham promoted the growth of a 'lay' moral theory represented by his insistence on reason as the norm of morality and on the duty of doing what one in good faith believes to be the right thing to do.

That there is truth in the contention that two moral theories are implicit in Ockham's ethical teaching can hardly, I think, be denied. He built on the substructure of the Christian-Aristotelian tradition, and he retained a considerable amount of it, as is shown by what he says about the virtues, right reason, natural rights and so on. But he added to this substructure a superstructure which consisted in an ultra-personal conception of the moral law; and he does not seem fully to have realized that the addition of this superstructure demanded a more radical recasting of the substructure than he actually carried out. His personal conception of the moral law was not without precedents in Christian thought; but the point is that in the twelfth and thirteenth centuries a moral theory had been elaborated in close association with metaphysics, which ruled out any view of the moral law as dependent simply and solely on the divine will. In retaining a good deal of the former moral theory, while at the same time asserting an authoritarian interpretation of the moral law, Ockham was inevitably involved in difficulties. Like other Christian mediaeval thinkers he accepted, of course, the existence of an actual moral order; and in his discussion of such themes as the function of reason or the existence of natural rights[49] he implied that reason can discern the precepts, or at least the fundamental precepts, of the moral law which actually obtains. At the same time he insisted that the moral order which actually obtains is due to the divine choice, in the sense that God could have established a different moral order and that He could even now order a man to do something contrary to the moral law which He has established. But, if the present moral order is dependent simply and solely on the divine choice, how could we know what it is save through God's revelation? It would seem that there can be only a revealed ethic. Yet Ockham does not appear to have said that there can be only a revealed ethic: he seems to have thought that men, without revelation, are able to discern the moral law in some sense. In this case they can presumably discern a prudential code or a set of hypothetical imperatives. Without revelation men could see that certain acts fit human nature and human society and that other acts are harmful; but they could not discern an immutable natural law, since there is no such immutable natural law, nor could they know, without revelation, whether the acts they thought right were really the acts ordered by God. If reason cannot prove conclusively God's existence, it obviously cannot prove that God has ordered this rather than that. If, therefore, we leave Ockham's theology out of account, it would seem that we are left with a non-metaphysical and non-theological morality, the precepts of which cannot be known as necessary or immutable precepts. Hence perhaps Ockham's insistence on the following of conscience, even an erroneous conscience. Left to himself, that is, without revelation, man might perhaps elaborate an ethic of the Aristotelian type; but he could not discern a natural law of the type envisaged by St. Thomas, since Ockham's authoritarian conception of the moral law, coupled with his 'nominalism', would rule this out. In this sense, then, one is probably justified in saying that two moralities are implicit in Ockham's teaching, namely an authoritarian ethic and a 'lay' or non-theological ethic.

It is one thing, however, to say that the two ethical systems are implicit in Ockham's moral teaching; and it is another thing to suggest that he intended to promote an ethic divorced from theology. One could say with far more justice that he intended the very opposite; for he evidently considered that his predecessors had obscured the doctrines of the divine omnipotence and liberty through their theories of an immutable natural law. As far as the interpretation of Ockham's own mind is concerned, it is clear that it is the personal side of his moral theory which has to be stressed. One has only to look at a passage like the following wherein he says that the reason why an act elicited contrary to the dictate of conscience is a wrong act is that 'it would be elicited contrary to the divine precept and the divine will which wills that an act should be elicited in conformity with right reason'.[50] In other words, the ultimate and sufficient reason why we ought to follow right reason or conscience is that God wills that we should do so. Authoritarianism has the last word. Again, Ockham speaks of an act 'which is intrinsically and necessarily virtuous *stante ordinatione divina*'.[51] In the same section he says that 'in the present order (*stante ordinatione quae nunc est*) no act is perfectly virtuous unless it is elicited in conformity with right reason'. Such remarks are revealing. A necessarily virtuous act is only relatively so, that is, if God has decreed that it should be virtuous. Given the order instituted by God, it follows logically that certain acts are good and others bad; but the order itself is dependent on God's choice. It possesses a certain stability, and Ockham did not imagine that God is constantly changing His orders, so to speak; but he insists that its stability is not absolute.

One can, then, sum up Ockham's position on more or less the following lines. The human being, as a free created being which is entirely dependent on God, is morally obliged to conform his will to the divine will in regard to that which God commands or prohibits. Absolutely speaking, God could command or prohibit any act, provided that a contradiction is not involved. Actually God has established a certain moral law. As a rational being man can see that he ought to obey this law. But he may not know what God has commanded; and in this case he is morally obliged to do what he honestly believes to be in accordance with God's commands. To act otherwise would be to act contrary to what is believed to be the divine ordinance; and to do this is to sin. It is not clear what Ockham thought of the moral situation of the man who has no knowledge of revelation, or even no knowledge of God's existence. He appears to imply that reason can discern something of the present moral order; but, if he did mean this, it is difficult to see how this idea can be reconciled with his authoritarian conception of morality. If the moral law is dependent simply on the divine choice, how can its content be known apart from revelation? If its content can be known apart from revelation, how can it be dependent simply on the divine choice? It would seem that the only way of escaping this difficulty is to say that what can be known apart from revelation is simply a provisional code of morality, based on non-theological considerations. But that Ockham actually had this notion clearly in mind, which would imply the possibility of a purely philosophic and second-rank ethic, as distinct from the divinely-imposed and obligatory ethic, I should not care to affirm. He thought in terms of the ethical code commonly accepted by Christians, though he went on to assert that it was dependent on the free divine choice. Very probably he did not clearly realize the difficulties created by his authoritarian conception.

Chapter Eight

OCKHAM (6)

The dispute on evangelical poverty, and the doctrine of natural rights – Political sovereignty is not derived from the spiritual power – The relation of the people to their ruler – How far were Ockham's political ideas novel or revolutionary? – The pope's position within the Church.

1. It would be a mistake to suppose that Ockham was a political philosopher in the sense of a man who reflects systematically on the nature of political society, sovereignty and government. Ockham's political writings were not written to provide an abstract political theory; they were immediately occasioned by contemporary disputes involving the Holy See, and Ockham's immediate object was to resist and denounce what he regarded as papal aggression and unjustified absolutism; he was concerned with relations between pope and emperor and between the pope and the members of the Church rather than with political society and political government as such. Ockham shared in the respect for law and custom and in the dislike for arbitrary and capricious absolutism which were common characteristics of the mediaeval philosophers and theologians: it would be wrong to suppose that he set out to revolutionize mediaeval society. It is true, of course, that Ockham was led to lay down general principles on the relations of Church and State and on political government; but he did this mainly in the course of conducting controversies on concrete and specific points of dispute. For example, he published the *Opus nonaginta dierum* about the year 1332 in defence of the attitude of Michael of Cesena in regard to the dispute on evangelical poverty. Pope John XXII had condemned as heretical a doctrine on evan-

gelical poverty which was held by many Franciscans and had deprived Michael of his post as General of the Franciscan Order. Counterblasts from Michael, who, together with Bonagratia of Bergamo and Ockham had taken refuge with the emperor, Ludwig of Bavaria, elicited from the pope the bull *Quia vir reprobus* (1329) in which Michael's doctrines were again censured and the Franciscans were rebuked for daring to publish tracts criticizing papal pronouncements. Ockham retaliated by subjecting the bull to close scrutiny and trenchant criticism in the *Opus nonaginta dierum*. This publication was occasioned, therefore, not by any purely theoretical consideration of the position of the Holy See, but by a concrete dispute, that concerning evangelical poverty; it was not composed by a political philosopher in hours of cool reflection but by a participant in a heated controversy. Ockham criticized the papal pronouncements as themselves heretical and was able to refer to the erroneous opinion of John XXII concerning the beatific vision. He was thus writing primarily as a theologian.

But though Ockham wrote the *Opus nonaginta dierum* for the specific purpose of defending his Franciscan colleagues against papal condemnation, and though he devoted a good deal of his attention to discovering heresies and errors in the pope's pronouncements, he discussed the poverty question in the manner which one would expect of a philosopher, a man accustomed to close and careful reasoning. The result is that one can find in the work Ockham's general ideas on, for example, the right of property, though it must be confessed that it is not easy to settle the question exactly which of the opinions discussed are Ockham's own opinions, since he writes in a much more restrained and impersonal manner than one might expect in a polemical writer involved in a heated controversy.

Man has a natural right to property. God gave to man the power to dispose of the goods of the earth in the manner dictated by right reason, and since the Fall right reason shows that the personal appropriation of temporal goods is necessary.[1] The right of private property is thus a natural right, willed by God, and, as such, it is inviolable, in the sense that no one can be despoiled of this right by an earthly power. The State can regulate the exercise of the right of private property, the way in which property is transferred in society, for example; but it cannot deprive men of the right against their will. Ockham does not deny that a criminal, for instance, can legitimately be deprived of his freedom to acquire and possess property; but the right of property, he insists, is a natural right which does not depend in its essence on the positive conventions of society; and without fault on his own part or some reasonable cause a man cannot be forcibly deprived of the exercise of the right, still less of the right itself.

Ockham speaks of a right (*ius*) as being a legitimate power (*potestas licita*), a power in conformity with right reason (*conformis rationi rectae*), and he distinguishes legitimate powers which are anterior to human convention from those which depend on human convention. The right of private property is a legitimate power which is anterior to human convention, since right reason dictates the institution of private property as a remedy for the moral condition of man after the Fall. Inasmuch as a man is permitted to own property and use it and to resist anyone who tries to wrest his property from him, he has a right to private property, for that permission (*licentia*) comes from the natural law. But not all natural rights are of the same kind. There are, first, natural rights which are valid until a contrary convention is made. For example, the Roman people have, according to Ockham, the right to elect their bishop: this follows from the fact that they are under an obligation to have a bishop. But the Roman people may cede this right of election to the Cardinals, though the right of the Roman people must again be exercised if for any reason election by the Cardinals becomes impossible or impracticable. Conditional natural rights of this sort are examples of what Ockham calls rights flowing from the natural law understood in the third sense.[2] Secondly, there are natural rights which obtained in the state of humanity before the Fall, though 'natural right' in this sense means simply the consequence of a perfection which once existed and no longer exists; it is conditional on a certain state of human perfection. Thirdly, there are rights which share in the immutability of moral precepts, and the right of private property is one of these rights. In the *Breviloquium* Ockham declares that 'the aforementioned power of appropriating temporal things falls under a precept and is reckoned to belong to the sphere of morality (*inter pure moralia computatur*)'.

But a further distinction is required. There are some natural rights in the third sense named (Ockham's *primus modus*) which are so bound up with the moral imperative that nobody is entitled to renounce them, since renunciation of the right would be equivalent to a sin against the moral law. Thus everyone has the duty of preserving his own life, and he would sin against the moral law by starving himself to death. But if he is obliged to maintain his life, he has a right to do so, a right which he cannot renounce. The right of private property, however, is not of this kind. There is, indeed, a precept of right reason that temporal goods should be appropriated and owned by men; but it is not necessary for the fulfilment of the precept that every individual man should exercise the right of private property, and he can, for a just and reasonable cause, renounce all rights to the possession of property. Ockham's main point in this connection is that the renunciation must be voluntary, and that when it is voluntary it is legitimate.

Pope John XXII had maintained that the distinction between merely using temporal things and having the right to use them was unreal. His principle was that 'He who, without a right, uses something uses it unjustly'. Now, the Franciscans were admittedly entitled to use temporal things like food and clothing. Therefore they must have a right over them, a right to use them, and it was unreal to pretend that it was the Holy See which possessed all these things without the Franciscans having any right at all. The reply was made that it is quite possible to renounce a right to property and at the same time to use legitimately those things of which the ownership has been renounced. The Franciscans renounced all rights of property, even the right of use: they were not like tenants who, without owning a field, have the right to use it and enjoy its fruits, but they enjoyed simply a 'precarious' use of temporal things over which they had no property rights at all. We must distinguish, says Ockham, between *usus iuris*, which is the right of using temporal things without the right over their substance, and *usus facti*, which springs from a mere permission to use the things of another, a permission which is at any moment revocable.[3] The pope had said that the Franciscans could not use food, for example, legitimately without at the same time having a right to do so, without, that is to say, possessing the *usus iuris*; but this is not true, said Ockham; the Franciscans have not the *usus iuris* but only the *usus facti*; they have the *usus nudus* or mere use of temporal things. Mere permission to use them does not confer a right to use them, for the permission is always revocable. The

Franciscans are *usuarii simplices* in a strict sense; their use of temporal things is permitted or tolerated by the Holy See, which possesses both the *dominium perfectum* and the *dominium utile* (or, in Ockham's phrase, *usus iuris*) over these things. They have renounced all property rights whatsoever, and this is true evangelical poverty, after the example of Christ and the Apostles, who neither individually nor in common possessed any temporal things (an opinion which John XXII declared to be heretical).

The actual dispute concerning evangelical poverty does not concern the history of philosophy; but it has been mentioned in order to show how Ockham's preoccupation with a concrete dispute led him to institute an inquiry concerning rights in general and the right of property in particular. His main point was that the right of private property is a natural right, but that it is a right which a man may voluntarily renounce, and that this renunciation may even include the right of use. From the philosophical point of view the chief interest of the discussion lies in the fact that Ockham insisted on the validity of natural rights which are anterior to human conventions, especially in view of the fact that he made the natural law dependent on the divine will. It may appear a gross inconsistency to say on the one hand that the natural law depends on the divine will and on the other hand that there are certain natural rights which share in the fixity of the natural law, and when Ockham asserts, as he does, that the natural law is immutable and absolute he would seem to be underlining the self-contradiction. It is true that, when Ockham asserts the dependence of the moral law on the divine will, he refers primarily to the possibility that God might have created a moral order different from the one He has actually instituted, and, if this were all that he meant, self-contradiction might be avoided by saying that the moral law is absolute and unalterable in the present order. But Ockham meant more than that; he meant that God can dispense from the natural law, or order acts contrary to the natural law, even when the present moral order has been constituted. It may be that the idea of the moral law's dependence on the divine will is more evident in the commentary on the *Sentences* than in Ockham's political works and that the idea of the immutability of the moral law is more evident in the political works than in the commentary on the *Sentences*; but the former idea appears, not only in the commentary, but also in the political works. In the *Dialogus*, for example, he says that there can be no exception from the precepts of the natural law in the strict sense 'unless God specially excepts someone'.[4] The same theme recurs in the *Octo quaestionum decisiones*,[5] and in the *Breviloquium*. The most one can say, then, by way of apology for Ockham, in regard to his consistency or lack of it, is that for him the natural law is unalterable, given the present order created by God, unless God intervenes to alter it in any particular instance. As a pure philosopher Ockham speaks on occasion as though there were absolute moral laws and human rights; but as a theologian he was determined to maintain the divine omnipotence as he understood it; and as he was theologian and philosopher in one it was scarcely possible for him to reconcile the absolute character of the moral law with his interpretation of the divine omnipotence, an omnipotence known by revelation but unprovable by the philosopher.

2. The dispute about evangelical poverty was not the only dispute in which Ockham was engaged; he was also involved in a dispute between the Holy See and the emperor. In 1323 Pope John XXII attempted to intervene in an imperial election, maintaining that papal confirmation was required, and when Ludwig of Bavaria was elected, the pope denounced the election. But in 1328 Ludwig had himself crowned at Rome, after which he declared the Avignon Pope to be deposed and appointed Nicholas V. (This antipope, however, had to make his submission in 1330, when Ludwig had departed for Germany.) The quarrel between pope and emperor lasted on after the death of John XXII in 1334 through the reign of Benedict XII into that of Clement VI, during whose pontificate Ockham died in 1349.

The immediate point at issue in this dispute was the emperor's independence of the Holy See; but the controversy had, of course, a greater importance than that attaching to the question whether or not an imperial election required papal confirmation; the broader issue of the proper relation between Church and State was inevitably involved. Further, the question of the right relation of sovereign to subjects was also raised, though it was raised primarily in regard to the pope's position in the Church. In this controversy Ockham stoutly supported the independence of the State in relation to the Church and in regard to the Church itself he strongly attacked papal 'absolutism'. His most important political work is the *Dialogus*, the first part of which was composed in the reign of John XXII. The *De potestate et iuribus romani imperii,* written in 1338 during the reign of Benedict XII, was subsequently incorporated in the *Dialogus* as the second treatise of the third part. The first treatise of the third part, the *De potestate papae et cleri,* was written with the purpose of dissociating its author from Marsilius of Padua, and it elicited from the latter the *Defensor minor.* The *Octo quaestionum decisiones super potestatem summi pontificis* was directed, partly at least, against the *De iure regni et imperii* of Leopold of Babenberg, while in the *Breviloquium de principatu tyrannico* Ockham gave a clear exposition of his political views. His last work, *De pontificum et imperatorum potestate,* was a diatribe against the Avignon papacy. Other polemical works include the *Compendium errorum papae,* an early publication which sums up Ockham's grievances against John XXII, and the *An princeps pro suo succursu, scilicet guerrae, possit recipere bona ecclesiarum, etiam invito papa,* which was written perhaps between August 1338 and the end of 1339 and was designed to show that Edward III of England was justified in taking subsidies from the clergy, even contrary to the pope's wishes or directions, in his war against the French.

Turning first to the controversy concerning the relations between Church and State one can remark that for the most part Ockham's thought moved within the older mediaeval political outlook. In other words, he gave little consideration to the relation of national monarch to emperor, and he was more concerned with the particular relations between pope and emperor than between Church and State in general. In view of his position as a refugee at the court of Ludwig of Bavaria this was only to be expected, though it is true, of course, that he could not discuss the immediate issue which interested him personally without extending his attention to the wider and more general issue. And, if one looks at Ockham's polemics from the point of view of their influence and in regard to the historical development of Europe, one can say that he did, in effect, concern himself with the relations of Church and State, for the position of the emperor in relation to a national monarch like the king of England was little more than a certain pre-eminence of honour.

In maintaining a clear distinction between the spiritual and temporal powers Ockham was not, of course, propounding any revolutionary theory. He insisted that the supreme head in the spiritual sphere, namely the pope, is not the source of imperial power and authority, and also that papal confirmation is not required in order to validate an imperial election. If the pope arrogates to himself, or attempts to assume, power in the temporal sphere, he is invading a territory over which he has no jurisdiction. The authority of the emperor derives, not from the pope, but from his election, the electors standing in the place of the people. There can be no doubt but that Ockham regarded political power as deriving from God through the people, either immediately, in the event of the people directly choosing a sovereign, or mediately, if the people have agreed, explicitly or implicitly, to some other way of transmitting political authority. The State needs a government and the people cannot avoid choosing a sovereign of some kind, whether emperor, monarch or magistrates; but in no case is the authority derived from, or dependent on, the spiritual power. That Ockham did not intend his denial of the pope's supreme power in temporal matters to apply only in favour of the emperor is made abundantly clear; for example, by the *An princeps pro suo succursu*. All legitimate sovereigns enjoy authority which is not derived from the pope.

3. But, as we have already seen, if Ockham supported the independence of temporal princes in relation to the Church, so far as temporal matters were concerned, he did not reject the temporal authority of the papacy in order to support political absolutism. All men are born free, in the sense that they have a right to freedom, and, though the principle of authority, like the principle of private property, belongs to the natural law, they enjoy a natural right to choose their rulers. The method of choosing a ruler and of transmitting authority from one ruler to his successor depends on human law, and it is obviously not necessary that every successive ruler should be elected; but the fundamental freedom of man to choose and appoint the temporal authority is a right which no power on earth can take from him. The community can, of course, of its own free will establish a hereditary monarchy; but in this case it voluntarily submits itself to the monarch and his legitimate successors, and if the monarch betrays his trust and abuses his authority, the community can assert its freedom by deposing him. 'After the whole world spontaneously consented to the dominion and empire of the Romans, the same empire was a true, just and good empire'; its legitimacy rested on its free acceptance by its subjects.[6] Nobody should be placed over the community ex-

cept by its choice and consent; every people and State is entitled to elect its head if it so wills.[7] If there were any people without a ruler in temporal affairs, the pope would have neither the duty nor the power of appointing rulers for that people, if they wished to appoint their own ruler or rulers.[8]

4. These two important points, namely the independence of the temporal power and the freedom of the people to settle their own form of government if they so choose, were not in themselves novelties. The idea of the two swords, for example, represented the common mediaeval outlook, and when Ockham protested against the tendency of certain popes to arrogate to themselves the position and rights of universal temporal monarchs, he was simply expressing the conviction of most mediaeval thinkers that the spiritual and temporal spheres must be clearly distinguished. Again, all the great mediaeval theologians and philosophers believed in natural rights in some sense and would have rejected the notion that princes possess absolute and unrestricted power. The mediaevals had a respect for law and custom and thoroughly disliked arbitrary power; and the idea that rulers must govern within the general framework of law expressed the general mediaeval outlook. It is difficult to say exactly how St. Thomas Aquinas regarded the problem of the derivation of the sovereign's authority; but he certainly thought of it as limited, as having a definite purpose, and he certainly considered that subjects are not bound to submit to tyrannical government. He recognized that some governments do, or may, derive their authority immediately from the people (ultimately from God); and, though there is no very clear indication that he regarded all governments as necessarily deriving their authority in this manner, he maintained that there can be a resistance to tyranny which is justified and is not to be accounted sedition. A ruler has a trust to fulfil, and if he does not fulfil it but abuses his trust, the community is entitled to depose him. There is good reason, then, for saying, as has been said, that in regard to dislike of arbitrary power and in regard to insistence on law, the principles of Ockham did not substantially differ from those of St. Thomas.

However, even though Ockham's insistence on the distinction of the spiritual and temporal powers and on the fundamental rights of subjects in a political community was not novel, still less revolutionary, if considered as expressing abstract principles, it does not follow that the manner in which he conducted his controversy with the papacy was not part of a general movement which can be called revolutionary. For the dispute between Ludwig of Bavaria and the papacy was one incident in a general movement of which the dispute between Philip the Fair and Boniface VIII had been an earlier symptom; and the direction of the movement, if looked at from the point of view of concrete historical development, was towards the complete independence of the State from the Church, even in spiritual matters. Ockham's thought may have moved within the old categories of papacy and empire, but the gradual consolidation of centralized national States was leading to a breakdown of the balance between the two powers and to the emergence of a political consciousness which found partial expression in the Reformation. Moreover, Ockham's hostility to papal absolutism even within the spiritual sphere, when viewed in the light of his general remarks on the relation of subjects to rulers, was bound to have implications in the sphere of political thought as well. I now turn to his ideas on the pope's position within the Church; though it is worth while noticing beforehand that, though Ockham's ideas on Church government concerned the ecclesiastical sphere and heralded the Conciliar Movement which was to be proximately occasioned by the Great Schism (1378–1417), these ideas were also part of the wider movement which ended in the disintegration of mediaeval Christendom.

5. It is entirely unnecessary to say more than a few words on the subject of Ockham's polemic against the position of the pope within the Church, as this subject belongs to Church history, not to the history of philosophy; but, as already mentioned, the further implications of his ideas on the subject make it desirable to say something about them. Ockham's main contention was that papal absolutism within the Church was unjustified, that it was detrimental to the good of Christendom, and that it should be checked and limited.[9] The means which Ockham suggested for limiting papal power was the establishment of a General Council. Possibly drawing on his experience and knowledge of the constitutions of the mendicant Orders he envisaged religious corporations such as parishes, chapters and monasteries sending chosen representatives to provincial synods. These synods would elect representatives for the General Council, which should include layfolk as well as clergy. It is to be noted that Ockham did not look on the General Council as an organ of

infallible doctrinal pronouncements, even if he thought that it was more likely to be right than the pope alone, but as a limitation to and a check on papal absolutism: he was concerned with ecclesiastical politics, with constitutionalizing the papacy, rather than with purely theological matters. He did not deny that the pope is the successor of St. Peter and the Vicar of Christ, nor did he wish, in principle, to destroy the papal government of the Church; but he regarded the Avignon papacy as going beyond its brief, so to speak, and as being unfit to govern without decisive checks and limitations. No doubt he held heterodox opinions; but his motive in making these suggestions was that of combating the actual exercise of arbitrary and unrestrained power, and that is why his ideas on the constitutionalization of the papacy had implications in the political sphere, even if his ideas, when looked at in relation to the immediate future, must be regarded as heralding the Conciliar Movement.

Chapter Nine

THE OCKHAMIST MOVEMENT: JOHN OF MIRECOURT AND NICHOLAS OF AUTRECOURT

The Ockhamist or nominalist movement – John of Mirecourt – Nicholas of Autrecourt – Nominalism in the universities – Concluding remarks.

1. The phrase 'Ockhamist Movement' is perhaps something of a misnomer. For it might be understood as implying that William of Ockham was the sole fountainhead of the 'modern' current of thought in the fourteenth century and that the thinkers of the movement all derived their ideas from him. Some of these thinkers, like the Franciscan Adam Wodham or Goddam (d. 1358), had indeed been pupils of Ockham, while others, like the Dominican Holkot (d. 1349), were influenced by Ockham's writings without, however, having actually been his pupils. But in some other cases it is difficult to discover how far a given philosopher owed his ideas to Ockham's influence. However, even if from one point of view it may be preferable to speak of the 'nominalist movement' rather than of the 'Ockhamist Movement', it cannot be denied that Ockham was the most influential writer of the movement; and it is only just that the movement should be associated with his name. The names 'nominalism' and 'terminism' were used synonymously to designate the *via moderna;* and the salient characteristic of terminism was the analysis of the function of the term in the proposition, namely the doctrine of *suppositio* or standing-for. As has already been indicated, the theory of *suppositio* can be found in logicians before Ockham; in the writings of Peter of Spain, for example; but it was Ockham who developed the terminist logic in that conceptualist and 'empiricist'

direction which we have come to associate with nominalism. One is justified, therefore, in my opinion, in speaking of the 'Ockhamist Movement', provided that one remembers that the phrase is not meant to imply that Ockham was the direct source of all the developments of that movement.

The development of the terminist logic forms one of the aspects of the movement. In this connection one may mention Richard Swineshead and William Heytesbury, both of whom were associated with Merton College, Oxford. The latter, whose logical writings enjoyed a wide circulation, became chancellor of the university of Oxford in 1371. Another popular logician of the fourteenth century was Richard Billingham. But the technical logical studies of the nominalists and of those influenced by the nominalist movement were frequently associated, as were those of Ockham himself, with a destructive attack on the traditional metaphysics, or rather on the proofs offered in the traditional metaphysics. Sometimes these attacks were based on the view that the traditional lines of proof did not amount to more than probable arguments. Thus according to Richard Swineshead the arguments which had been employed to prove the unicity of God were not demonstrations but dialectical arguments, that is to say, arguments which did not exclude the possibility of the opposite being true or which could not, in the language of the time, be reduced to the principle of contradiction. Sometimes emphasis was placed on our supposed inability to know any substance. If we can have no knowledge of any substance, argued Richard Billingham, we cannot prove the existence of God. Monotheism is a matter of faith, not of philosophical proof.

The relegation of propositions like 'God exists', where the term 'God' is understood as denoting the supreme unique Being, to the sphere of faith does not mean that any philosopher doubted the truth of these propositions: it simply means that he did not think that such propositions can be proved. Nevertheless, this sceptical attitude in regard to metaphysical arguments was doubtless combined, in the case of different philosophers, with varying degrees of insistence on the primacy of faith. A lecturer or professor in the faculty of arts might question the validity of metaphysical arguments on purely logical grounds, while a theologian might also be concerned to emphasize the weakness of the human reason, the supremacy of faith and the transcendent character of revealed truth. Robert Holkot, for example, postulated a 'logic of faith', distinct from and superior to natural logic. He certainly denied the demonstrative character of theistic arguments. Only analytic propositions are absolutely certain. The principle of causality, employed in traditional arguments for God's existence, is not an analytic proposition. From this it follows that philosophical arguments for God's existence cannot amount to more than probable arguments. Theology, however, is superior to philosophy; and in the sphere of dogmatic theology we can see the operation of a logic which is superior to the natural logic employed in philosophy. In particular, that the principle of contradiction is transcended in theology is clear, thought Holkot, from the doctrine of the Trinity. My point is, then, not that the theologians who were influenced by the nominalist criticism of metaphysical 'demonstrations' did not support their criticism by an appeal to logic, but rather that this relative scepticism in philosophy must not be taken without more ado as involving a sceptical attitude towards theological statements considered as statements of fact or as a conscious relegation of dogmatic theology to the sphere of conjecture.

Acceptance of this or that nominalist position did not mean, of course, that a given thinker adopted all the positions maintained by William of Ockham. John of Rodington (d. 1348), for example, who became Provincial of the English Franciscans, doubted the demonstrative character of arguments for God's unicity: but he rejected the notion that the moral law depends simply on the divine will. John of Bassolis (d. 1347), another Franciscan, also questioned the demonstrative character of metaphysical proofs for God's existence, unicity and infinity; but he combined this critical attitude with an acceptance of various Scotist positions. Scotism was naturally a powerful influence in the Franciscan Order, and it produced philosophers like Francis of Meyronnes (d. *c.* 1328), Antoine André (d. *c.* 1320), the *Doctor dulcifluus*, and Francis de Marcia, the *Doctor succinctus*. It is only to be expected, then, that we should find the Scotist and Ockhamist lines of thought meeting and mingling in thinkers like John of Ripa, who lectured at Paris in the early part of the second half of the fourteenth century, and Peter of Candia (d. 1410). Further, in some cases where a thinker was influenced both by the writings of St. Augustine and by Ockhamism, it is not always easy to judge which influence was the stronger on any given point. For example, Thomas Bradwardine (*c.* 1290–1349) appealed to St. Augustine in support of his doctrine of theological determinism; but it is difficult to say how far he was influenced by Augustine's writings taken by themselves and how far he was influenced in his interpretation of Augustine by the Ockhamist emphasis on the divine omnipotence and the divine will. Again, Gregory of Rimini (d. 1358), who became General of the Hermits of St. Augustine, appealed to Augustine in support of his doctrines of the primacy of intuition and the 'sign' function of universal terms. But there is difficulty in deciding to what extent he simply adopted Ockhamist positions and then tried to cover them with the mantle of St. Augustine because he himself was a member of the Augustinian Order, and to what extent he really believed that he found in St. Augustine's writings positions which had been suggested to him by Ockham's philosophy. The Dominican Robert Holkot even tried to show that some of his clearly Ockhamist tenets were really not alien to the mind of St. Thomas Aquinas.

Enough has been said to show that Ockhamism or nominalism, which was associated particularly with the secular clergy, penetrated deeply into the religious Orders. Its influence was felt not only in the Franciscan Order, to which Ockham himself had belonged, but also in the Dominican and other Orders. At the same time, of course, the traditional lines of thought were still maintained, especially in an Order which possessed an official Doctor, as the Dominican Order possessed St. Thomas. Take, for example, the Hermits of St. Augustine, who looked on Giles of Rome as their Doctor. We have seen that Gregory of Rimini, who was General of the Order from 1357 until 1358, was influenced by Ockhamism; but Thomas of Strasbourg, who preceded Gregory as General (1345–1357), had tried to protect the Order from nominalist influence in the name of fidelity to Giles of Rome. In point of fact it did not prove possible to keep out or stamp out the influence of nominalism; but the fact that the Order possessed an official Doctor doubtless encouraged a certain moderation in the degree to which the more extreme nominalist positions were accepted by the sympathizers with the *via moderna*.

One common factor among the nominalists or Ockhamists was, as we have seen, the emphasis they laid on the theory of *suppositio*, the analysis of the different ways in which the terms in a proposition stand for things. It is obvious, however, that one is justified in speaking about 'nominalism' or, if preferred, conceptualism only in the case of philosophers who, like Ockham, maintained that a general term or class-name stands in the proposition for individual things, and for individual things alone. Together with this doctrine, namely that universality belongs only to terms in their logical function, the nominalists also tended to maintain that only those propositions which are reducible to the principle of contradiction are absolutely certain. In other words, they held that the truth of a statement is not absolutely certain unless the opposite cannot be stated without contradiction. Now, no statement of a causal relationship can, they thought, be a statement of this kind. In other words, their theory of universals led the nominalists to an empiricist analysis of the causal relation. Moreover, in so far as the inference from phenomena to substance was an inference from effect to cause, this analysis affected also the nominalist view of the substance-accident metaphysic. If, then, on the one hand only analytic propositions, in the sense of propositions reducible to the principle of contradiction, are absolutely certain, while on the other hand statements about causal relations are empirical or inductive generalizations which enjoy at best only a very high degree of probability, it follows that the traditional metaphysical arguments, resting on the employment of the principle of causality and on the substance-accident metaphysic, cannot be absolutely certain. In the case, then, of statements about God's existence, for example, the nominalists maintained that they owed their certainty not to any philosophical arguments which could be adduced in their favour but to the fact that they were truths of faith, taught by Christian theology. This position naturally tended to introduce a sharp distinction between philosophy and theology. In one sense, of course, a sharp distinction between philosophy and theology had always been recognized, namely in the sense that a distinction had always been recognized between accepting a statement as the result simply of one's own process of reasoning and accepting a statement on divine authority. But a thinker like Aquinas had been convinced that it is possible to prove the 'preambles of faith', such as the statement that a God exists who can make a revelation. Aquinas was also convinced, of course, that the act of faith involves supernatural grace; but the point is that he recognized as strictly provable certain truths which are logically presupposed by the act of faith, even if in most actual cases supernatural faith is operative long before a human being comes to understand, if he ever does advert to or understand, the proofs in question. In the nominalist philosophy, however, the 'preambles of faith' were not regarded as strictly provable, and the bridge between philosophy and theology (so far, that is, as one is entitled to speak of a 'bridge' when faith demands supernatural grace) was thus broken. But the nominalists were not concerned with 'apologetic' considerations. In the Christian Europe of the Middle Ages apologetics were not a matter of such concern as they became for theologians and Catholic philosophers of a later date.

In the foregoing summary of the positions of the nominalists I have used the word 'nominalist' to mean the thoroughgoing nominalist or the thinker who developed the potentialities of nominalism or the 'ideal' nominalist, the nominalist *pur sang.* I have remarked earlier that not all those thinkers who were positively affected by the Ockhamist movement and who may in certain respects be called 'nominalists' adopted all the positions of Ockham. But it will be of use, I hope, to give some account of the philosophical ideas of two thinkers associated with the movement, namely John of Mirecourt and Nicholas of Autrecourt, the latter of whom particularly was an extremist. Acquaintance with the philosophy of Nicholas of Autrecourt is an effective means, if further means are still needed, of dispelling the illusion that there was no variety of opinions in mediaeval philosophy about important topics. After outlining the thought of these two men I shall conclude the chapter with some remarks on the influence of nominalism in the universities, especially in the new universities which were founded in the latter part of the fourteenth century and during the fifteenth.

2. John of Mirecourt, who seems to have been a Cistercian (he was called *monachus albus,* 'the white monk'), lectured on the *Sentences* of Peter Lombard at the Cistercian College of St. Bernard in Paris. Of these lectures, which were given in 1344–5, there exist two versions. As a number of his propositions were immediately attacked, John of Mirecourt issued an explanation and justification of his position; but none the less some 41 propositions were condemned in 1347 by the chancellor of the university and the faculty of theology. This led to the publication by John of another work in defence of his position. These two 'apologies', the first explaining or defending 63 suspected propositions, the second doing the same for the 41 condemned propositions, have been edited by F. Stegmüller.[1]

Two types of knowledge are distinguished by John of Mirecourt; and he distinguishes them according to the quality of our assent to different propositions. Sometimes our assent is 'evident', which means, he says, that it is given without fear, actual or potential, of error. At other times our assent is given with fear, actual or potential, of error, as, for example, in the case of suspicion or of opinion. But it is necessary to make a further distinction. Sometimes we give an assent without fear of error because we see clearly the evident truth of the proposition to which we assent. This happens in the case of the principle of contradiction and of those principles and conclusions which are ultimately reducible to the principle of contradiction. If we see that a proposition rests upon or is reducible to the principle of contradiction, we see that the opposite of that proposition, its negation that is to say, is inconceivable and impossible. At other times, however, we give an assent without fear of error to propositions the truth of which is not intrinsically evident, though it is assured in virtue of irrefutable testimony. The revealed truths of faith are of this kind. We know, for example, only by revelation that there are three Persons in one God.

Leaving out of account the revealed truths of faith we have, then, so far, propositions to which we assent without fear of error because they are reducible to the primary self-evident principle, the principle of contradiction, and propositions to which we assent with fear of error (for example, 'I think that that object in the distance is a cow'). Assents of the first kind are called by John of Mirecourt *assensus evidentes*, assents of the second kind *assensus inevidentes*. But we must now distinguish two kinds of *assensus evidentes*. First of all, there are evident assents in the strictest and most proper meaning of the phrase. Assent of this kind is given to the principle of contradiction, to principles which are reducible to the principle of contradiction and to conclusions which rest upon the principle of contradiction. In the case of such propositions we have *evidentia potissima*. Secondly, there are assents which are indeed given without fear of error but which are not given in virtue of the proposition's intimate connection with the principle of contradiction. If I give my assent to a proposition based on experience (for example, 'there are stones') I give it without fear of error but I give it in virtue of my experience of the external world, not in virtue of the proposition's reducibility to the principle of contradiction. In the case of such propositions we have, not *evidentia potissima*, but *evidentia naturalis*. John of Mirecourt defines this 'natural evidence' as the evidence by which we give our assent to a thing's existence without any fear of error, this assent being brought about by causes which naturally necessitate our assent.

The above account of John's doctrine on human assents comes from his first apology. He is there explaining the 44th proposition, which had been made an object of attack. The proposition runs as follows: 'It has not been demonstratively proved from propositions which are self-evident or which possess an evidence reducible by us to the certitude of the primary principle that God exists, or that there is a most perfect being, or that one thing is the cause of another thing, or that any created thing has a cause without this cause having its own cause and so on to infinity, or that a thing cannot as a total cause produce something nobler than itself, or that it is impossible for something to be produced which is nobler than anything which (now) exists.' In particular, then, the proofs of God's existence do not rest on self-evident propositions or on propositions which we are capable of reducing to the principle of contradiction, which is the primary self-evident principle. John's adversaries interpreted his doctrine as meaning that no proof of God's existence is of such a kind that it compels assent once it is understood, and that we are not certain, so far as philosophy goes, of God's existence. In answer John observes that the proofs of God's existence rest on experience and that no proposition which is the result of experience of the world is reducible by us to the principle of contradiction. It is clear from his teaching in general, however, that he made one exception to this general rule, namely in the case of the proposition which asserts the existence of the thinker or speaker. If I say that I deny or even doubt my own existence I am contradicting myself, for I cannot deny or even doubt my existence without affirming my existence. On this point John of Mirecourt followed St. Augustine. But this particular proposition stands by itself. No other proposition which is the result of sense-experience, or experience of the external world, is reducible by us to the principle of contradiction. No proposition of this kind, then, enjoys *evidentia potissima*. But John denied that he meant that all such propositions are doubtful. They do not enjoy *evidentia potissima* but they enjoy *evidentia naturalis*. Although propositions founded on experience of the external world are not evident in the same way as the principle of contradiction is evident, 'it does not follow from this that we must doubt about them any more than about the first principle. From this it is clear that I do not intend to deny any experience, any knowledge, any evidence. It is even clear that I hold altogether the opposite opinion to those who would say that it is not evident to them that there is a man or that there is a stone, on the ground that it might appear to them that these things are so without their being really so. I do not mean to deny that these things are evident to us and known by us, but only that they are not known to us by the supreme kind of knowledge (*scientia potissima*).'

Analytic propositions, that is to say propositions which are reducible by analysis to the self-evident principle of contradiction, are thus absolutely certain, and this absolute certainty attaches also to each one's affirmation of his own existence. Apart from this last affirmation all propositions which are the result of and express experimental knowledge of the world enjoy only 'natural evidence'. But what does John of Mirecourt mean by 'natural evidence'? Does this mean simply that we spontaneously give our assent in virtue of a natural unavoidable propensity to assent? If so, does it or does it not follow that the propositions to which we give this kind of assent are certain? John admits that error is possible in the case of some empirical propositions: he could hardly do otherwise. On the other hand he asserts that 'we cannot err in many things (propositions) which accord with our experiences'. Again, he could hardly say anything else, unless he were prepared to admit that his adversaries had interpreted his doctrine correctly. But it seems to be clear that John of Mirecourt accepted the Ockhamist doctrine that sensitive knowledge of the external world could be miraculously caused and conserved by God in the absence of the object. This theme was treated by him at the beginning of his commentary on the *Sentences*. It is probably safe to say, then, that for him 'natural evidence' meant that we naturally assent to the existence of what we sense, though it would be possible for us to be in error, if, that is to say, God were to work a miracle. There is no contradiction in the idea of God working such a miracle. If, therefore, we use the word 'certain' in the sense not only of feeling certain but also of having objective and evident certainty, we are certain of the principle of contradiction and of propositions reducible thereto and each one is certain of his own existence, the infallible character of the intuition of one's own existence being shown by the connection of the proposition affirming one's own existence with the principle of contradiction; but we are not certain of the existence of external objects, however certain we may *feel*. If we care to bring in Descartes' hypothetical 'evil genius', we can say that for John of Mirecourt we are not certain of the existence of the external world, unless God assures us that it exists. All proofs, then, of God's existence which rest upon our knowledge of the external world are uncertain; at least they are not 'demonstrative', in the sense of being reducible to the principle of contradiction or of resting on it. In his first apology John openly says that the opposite of the proposition 'God exists' implies a contradiction; but he goes on to observe that a proposition of this kind does not enjoy the evidence which attaches to the first principle. Why not? Because we arrive at the knowledge expressed in such propositions by reflection on the data of sense-experience, in which we can err, although 'we cannot err in many things (propositions) which accord with our experiences'. Does he mean that we can err in particular empirical judgments, but that we cannot err in regard to a conclusion like the existence of God which follows on the totality of sense-experience rather than on particular empirical judgments? In this case what of the possibility of our having sense-experience when no object is present? This is, no doubt, a limiting possibility and we have no reason to suppose that it is an actuality so far as the totality of sense-experience is concerned; but none the less it remains a possibility. I do not see how the traditional proofs of God's existence can have more than moral certainty or, if you like, the highest degree of probability on John's premisses. In his apology he may make an attempt to justify his position by having it both ways; but it seems clear that for him the proofs of God's existence cannot be demonstrative in the sense in which he understands demonstrative. Leaving out of account the question whether John was right or wrong in what he said, he would have been more consistent, I think, if he had openly admitted that for him the proofs of God's existence, based on sense-experience, are not absolutely certain.

The principle of causality, according to John of Mirecourt, is not analytic; that is to say, it cannot be reduced to the principle of contradiction or be shown to depend upon it in such a way that the denial of the principle of causality involves a contradiction. On the other hand it does not follow that we have to doubt the truth of the principle of causality: we have 'natural evidence', even if we have not got *evidentia potissima.* Again the question arises exactly what is meant by 'natural evidence'. It can hardly mean objectively irrefutable evidence, for if the truth of the principle of causality were objectively so clear that it could not possibly be denied and that its opposite was inconceivable, it would surely follow that its evidence is reducible to the evidence of the principle of contradiction. When John speaks of 'causes naturally necessitating assent', it looks very much as though he meant that, though we can conceive the possibility of the principle of causality not being true, we are obliged by nature to think and act in the concrete as though it were true. From this it would appear to follow that for all practical purposes the proofs of God's existence which rest on the validity of the principle of causality are 'evident', but that none the less we can conceive of their not being cogent. Perhaps this means little more than that the proofs of God's existence cannot compel assent in the same way as a mathematical theorem, for example, can compel assent. John's opponents understood him as meaning that one cannot prove God's existence and that God's existence is therefore uncertain; but when he denied that the proofs are demonstrative he was using the word 'demonstrative' in a special sense, and, if his apology represents his real teaching, he did not mean to say that we must be sceptical concerning God's existence. There can, indeed, be little question of his having intended to teach scepticism; but on the other hand it is clear that he did not regard the proofs of God's existence as possessing the same degree of cogency which St. Thomas would have attributed to them.

In criticizing in this way the proofs of God's existence John of Mirecourt showed himself to be a thinker who had his place in the Ockhamist movement. He showed the same thing by his doctrine concerning the moral law. Proposition 51, as contained in the first apology, runs as follows. 'God can cause any act of the will in the will, even hatred of Himself; I doubt, however, whether anything which was created in the will by God alone would be hatred of God, unless the will conserved it actively and effectively.' According to the way of speaking common among the Doctors, says John, hatred of God involves a deformity in the will, and we must not allow that God could, as total cause, cause hatred of

Himself in the human will. Absolutely speaking, however, God could cause hatred of Himself in the will, and if He did so, the man in question would not hate God culpably. Again, in the second apology the 25th condemned proposition is to the effect that 'hatred of the neighbour is not demeritorious except for the fact that it has been prohibited by God'. John proceeds to explain that he does not mean that hatred of the neighbour is not contrary to the natural law; he means that a man who hates his neighbour runs the risk of eternal punishment only because God has prohibited hatred of the neighbour. In regard to the 41st proposition of the first apology John similarly observes that nothing can be 'demeritorious' unless it is prohibited by God. It can, however, be contrary to the moral law without being demeritorious.

Needless to say, John of Mirecourt had no intention of denying our duty to obey the moral law; his aim was to emphasize the supremacy and omnipotence of God. Similarly he seems, though extremely tentatively, to have favoured the opinion of St. Peter Damian that God could bring it about that the world should never have been, that is to say, that God could bring it about that the past should not have happened. He allows that this undoing of the fact cannot take place *de potentia Dei ordinata*; but, whereas one might well expect him to appeal to the principle of contradiction in order to show that the undoing of the past is absolutely impossible, he says that this absolute impossibility is not evident to him. 'I was unwilling to lay claim to knowledge which I did not possess' (first apology, proposition 5). He does not say that it is possible for God to bring it about that the past should not have happened; he says that the impossibility of God's doing this is not evident to him. John of Mirecourt was always careful in his statements.

He shows a similar care in the way he hedges over those statements which appear to teach theological determinism and which may betray the influence of Thomas Bradwardine's *De Causa Dei*. According to John, God is the cause of moral deformity, of sin that is to say, just as He is the cause of natural deformity. God is the cause of blindness by not supplying the power of vision; and He is the cause of moral deformity by not supplying moral rectitude. John qualifies this statement, however, by observing that it is perhaps true that while a natural defect can be the total cause of natural deformity, a moral defect is not the total cause of moral deformity because moral deformity (sin), in order to exist, must proceed from a will (first apology, proposition 50). In his commentary on the *Sentences*[2] he first observes that it seems to him possible to concede that God is the cause of moral deformity, and then remarks that the common teaching of the Doctors is the very opposite. But they say the opposite since, in their eyes, to say that God is the cause of sin is to say that God acts sinfully, and that it is impossible for God to act sinfully is clear to John too. But it does not follow from this, he insists, that God cannot be the cause of moral deformity. God causes the moral deformity by not supplying moral rectitude; but the sin proceeds from the will, and it is the human being who is guilty. Therefore, if John says that God is not the total cause of sin, he does not mean that God causes the positive element in the act of the will while the human being causes the privation of right order: for him God can be said to cause both, though the privation of right order cannot be realized except in and through a will. The will is the 'effective' cause, not God, though God can be called the 'efficacious' cause in that He wills efficaciously that there should be no rectitude in the will. Nothing can happen unless God wills it, and if God wills it, He wills it efficaciously, for His will is always fulfilled. God causes the sinful act even in its specification as a sinful act of a certain kind; but He does not cause it sinfully.

John considered that the real distinction between accidents and substances is known only by faith. 'I think that except for the faith many would perhaps have said that everything is a substance.'[3] Apparently he affirmed (at least he was understood as affirming) that 'it is probable, as far as the natural light of reason is concerned, that there are no accidents distinct from substance, but that everything is a substance; and except for the faith, this would be or could be probable' (43rd proposition of first apology). For example, 'it can be said with probability that thinking or willing is not something distinct from the soul, but that it is the soul itself' (proposition 42). John defends himself by saying that the reasons for affirming a distinction between substance and accident have more force than the reasons which can be given for denying a distinction; but he adds that he does not know if the arguments for affirming it can rightly be called demonstrations. It is clear that he did not think that these arguments amounted to demonstrations; he accepted the distinction as certain only on faith.

It is difficult to ascertain with any degree of certainty

precisely what John of Mirecourt's personal opinions actually were, owing to the way in which he explains away in his apologies what he had said in his lectures on the *Sentences*. When John protests that he is simply retailing other people's opinions or when he remarks that he is merely putting forward a possible point of view without affirming that it is true, is he thoroughly sincere or is he being diplomatic? One can scarcely give any definite answer. However, I turn now to an even more extreme and thoroughgoing adherent of the new movement.

3. Nicholas of Autrecourt, who was born about the year 1300 in the diocese of Verdun, studied at the Sorbonne between 1320 and 1327. In due course he lectured on the *Sentences*, on Aristotle's *Politics*, etc. In 1338 he obtained a Prebend's stall in the Cathedral of Metz. Already in his introductory lecture on the *Sentences* of Peter Lombard, Nicholas had indicated his departure from the thought of previous philosophers, and a continuation of this attitude resulted in a letter from Pope Benedict XII to the Bishop of Paris on November 21st, 1340, in which the latter was instructed to see that Nicholas, together with certain other offenders, put in a personal appearance at Avignon within a month. The pope's death led to a postponement of the investigation of Nicholas's opinions; but after the coronation of Clement VI on May 19th, 1342, the matter was taken up again. The new pope entrusted the examination of Nicholas's opinions to a commission under the presidency of Cardinal William Curti, and Nicholas was invited to explain and defend his ideas. He was given the opportunity of defending himself in the pope's presence, and his replies to the objections brought against his doctrine were taken into account. But when it became clear what the verdict would be Nicholas fled from Avignon; and it is possible, though not certain, that he took refuge for the time being at the court of Ludwig of Bavaria. In 1346 he was sentenced to burn his writings publicly at Paris and to recant the condemned propositions. This he did on November 25th, 1347. He was also expelled from the teaching body of the university of Paris. Of his later life little is known, save for the fact that he became an official of the Cathedral of Metz on August 6th, 1350. Presumably he lived 'happily ever after'.

Of Nicholas's writings we possess the first two letters of a series of nine which he wrote to the Franciscan Bernard of Arezzo, one of his principal critics, and a large part of a letter which he wrote to a certain Aegidius (Giles). We also possess a letter from Aegidius to Nicholas. In addition, the lists of condemned propositions contain excerpts from other letters of Nicholas to Bernard of Arezzo together with some other fragments. All these documents have been edited by Dr. Joseph Lappe.[4] We possess also a treatise by Nicholas which begins *Exigit ordo executionis* and which is referred to as the *Exigit*. It has been edited by J. R. O'Donnell, together with Nicholas's theological writing *Utrum visio creaturae rationalis beatificabilis per Verbum possit intendi naturaliter*.[5] There is further a note by John of Mirecourt about Nicholas's doctrine on causality.[6]

At the beginning of his second letter to Bernard of Arezzo Nicholas remarks that the first principle to be laid down is that 'contradictions cannot be true at the same time'.[7] The principle of contradiction, or rather of non-contradiction, is the primary principle, and its primacy is to be accepted both in the negative sense, namely that there is no more ultimate principle, and in the positive sense, namely that the principle positively precedes and is presupposed by every other principle. Nicholas is arguing that the principle of non-contradiction is the ultimate basis of all natural certitude, and that while any other principle which is put forward as the basis of certitude is reducible to the principle of non-contradiction, the latter is not reducible to any other principle. If any principle other than the principle of non-contradiction is proposed as the basis of certitude, that is, if a principle which is not reducible to the principle of non-contradiction is proposed as the basis of certitude, the proposed principle may appear to be certain but its opposite will not involve a contradiction. But in this case the apparent certitude can never be transformed into genuine certitude. It is only the principle of non-contradiction which bears its own guarantee on its face, so to speak. The reason why we do not doubt the principle of non-contradiction is simply that it cannot be denied without contradiction. In order, then, for any other principle to be certain, its denial must involve a contradiction. But in that case it is reducible to the principle of non-contradiction, in the sense that it is certain in virtue of that principle. The principle of non-contradiction must therefore be the primary principle. It is to be remarked that it is not the truth of the principle of non-contradiction which is in question but its primacy. Nicholas tries to show that any genuine certitude rests ultimately on this principle, and he does it by showing that any principle which did not rest on, or was not reducible to, the principle of non-contradiction would not be genuinely certain.

Any certitude which we have in the light of the principle of non-contradiction is, says Nicholas, genuine certitude, and not even the divine power could deprive it of this character. Further, all genuinely certain propositions possess the same degree of evidence. It makes no difference whether a proposition is immediately or mediately reducible to the principle of non-contradiction. If it is not reducible to the principle of non-contradiction, it is not certain; and if it is reducible, it is equally certain, whether it is immediately or mediately reducible. In geometry, for example, a proposition is not less certain because it happens to be the conclusion of a long chain of reasoning, provided that it is rightly demonstrated in the light of the primary principle. Apart from the certitude of faith there is no other certitude than the certitude of the principle of non-contradiction and of propositions which are reducible to that principle.

In a syllogistic argument, then, the conclusion is certain only if it is reducible to the principle of non-contradiction. What is the necessary condition of this reducibility? The conclusion, says Nicholas, is reducible to the primary principle only if it is identical with the antecedent or with a part of what is signified by the antecedent. When this is the case it is impossible to affirm the antecedent and deny the conclusion or to deny the conclusion and affirm the antecedent without contradiction. If the antecedent is certain, the conclusion is also certain. For example, in the inference 'all X's are Y, therefore this X is Y' the conclusion is identical with part of what is signified by the antecedent. It is impossible, without contradiction, to affirm the antecedent and deny the conclusion. That is, if it is certain that all X's are Y, it is certain that any particular X is Y.

How does this criterion of certitude affect factual knowledge? Bernard of Arezzo maintained that because God can cause an intuitive act in the human being without the cooperation of any secondary cause we are not entitled to argue that a thing exists because it is seen. This view was similar to that of Ockham, though Bernard apparently did not add Ockham's qualification that God could not produce in us evident assent to the existence of a non-existent thing, since this would involve a contradiction. Nicholas maintained, though, that Bernard's view led to scepticism, for on his view we should have no means of achieving certitude concerning the existence of anything. In the case of immediate perception the act of perception is not a sign from which we infer the existence of something distinct from the act. To say, for example, that I perceive a colour is simply to say that the colour appears to me: I do not see the colour and then infer its existence. The act of perceiving a colour and the act of being aware that I perceive a colour are one and the same act: I do not perceive a colour and then have to find some guarantee that I actually do perceive a colour. Immediate cognition is its own guarantee. A contradiction would be involved in saying that a colour appears and at the same time that it does not appear. In his first letter to Bernard, Nicholas says, therefore, that in his opinion 'I am evidently certain of the objects of the five senses and of my acts.'[8] Against what he regarded as scepticism, then, Nicholas maintained that immediate cognition, whether it takes the form of sense-perception or of perception of our interior acts, is certain and evident; and he explained the certitude of this knowledge by identifying the direct act of perception and the self-conscious awareness of this act of perception. In this case a contradiction would be involved in affirming that I have an act of perception and in denying that I am aware that I have an act of perception. The act of perceiving a colour is the same as the appearing of the colour to me, and the act of perceiving the colour is identical with the act of being aware that I perceive a colour. To say that I perceive a colour and to say that the colour does not exist or that I am not aware that I perceive a colour would involve me in a contradiction.

Nicholas thus admitted as certain and evident not only analytic propositions but also immediate perception.[9] But he did not think that from the existence of one thing we can infer with certainty the existence of another thing. The reason why we cannot do this is that in the case of two things which are really different from one another it is possible without logical contradiction to affirm the existence of the one thing and deny the existence of the other. If *B* is identical either with the whole of A or with part of A, it is not possible without contradiction to affirm the existence of A and deny that of *B*; and if the existence of A is certain the existence of *B* is also certain. But if *B* is really distinct from A no contradiction is involved in affirming A's existence and yet at the same time denying the existence of *B*. In the second letter to Bernard of Arezzo Nicholas makes the following assertion. 'From the fact that something is known to exist it cannot be inferred evidently, with, that is, evidence reducible to the first principle or to the certitude of the first principle, that another thing exists.'[10]

Bernard of Arezzo tried to counter Nicholas's assertion by what he evidently regarded as common-sense examples to the contrary. For instance, there is a white colour. But a white colour cannot exist without a substance. Therefore there is a substance. The conclusion of this syllogism is, said Bernard, certain. Nicholas's answer was on the following lines. If it is assumed that whiteness is an accident, and if it is assumed that an accident inheres in a substance and cannot exist without it, the conclusion is indeed certain. In the first place, however, the example would be irrelevant to the discussion. For what Nicholas asserted was that one cannot infer with certainty the existence of one thing from the existence of another. In the second place the assumptions that whiteness is an accident and that an accident necessarily inheres in a substance render the argument hypothetical. If whiteness is an accident and if an accident necessarily inheres in a substance, then, given this whiteness, there is a substance in which it inheres. But Nicholas would not admit that there is any compelling reason why these assumptions should be accepted. Bernard's argument conceals its assumptions. It does not show that one can argue with certainty from the existence of one thing to the existence of another thing, for Bernard has assumed that whiteness inheres in a substance. The fact that one sees a colour warrants one's concluding that a substance exists, only if one has assumed that a colour is an accident and that an accident necessarily inheres in a substance. But to assume this is to assume what has to be proved. Bernard's argument is therefore a concealed vicious circle.

Nicholas commented in a similar manner on another example brought by Bernard in order to show that one can argue with certainty from the existence of one thing to the existence of another thing. Fire is applied to tow, and there is no obstacle; therefore there will be heat. Either, said Nicholas, the consequent is identical with the antecedent or with part of it or it is not. In the first case the example would be irrelevant. For the argument would not be an argument from the existence of one thing to the existence of another thing. In the second case there would be two different propositions of which the one could be affirmed and the other denied without contradiction. 'Fire is applied to tow and there is no obstacle' and 'there will not be heat' are not contradictory propositions. And if they are not contradictory propositions the conclusion cannot be certain with the certitude which comes from reducibility to the first principle. Yet this, as has been agreed, is the only certitude.

From this position of Nicholas, that the existence of one thing cannot with certainty be inferred from that of another, it follows that no proposition which asserts that because A happens *B* will happen or that because *B* exists A exists, where A and *B* are distinct things, is or can be certain. Apart, then, from the immediate perception of sense-data (colours, for example) and of our acts no empirical knowledge is or can be certain. No causal argument can be certain. We doubtless believe in necessary connections in nature; but logic cannot detect them, and propositions which state them cannot be certain. What, then, is the reason of our belief in causal connections? Nicholas apparently explained this in terms of the experience of repeated sequences which gives rise to the expectation that if *B* has followed A in the past it will do so again in the future. Nicholas, it is true, affirmed that we cannot have probable knowledge that *B* will follow A in the future, unless we have evident certitude that at some time in the past *B* has followed A; but he did not mean that we cannot have probable knowledge that *B* will follow A in the future, unless we have evident certitude in the past of a necessary causal connection between A and *B*. What he meant, in terms of his own example in his second letter to Bernard, was that I cannot have probable knowledge that if I put my hand to the fire it will become warm, unless I have evident certitude of warmth in my hand having followed my putting my hand to the fire in the past. 'If it was once evident to me when I put my hand to the fire that I became warm, it is now probable to me that if I put my hand to the fire I should become warm.'[11] Nicholas considered that repeated experience of the coexistence of two things or of the regular sequence of distinct events increases the probability, from the *subjective* point of view, of similar experiences in the future; but repeated experience does not add anything to the objective evidence.[12]

It is clear that Nicholas considered that the possibility of God acting immediately as a causal agent, without, that is, using any secondary cause, rendered it impossible to argue with absolute certainty from the existence of one created thing to the existence of another created thing. He also argued against Bernard that on the principles enunciated by the latter it would be equally impossible. But the main interest of Nicholas's discussion of causality lies in the fact that he did not simply argue from the universally admitted doctrine of the divine omnipotence (universally admitted as a theological doctrine at any rate) but approached the question on a purely philosophical level.

It is to be noted that Nicholas did not deny that we can have certitude concerning the coexistence of appearances of *A* and *B*. All that is required is that we should actually have the two perceptions at once. But he did deny that one can infer with certainty the existence of the non-apparent from the existence of an appearance. He would not allow, then, that one can infer with certainty the existence of any substance. In order to know with certainty the existence of any material substance we should have either to perceive it directly, intuitively, or to infer its existence with certainty from the appearances or phenomena. But we do not perceive material substances, according to Nicholas. If we did, even the uneducated (the *rustici*) would perceive them. And this is not the case. Moreover, we cannot infer their existence with certainty, for the existence of one thing cannot be logically deduced from the existence of another thing.

In his ninth letter to Bernard, Nicholas asserted that 'these inferences are not evident: there is an act of understanding: therefore there is an intellect; there is an act of willing: therefore there is a will'.[13] This statement suggests that according to Nicholas we have no more certainty of the soul's existence as a substance than we have of material substances. Elsewhere, however, he states that 'Aristotle never had evident knowledge of any substance other than his own soul, understanding by "substance" something different from the objects of our five senses and from our formal experience.'[14] Again, 'we have no certitude concerning a substance joined to matter other than our soul'.[15] Statements like this have led some historians to conclude that Nicholas admitted that we have certitude about the knowledge of the soul as a spiritual substance. They accordingly interpret his remarks about our not being entitled to infer the existence of the intellect from the existence of acts of understanding and the existence of the will from the existence of acts of volition as an attack on the faculty psychology. This is certainly a possible interpretation, though it might be considered odd if Nicholas directed his attack simply against the theory of distinct faculties which had already been subjected to criticism by William of Ockham, for example. But the *Exigit*[16] seems to imply, though it does not say so clearly, that we have no direct awareness of the soul. And in this case it would appear to follow, on Nicholas's premisses, that we have no natural knowledge of the soul's existence as a substance. The statement that Aristotle had no certain knowledge of any substance other than his own soul may be analogous to the assertion in the fifth letter to Bernard of Arezzo that we do not know with certainty that there is any efficient cause other than God. For his general position shows that in Nicholas's opinion we have no natural or philosophical certain knowledge that even God is an efficient cause. It is true that if the parallel between the two statements is pushed, it would seem to follow that Aristotle, according to Nicholas, enjoyed the certainty of faith about the existence of his soul as a spiritual substance; and Nicholas cannot possibly have meant to say this. But it is not necessary to interpret his remarks so strictly. However, it is difficult to be sure whether he did or did not make an exception in favour of our knowledge of our own souls from his general view that we have no certain knowledge of the existence of substances considered as distinct from phenomena.

It is evident that in his critique of causality and substance Nicholas anticipated the position of Hume; and the similarity is all the more striking if he did in fact deny that we have any certain knowledge of the existence of any substance, material or spiritual. But Dr. Weinberg is undoubtedly right, I think, in pointing out that Nicholas was not a phenomenalist. Nicholas thought that one cannot infer with certainty the existence of a non-apparent entity from the existence of phenomena; but he certainly did not think this means that one can infer its non-existence. In the sixth letter to Bernard he laid it down that 'from the fact that one thing exists, it cannot be inferred with certainty that another thing does not exist'.[17] Nicholas did not say that only phenomena exist or that affirmations of the existence of metaphenomenal entities are nonsensical. All he said was that the existence of phenomena does not enable us to infer with certainty the existence of the metaphenomenal or non-apparent. It is one thing to say, for example, that we are unable to prove that there is anything in a material object other than what appears to the senses, and it is another thing to say that there actually is no substance. Nicholas was not a dogmatic phenomenalist. I do not mean to imply by this that Hume was a dogmatic phenomenalist, for he was not, whatever objections his (and Nicholas's) critical analyses of causality and substance may be open to. My point is simply that one must not conclude from Nicholas's denial of the demonstrability of the existence of substances that he actually denied the existence of all substances or said that their non-existence could be proved.

It is obvious enough that Nicholas's critique of causality and substance had important repercussions in regard to his attitude towards the traditional philosophical theology. Although Nicholas does not say so in clear and explicit terms, it would seem to follow from his general principles that it is not possible to prove the existence of God as efficient cause. In the fifth letter to Bernard he remarks that God may be the sole efficient cause, since one cannot prove that there is any natural efficient cause. But to say that God may be the sole efficient cause is not to say that He is the sole efficient cause or, indeed, that He can be proved to be an efficient cause at all. Nicholas meant merely that for all we know or can establish to the contrary God may be the sole efficient cause. As to our being able to prove that God actually is efficient cause, this is excluded by the general principle that we cannot infer with certainty the existence of one thing from the existence of another thing.

The causal or cosmological argument for God's existence could not, then, be a demonstrative argument on Nicholas's premisses. Nor could St. Thomas's fourth or fifth arguments be admitted as proofs yielding certain conclusions. We cannot, says Nicholas in the fifth letter to Bernard, prove that one thing is or is not nobler than another thing. Neither inspection of one thing nor comparison of two or more things is able to prove a hierarchy of degrees of being from the point of view of value. 'If anything whatever is pointed out, nobody knows evidently that it may not exceed all other things in value.'[18] And Nicholas does not hesitate to draw the conclusion that if by the term 'God' we understand the noblest being, nobody knows with certainty whether any given thing may not be God. If, then, we cannot establish with certainty an objective scale of perfection, St. Thomas's fourth argument obviously cannot be considered a demonstrative argument. As to the argument from finality, St. Thomas's fifth argument, this is ruled out by Nicholas's statement in the same letter that 'no one knows evidently that one thing is the end (that is, final cause) of another'.[19] One cannot establish by inspection or analysis of any one thing that it is the final cause of another thing, nor is there any way of demonstrating it with certainty. We see a certain series of events, but final causality is not demonstrable.

Nicholas did, however, admit a probable argument for God's existence. Assuming as probable that we have an idea of the good as a standard for judging about the contingent relations between things,[20] and assuming that the order of the universe is such that it would satisfy a mind operating with the criterion of goodness and fitness, we can argue first that all things are so interconnected that one thing can be said to exist for the sake of another and secondly that this relationship between things is intelligible only in the light of the hypothesis that all things are subjected to an ultimate end, the supreme good or God. It might well appear that an argument of this kind would be no more than an entirely unfounded hypothesis, and that it could not, on Nicholas's own principles, amount to a probable argument. But Nicholas did not deny that we can have some sort of evidence enabling us to form a conjectural hypothesis which may be more or less probable, though it may not be certain as far as we are concerned. It might be true; it might even be a necessary truth; but we could not know that it was true, though we could believe it to be true. Besides theological belief, that is, faith in revealed truths, there is room for a belief which rests on arguments that are more or less probable.

Nicholas's probable argument for God's existence was part of the positive philosophy which he put forward as probable. It is not, in my opinion, worth while going into this philosophy in any detail. Apart from the fact that it was proposed as a probable hypothesis, its various parts are by no means always consistent with one another. One may mention, however, that for Nicholas the corruptibility of things is probably inconsistent with the goodness of the universe. Positively expressed this means that things are probably eternal. In order to show that this supposition cannot be ruled out by observation Nicholas argued that the fact that we see B succeeding A does not warrant our concluding that A has ceased to exist. We may not see A any more, but we do not see that A does not exist any more. And we cannot establish by reasoning that it does not any longer exist. If we could, we could establish by reasoning that nothing exists which is not observed, and this we cannot do. The Aristotelian doctrine of change is by no means certain. Moreover, the corruption of substances can be explained much better on an atomistic hypothesis than on Aristotelian principles. Substantial change may mean simply that one collocation of atoms is succeeded by another, while accidental change many mean the addition of fresh atoms to an atomic complex or the subtraction of some atoms from that complex. It is probable that the atoms are eternal and that precisely the same combinations occur in the periodic cycles which eternally recur.

As to the human soul, Nicholas maintained the hypothesis of immortality. But his suggestions on this matter are closely connected with a curious explanation of knowledge. As all things are eternal, it may be supposed that in knowledge the soul or mind enters into a temporary union with the object of knowledge. And the same can be said of imagination. The soul enters into a state of conjunction with images, but the images themselves are eternal. This hypothesis throws light, in Nicholas's opinion, on the nature of immortality. We may suppose that to good souls noble thoughts come after death, while to bad souls come evil thoughts. Or we may suppose that good souls enter into union with a better collection of atoms and are disposed to better experiences than they received in their previous embodied states, while evil souls enter into union with worse atoms and are disposed to receive more evil experiences and thoughts than in their previous embodied states. Nicholas claimed that this hypothesis allowed for the Christian doctrine of rewards and punishments after death; but he added a prudential qualification. His statements were, he said, more probable than the statements which had for a long time seemed probable. None the less, someone might turn up who would deprive his own statements of probability; and in view of this possibility the best thing to do is to adhere to the Biblical teaching on rewards and punishments. This line of argument was called in the *Articles of Cardinal Curti* a 'foxy excuse' (*excusatio vulpina*).[21]

Nicholas's positive philosophy was obviously at variance on some points with Catholic theology. And indeed Nicholas did not hesitate to say that his statements were more probable than the contradictory assertions. But one must interpret this attitude with some care. Nicholas did not state that his doctrines were true and the opposite doctrines false: he said that if the propositions which were contradictory to his own were considered simply in regard to their probability, that is, as probable conclusions of reason, they were less probable than his own statements. For example, the theological doctrine that the world has not existed from eternity is for him certainly true, if it is considered as a revealed truth. But if one attends simply to the philosophical arguments which can be adduced in favour of its truth, one must admit, according to Nicholas, that they are less probable than the philosophical arguments which can be adduced in favour of the contradictory proposition. One is not entitled, however, to conclude that the contradictory proposition is not true. For all we know it may even be a necessary truth. Probability has to be interpreted in terms of the natural evidence available to us at any given moment, and a proposition may be for us more probable than its contradictory even though it is in fact false and its contradictory true. Nicholas did not propose a double-truth theory; nor did he deny any defined doctrines of the Church. What his subjective attitude was is a matter about which we cannot be sure. Pierre d'Ailly asserted that a number of Nicholas's propositions were condemned out of envy or ill-will; and Nicholas himself maintained that some statements were attributed to him which he did not hold at all or which he did not hold in the sense in which they were condemned. It is difficult to judge how far one is justified in taking his protestations at their face-value and how far one should assume that his critics were justified in dismissing these protestations as 'foxy' excuses. There can be little doubt, I think, that he was sincere in saying that the philosophy which he put forward as 'probable' was untrue in so far as it conflicted with the teaching of the Church. At least there is no real difficulty in accepting his sincerity on this point, since apart from any other consideration it would have been quite inconsistent with the critical side of his philosophy if he had regarded the conclusions of his positive philosophy as certain. On the other hand, it is not so easy to accept Nicholas's protestation that the critical views expounded in his correspondence with Bernard of Arezzo were put forward as a kind of experiment in reasoning. His letters to Bernard hardly give that impression, even if the possibility cannot be excluded that the explanation which he offered to his judges represented his real mind. After all, he was by no means the only philosopher of his time to adopt a critical attitude towards the traditional metaphysics, even if he went further than most.

It is, however, quite clear that Nicholas meant to attack

the philosophy of Aristotle and that he considered his own positive philosophy to be a more probable hypothesis than the Aristotelian system. He declared that he was himself very astonished that some people study Aristotle and the Commentator (Averroes) up to a decrepit old age and forsake moral matters and the care of the common good in favour of the study of Aristotle. They do this to such an extent that when the friend of truth rises up and sounds a trumpet to rouse the sleepers from slumber they are greatly afflicted and rush upon him like armed men to deadly combat.[22]

Mention of 'moral matters' and of the 'common good' leads one to inquire what Nicholas's ethical and political teaching was. We have not much to go upon here. But it seems clear that he maintained the Ockhamist theory of the arbitrary character of the moral law. There is a condemned proposition of his to the effect that 'God can order a rational creature to hate Him, and that the rational creature merits more by obeying this precept than by loving God in obedience to a precept. For he would do so (that is, hate God) with greater effort and more against his inclination.'[23] As to politics, Nicholas is said to have issued a proclamation that whoever wanted to hear lectures on Aristotle's *Politics* together with certain discussions about justice and injustice which would enable a man to make new laws or to correct laws already in existence, should repair to a certain place where he would find Master Nicholas of Autrecourt, who would teach him all these things.[24] How far this proclamation constitutes evidence of Nicholas's serious concern for the common welfare and how far it is the expression of a love of notoriety it is difficult to say.

I have given an account of the philosophical ideas of John of Mirecourt and Nicholas of Autrecourt in a chapter on the 'Ockhamist Movement'. Is this procedure justified? Nicholas's positive philosophy, which he put forward as probable, was certainly not the philosophy of William of Ockham; and in this respect it would be quite wrong to call him an 'Ockhamist'. As to his critical philosophy, it was not the same as that of Ockham, and Nicholas cannot be properly called an 'Ockhamist', if by this term is meant a disciple of Ockham. Moreover, the tone of Nicholas's writing is different from that of the Franciscan theologian. None the less, Nicholas was an extreme respresentative of that critical movement of thought which was a prominent feature of fourteenth-century philosophy and which finds expression in one aspect of Ockhamism. I have indicated earlier that I use the term 'Ockhamist Movement' to denote a philosophical movement which was characterized, in part, by a critical attitude towards the presuppositions and arguments of the traditional metaphysics, and if the term is used in this sense, one can, I think, justifiably speak of John of Mirecourt and Nicholas of Autrecourt as belonging to the Ockhamist movement.

Nicholas of Autrecourt was not a sceptic, if by this term we mean a philosopher who denies or questions the possibility of attaining any certain knowledge. He maintained that certainty is obtainable in logic and in mathematics and in immediate perception. In modern terms he recognized as certain both analytic propositions (the propositions which are now sometimes called 'tautologies') and basic empirical statements, though one must add the proviso that for Nicholas we can have evident immediate knowledge without that knowledge being expressed in a proposition. On the other hand, propositions involving the assertion of a causal relation in the metaphysical sense or propositions based on an inference from one existent to another he regarded not as certain propositions but rather as empirical hypotheses. One must not, however, turn Nicholas into a 'logical positivist'. He did not deny the significance of metaphysical or theological statements: on the contrary, he presupposed the certitude of faith and admitted revelation as a source of absolute certainty.

4. I announced my intention of concluding this chapter with some remarks on the influence of the new movement in the universities, especially in the universities which were founded in the latter part of the fourteenth century and during the fifteenth.

In 1389 a statute was passed at the university of Vienna requiring of students in the faculty of arts that they should attend lectures on the logical works of Peter of Spain, while later statutes imposed a similar obligation in regard to the logical works of Ockhamist authors like William Heytesbury. Nominalism was also strongly represented in the German universities of Heidelberg (founded in 1386), Erfurt (1392) and Leipzig (1409) and in the Polish university of Cracow (1397). The university of Leipzig is said to have owed its origin to the exodus of nominalists from Prague, where John Hus and Jerome of Prague taught the Scotist realism which they had learnt from John Wycliffe (*c.* 1320–84). Indeed, when the Council of Constance condemned the theological errors of John Hus in 1415, the nominalists were quick to argue that Scotist realism had also been condemned, though this was not actually the case.

In the first half of the fifteenth century a rather surprising revival of the philosophy of St. Albert the Great took place. The nominalists seem to have left Paris early in the century, partly owing to the conditions brought about by the Hundred Years War, though Ehrle was doubtless correct in connecting the revival of 'Albertism' with the return of the Dominicans to Paris in 1403. They had left the city in 1387. The supremacy of Albertism did not last very long, however, because the nominalists returned in 1437 after the city had been liberated from the English. On March 1st, 1474, King Louis XI issued a decree prohibiting the teaching of nominalism and ordering the confiscation of nominalist books; but in 1481 the ban was withdrawn.

In the fifteenth century, then, nominalism was strongly entrenched at Paris, Oxford and many German universities; but the older traditions continued to hold their ground in certain places. This was the case in the university of Cologne, which was founded in 1389. At Cologne the doctrines of St. Albert and St. Thomas were in possession. After the condemnation of John Hus the Prince Electors asked the university to adopt nominalism on the ground that the more old-fashioned realism easily led to heresy, even though it was not evil in itself. But in 1425 the university replied that while it remained open to anyone to adopt nominalism if he chose, the doctrines of St. Albert, St. Thomas, St. Bonaventure, Giles of Rome and Duns Scotus were above suspicion. In any case, said the university, the heresies of John Hus did not spring from philosophical realism but from the theological teaching of Wycliffe. Further, if realism were forbidden at Cologne the students would leave the university.

With the university of Cologne one must associate that of Louvain, which was founded in 1425. The statutes of 1427 required of candidates for the doctorate that they should take an oath never to teach the doctrines of Buridan, Marsilius of Inghen, Ockham or their followers; and in 1480 professors who expounded Aristotle in the light of the Ockhamist theories were threatened with suspension from office.

The adherents of the 'ancient way', therefore, were by no means completely routed by the nominalists. Indeed, in the middle of the fourteenth century realism gained a foothold at Heidelberg. Moreover, they could boast of some eminent names. Chief among them was John Capreolus (*c.* 1380–

1444), a Dominican who lectured for a time at Paris and later at Toulouse. He set out to defend the doctrines of St. Thomas against the contrary opinions of Scotus, Durandus, Henry of Ghent and all adversaries in general, including the nominalists. His great work, which was completed shortly before his death at Rodez and which earned for him the title of *Princeps thomistarum*, was the *Libri IV defensionum theologiae divi Thomae de Aquino*. Capreolus was the first of the line of distinguished Dominican Thomists and commentators on St. Thomas, which included at a later period men like Cajetan (d. 1534) and John of St. Thomas (d. 1644).

In the Italian universities a current of Averroistic Aristotelianism was represented at Bologna in the first half of the fourteenth century by thinkers like Thaddaeus of Parma and Angelo of Arezzo and passed to Padua and Venice where it was represented by Paul of Venice (d. 1429), Cajetan of Thiene (d. 1465), Alexander Achillini (d. 1512) and Agostino Nipho (d. 1546). The first printed edition of Averroes appeared at Padua in 1472. Something will be said later, in connection with the philosophy of the Renaissance, about the controversy between those who followed Averroes' interpretation of Aristotle and those who adhered to the interpretation given by Alexander of Aphrodisias, and about the condemnation of 1513. The Averroists have been mentioned here simply as an illustration of the fact that the *via moderna* should not be regarded as having swept all before it in the fourteenth and fifteenth centuries.

Nevertheless, nominalism possessed that attraction which comes from modernity and freshness, and it spread widely, as we have seen. A notable figure among fifteenth-century nominalists was Gabriel Biel (*c.* 1425–95), who taught at Tübingen and composed an epitome of Ockham's commentaries on the *Sentences* of Peter Lombard. Biel's work was a methodical and clear exposition of Ockhamism, and though he did not pretend to be more than a follower and exponent of Ockham he exercised a considerable influence. Indeed, the Ockhamists at the universities of Erfurt and Wittenberg were known as *Gabrielistae*. It is perhaps interesting to note that Biel did not interpret Ockham's moral theory as meaning that there is no natural moral order. There are objects or ends besides God which can be chosen in accordance with right reason, and pagan philosophers like Aristotle, Cicero and Seneca were able to accomplish morally good and virtuous acts. In virtue of his 'absolute power' God could, indeed, command acts opposed to the dictates of the natural reason; but this does not alter the fact that these dictates can be recognized without revelation.

5. Finally one may recall that the Ockhamist Movement or nominalism had various aspects. On the purely logical side it was partly a development of the logic of terms and of the theory of *suppositio* as found in pre-Ockhamist logicians like Peter of Spain. This terminist logic was used by William of Ockham in order to exclude all forms of realism. The problem of universals was treated from a logical rather than an ontological point of view. The universal is the abstract term considered according to its logical content, and this term stands in the proposition for individual things, which are the only things which exist.

This terminist logic had not of itself any sceptical consequences in regard to knowledge, nor did Ockham regard it as having any such consequences. But together with the logical aspect of nominalism one must take into account the analysis of causality and the consequences of this analysis in regard to the epistemological status of empirical hypotheses. In the philosophy of a man like Nicholas of Autrecourt we have seen a sharp distinction drawn between analytic or formal propositions, which are certain, and empirical hypotheses, which are not and cannot be certain. With Ockham this view, so far as he held it, was closely connected with his insistence on the divine omnipotence: with Nicholas of Autrecourt the theological background was very much less in evidence.

We have seen, too, how the nominalists (some more than others) tended to adopt a critical attitude towards the metaphysical arguments of the older philosophers. This attitude was fully explicit in an extremist like Nicholas of Autrecourt, since it was made to rest on his general position that one cannot infer with certainty the existence of one thing from the existence of another thing. Metaphysical arguments are probable rather than demonstrative.

But, whatever one may be inclined to think on one or two cases, this critical attitude in regard to metaphysical speculation was practically always combined with a firm theological faith and a firm belief in revelation as a source of certain knowledge. This firm belief is particularly striking in the case of Ockham himself. His view that it is possible to have what would be, from the psychological point of view, intuition of a non-existent thing and his theory about the ultimate dependence of the moral law on the divine choice were not expressions of scepticism but of the tremendous emphasis he placed on the divine omnipotence. If one attempts to turn the nominalists into rationalists or even sceptics in the modern sense, one is taking them out of their historical setting and severing them from their mental background. In the course of time nominalism became one of the regular currents in Scholastic thought; and a theological chair of nominalism was erected even in the university of Salamanca.

But nominalism suffered the fate of most philosophical schools of thought. It obviously began as something new; and whatever one's opinion concerning the various tenets of the nominalists may be, it can hardly be denied that they had something to say. They helped to develop logical studies and they raised important problems. But in the course of time a tendency to 'logic-chopping' showed itself, and this can perhaps be connected with their reserved attitude towards metaphysics. Logical refinements and exaggerated subtlety tended to drain off the energies of the later nominalists; and when philosophy received a fresh impetus at the time of the Renaissance this impetus did not come from the nominalists.

Chapter Ten

THE SCIENTIFIC MOVEMENT

Physical science in the thirteenth and fourteenth centuries – The problem of motion; impetus and gravity – Nicholas Oresme; the hypothesis of the earth's rotation – The possibility of other worlds – Some scientific implications of nominalism; and implications of the impetus theory.

1. For a long time it was widely supposed that there was no respect for experience in the Middle Ages and that the only ideas on science which the mediaevals possessed were adopted uncritically from Aristotle and other non-Christian writers. Science was assumed to have started again, after centuries of almost complete quiescence, at the time of the Renaissance. Then it was found that a considerable interest had been taken in scientific matters during the fourteenth century, that some important discoveries had been made at that time, that various theories had been fairly widely held which did not derive from Aristotle and that certain hypotheses which were usually associated with the Renaissance scientists had been proposed in the late Middle Ages. At the same time a better knowledge of late mediaeval philosophy suggested that the scientific movement of the fourteenth century should be connected with Ockhamism or nominalism, largely on the ground that Ockham and those who belonged more or less to the same movement of thought insisted on the primacy of intuition or of immediate experience in the acquisition of factual knowledge. It was not that Ockham himself was thought to have shown much interest in scientific matters; but his insistence on intuition as the only basis of factual knowledge and the empiricist side of his philosophy were thought to have given a powerful impetus

to scientific interests and investigations. This view of the matter could be fitted into the traditional outlook inasmuch as Ockham and the nominalists were supposed to have been resolute anti-Aristotelians.

It is not at all my intention to attempt to deny that there is truth in this interpretation of the facts. Although Ockham cannot possibly be called simply 'anti-Aristotelian' without qualification, since in some matters he regarded himself as the true interpreter of Aristotle, his philosophy was in certain important respects undoubtedly at variance with Aristotle's, and it is clear that some thinkers who belonged to the nominalist movement were extremely hostile to Aristotelianism. Moreover, it is probably true to say that Ockhamist insistence on experience as the basis of our knowledge of existent things favoured the growth of empirical science. It may be difficult to assess an epistemological theory's positive influence on the growth of science; but it is reasonable to think that the doctrine of the primacy of intuition would naturally encourage such growth rather than discourage it. Moreover, if one assumes that causes cannot be discovered by *a priori* theorizing but that recourse must be had to experience in order to discover them, this assumption is calculated to turn the mind towards the investigation of the empirical data. No doubt, it can be said with justice that science does not consist in 'intuition' or in merely observing the empirical data; but the point is not that Ockhamism provided a theory of scientific method but rather that it helped to create an intellectual climate which facilitated and tended to promote scientific research. For by directing men's minds to the facts or empirical data in the acquisition of knowledge it at the same time directed them away from passive acceptance of the opinions of illustrious thinkers of the past.

But though it would be improper to discount the connection of fourteenth-century science with Ockhamism it would be equally improper to attribute its growth to Ockhamism as a sufficient cause. In the first place it is not clear to what extent one can legitimately speak of the fourteenth-century physicists as 'Ockhamists', even if one uses the term in a wide sense. One of the leading figures who took an interest in physical theories was John Buridan, who was for a time rector of the university of Paris and died about 1360. This theologian, philosopher and physicist was influenced by the terminist logic and by certain views which were held by Ockham; but he was by no means an unqualified nominalist.

Apart from the fact that in his official capacity as rector he was associated with the condemnation of nominalist theories in 1340 he maintained, for example, in his writings that it is possible to prove the existence of one thing from the existence of another thing and that consequently it is possible to prove the existence of God. Albert of Saxony was rather more of an Ockhamist. Rector of the university of Paris in 1353 he became in 1365 the first rector of the university of Vienna. In the same year he was appointed bishop of Halberstadt. He died in that post in 1390. In logic he followed Ockham; but he was certainly not an extreme adherent of the *via moderna*. It is true that he held that the certitude given by experience cannot be absolute; but it would appear that his view of the hypothetical character of empirical statements was due more to the conviction that God can miraculously 'interfere' with the natural order than to any other consideration. Marsilius of Inghen (d. 1396), who was rector of the university of Paris in 1367 and 1371 and first rector of the university of Heidelberg in 1386, was indeed, a declared adherent of the *via moderna*; but he seems to have tempered the nominalist position on universals with a dose of realism, and he thought that the metaphysician can prove the existence and unicity of God. As for Nicholas Oresme, who taught at Paris and died as bishop of Lisieux in 1382, he was much more of a physicist than a philosopher, though he had, of course, theological and philosophical interests.

One can say then, I think, that the leading figures in the scientific movement of the fourteenth century had in most cases affiliations with the Ockhamist Movement. And if one is going to use the term 'nominalist' to denote those who adopted the Ockhamist or terminist logic, one can call them 'nominalists'. But it would be a mistake to suppose that they all adhered to Ockham's views on metaphysics; and it would be still more of a mistake to suppose that they shared the extremist philosophical position of a thinker like Nicholas of Autrecourt. Indeed, Buridan and Albert of Saxony both attacked Nicholas. It is fairly clear, however, that the *via moderna* in philosophy did stimulate, though it did not cause, the scientific developments of the fourteenth century.

That the nominalist movement cannot be accounted the sufficient cause of the growth of science in the fourteenth century is clear from the fact that fourteenth-century science was to a considerable extent a continuation of and growth from thirteenth-century science. I have mentioned that modern research has brought to light the reality of scientific progress in the fourteenth century. But research is also bringing to light the scientific investigations which were pursued in the thirteenth century. These investigations were stimulated mainly by the translations of Greek and Arabic scientific works; but they were none the less real. Mediaeval science was doubtless primitive and rudimentary if we compare it with the science of the post-Renaissance era; but there is no longer any excuse for saying that there was no science in the Middle Ages outside the fields of theology and philosophy. Not only was there a scientific development in the Middle Ages but there was also a continuity in some degree between the science of the late Middle Ages and the science of the Renaissance. It would be foolish to belittle the achievements of the Renaissance scientists or to make out that their hypotheses and discoveries were all anticipated in the Middle Ages. But it is also foolish to depict Renaissance science as being without historical antecedents and parentage.

In the thirteenth century a number of thinkers had insisted on the need for observation or 'experience' in scientific study. In the preceding volume of this history mention was made in this connection of St. Albert the Great (1206–80), Peter of Maricourt (exact dates unknown), Robert Grosseteste (*c.* 1175–1253) and of Roger Bacon (*c.* 1212–after 1292). Peter of Maricourt, who stimulated Bacon's interest in scientific matters, is notable for his *Epistola de magnete*, which was utilized by William Gilbert in the second half of the sixteenth century. Grosseteste wrote on optics and tried to improve the theory of refraction contained in Greek and Arabic writings. Optics constituted also one of Bacon's special interests. The Silesian scientist, mathematician and philosopher Witelo wrote on the same subject in his *Perspectiva.* This work was composed in dependence on the writings of the Islamic scientist Alhazen; and Kepler later supplied some developments on Witelo's ideas in his *Ad Vitellionem paralipomena* (1604). The Dominican Theodoric of Freiberg (d. *c.* 1311) developed a theory in explanation of the rainbow on an experimental basis, which was adopted by Descartes;[1] and another Dominican, Jordanus Nemorarius, made discoveries in mechanics.

But though the thirteenth-century physicists insisted on the need for observation in scientific research, and though a man like Roger Bacon was quick to see the practical purposes to which scientific discoveries could be put, they were by no means blind to the theoretical aspects of scientific method. They did not regard science as consisting in the mere accumulation of empirical data; nor did they concentrate simply on real or imagined practical results. They were interested in explaining the data. Aristotle had held that scientific knowledge is obtained only when one is in a position to show how the observed effects follow from their causes; and for Grosseteste and Bacon this meant in large part being able to give a mathematical deduction of the effects. Hence the great emphasis placed by Bacon on mathematics as the key to other sciences. Furthermore, whereas Aristotle had not given any very clear indication how a knowledge of the 'causes' is to be actually obtained, Grosseteste and Bacon showed how the elimination of explanatory theories which are incompatible with the facts helped one to arrive at this knowledge. In other words, they saw not only that an explanatory hypothesis could be arrived at by examining the common factors in different instances of the phenomenon under investigation, but also that it is necessary to verify this hypothesis by considering what results should follow if the hypothesis were true and by then experimenting in order to see if these expectations are actually fulfilled.

Fourteenth-century science was therefore not an entirely new development: it was a continuation of the scientific work of the preceding century, just as this work was itself a continuation of the scientific studies made by Greek and Arab physicists and mathematicians. But in the fourteenth century other problems came into prominence, especially the problem of motion. And the consideration of this problem in the fourteenth century might have suggested a conception of scientific hypotheses which, had it been subsequently accepted by Galileo, might have gone a long way towards preventing the latter's clash with the theologians.

2. In Aristotle's account of motion a distinction was made between natural and unnatural motion. An element like fire is naturally light and its natural tendency is to move upwards towards its natural place, while earth is heavy and has a natural movement downwards. But one can take a naturally heavy thing and throw it upwards, a stone, for example; and so long as the stone is moving upwards its motion is unnatural. Aristotle considered that this unnatural motion requires an explanation. The obvious answer to the question why the stone moves upwards is that it is thrown

upwards. But once the stone has left the hand of the person who throws it it continues to move upwards for some time. Aristotle's answer to the question why this happens was that the person who throws the stone and so starts it on its upward course moves not only the stone but also the surrounding air. This air moves the air higher up and each portion of the air which is moved carries the stone with it until the successive movements of portions of air become so weak that the stone's natural tendency to downward motion is able at length to reassert itself. The stone then begins to move towards its natural place.

This account of unnatural or violent motion was rejected by William of Ockham. If it is the air which moves a flying arrow, then if two arrows meet in flight we shall have to say that at that moment the same air is causing movements in opposite directions; and this cannot be the case.[2] On the other hand, one cannot suppose that a stone which is thrown upwards continues to move in virtue of some power or quality imparted to it. There is no empirical evidence of the existence of any such quality distinct from the projectile. If there were such a quality it could be conserved by God apart from the projectile; but it would be absurd to suppose that this can be done. Local motion does not involve anything beyond a 'permanent thing' and the term of the motion.[3]

Ockham thus rejected the idea of a quality impressed on the projectile by the agent as an explanation of motion; and to this extent he may be said to have anticipated the law of inertia. But the physicists of the fourteenth century were not content to say that a thing moves because it is in motion: they preferred to adopt the theory of impetus, which had been put forward by Philoponus in the early part of the sixth century and which had been already adopted by the Franciscan Peter John Olivi (*c.* 1248–98), who spoke of the impulse (*impulsus*) or 'inclination' that is given to the projectile by the moving agent. This quality or energy in virtue of which a stone, for example, continues to move after it has left the hand of the thrower until it is overcome by the resistance of the air and the weight of the stone was called *impetus* by the fourteenth-century physicists. They supported the theory empirically, in that they maintained that it was better adapted than the Aristotelian theory for 'saving the appearances'. For example, John Buridan held that Aristotle's theory of motion was unable to explain the movement of a spinning top, whereas this could be explained on the impetus theory. The spinning top, he said, stays in one place; it does not leave its place, which could then be filled by air which would move the top. But though the fourteenth-century physicists attempted to support the impetus theory empirically or to verify it, they did not confine themselves to purely physical considerations but introduced philosophical questions stated in the traditional categories. For example, in his *Abbreviationes super VIII libros physicorum* Marsilius of Inghen raised the question, to what category or *praedicamentum* should impetus be assigned. He did not supply any very definite answer to this question; but he clearly thought that there are different kinds of impetus. For some projectiles move upwards, others downwards, some straight forwards, others in a circle. Again, although Albert of Saxony declared that the question whether impetus is a substance or an accident is a question for the metaphysician rather than for the physicist, he himself asserted that it is a quality, that is to say an accident. In any case it is clear that these physicists regarded impetus as something distinct from and impressed upon the projectile or moving body: they did not follow William of Ockham in his denial of any such distinct reality.

An interesting application of the impetus theory was made in regard to the movement of the heavenly bodies. In his commentary on the *Metaphysics*[4] Buridan maintained that God imparted to the heavenly bodies an original impetus which is the same in kind as the impetus in virtue of which terrestrial bodies move. There is no need to suppose that the heavenly bodies are made of a special element (the quintessence or fifth element), which can only move with a circular motion. Nor is it necessary to postulate Intelligences of the spheres to account for the spheres' movements. Motion on earth and motion in the heavens can be explained in the same way. Just as a man imparts an impetus to the stone which he throws into the air, so God imparted impetus to the heavenly bodies when He created them. The reason why the latter continue to move while the stone eventually falls to the earth is simply that the stone encounters resistance whereas the heavenly bodies do not. The impetus of the stone is gradually overcome by the air's resistance and the force of gravity; and the operation of these factors results in the stone's eventually moving towards its natural place. But although the heavenly bodies are not composed of some special matter of their own these factors do not operate in their case: gravity, in the sense of a factor which makes a body tend towards the earth as its natural place, operates only in regard to bodies within the terrestrial sphere.

This theory of impetus was adopted, to all intents and purposes, by Albert of Saxony, Marsilius of Inghen and Nicholas Oresme. The first-named, however, tried to give a clear account of what is meant by gravity. He made a distinction between the centre of gravity in a body and the centre of its volume. These are not necessarily the same. In the case of the earth they are different, as the earth's density is not uniform; and when we talk about the 'centre of the earth' in connection with gravity it is the earth's centre of gravity which is meant. The tendency of a body to move towards its natural place may, then, be taken to mean its tendency to unite its own centre of gravity with the earth's centre of gravity or 'the centre of the earth'. A body's 'gravity' means this tendency. It is noteworthy that this 'explanation' is a physical account: it is not an account in terms of 'ultimate causes' but a positive account of what happens or is thought to happen.

3. The wider implications of the impetus theory will be briefly discussed later in this chapter. At the moment I wish to mention one or two other developments connected with problems of motion.

Nicholas Oresme, who was one of the most independent and outstanding of the mediaeval physicists, made several discoveries in the sphere of dynamics. He found, for example, that when a body moves with a uniformly increasing velocity the distance which it travels is equal to the distance travelled in the same time by a body which moves with a uniform velocity equal to that attained by the first body at the middle instant of its course. Furthermore, he tried to find a way of expressing successive variations of intensity which would make it easy to understand and compare them. The way he suggested was that of representing them by means of graphs, making use of rectangular co-ordinates. Space or time would be represented by a straight base line. On this line Nicholas erected vertical lines, the length of which corresponded to the position or the intensity of the variable. He then connected the ends of the vertical lines and so was able to obtain a curve which represented the fluctuations in intensity. This geometrical device obviously prepared the way for further mathematical developments. But to depict Nicholas as the founder of analytic geometry, in the sense of ascribing to him the developments of Descartes, would be an exaggeration. For the geometrical presentation suggested by Nicholas had to be superseded by the substitution of numerical equivalents. This does not mean, however, that his work was not of importance and that it did not represent an important stage in the development of applied mathematics. He does not appear, however, to have realized very clearly the difference between symbol and reality. Thus in his treatise *De uniformitate et difformitate intensionum* he implies that heat of varying intensity is actually composed of geometrical particles of pyramidal structure, a notion which recalls to mind the statement in Plato's *Timaeus* that the particles of fire possess pyramidal form, as pyramids have 'the sharpest cutting edges and the sharpest points in every direction'.[5] Indeed, in the treatise *Du ciel et du monde*,[6] he shows plainly enough his predilection for Plato.

One of the problems discussed by Nicholas was that of the earth's movement. The matter had apparently already been discussed at an earlier date, for Francis of Meyronnes, a Scotist who wrote early in the fourteenth century, asserts that 'a certain doctor' maintained that if it was the earth which moved rather than the heavens it would be a 'better arrangement' (*melior dispositio*). Albert of Saxony dismissed as insufficient the arguments offered in favour of the hypothesis that the earth rotates daily on its axis; but Nicholas Oresme, who discussed the hypothesis at some length, gave it a more favourable reception, even if in the end he preferred not to accept it.

In his treatise *Du ciel et du monde* Nicholas maintained first of all that direct observation cannot afford a proof that the heaven or firmament rotates daily while the earth remains at rest. For the appearances would be precisely the same if it were the earth and not the heaven which rotated. For this and other reasons 'I conclude that one could not show by any experience that the heaven was moved with a daily motion and the earth was not moved in this way.'[7] As to other arguments adduced against the possibility of the earth's daily rotation, replies can be made to them all. For example, from the fact that parts of the earth tend to their 'natural place' with a downward movement it does not follow that the earth as a whole cannot rotate: it cannot be shown that a body as a whole may not have one simple movement while its parts have other movements.[8] Again, even if the heaven does rotate, it does not necessarily follow that the earth is at rest. When a mill-wheel rotates, the centre does not remain at rest, except for a mathematical point which is not a body at all.[9] As to arguments drawn from the Scriptures, one must remember that the Scriptures speak according to a common mode of speech and that they are not necessarily to be regarded as making a scientific statement in some particular case. From the statement in the Bible that the sun was stopped in its course[10] one is no more entitled to draw the scientific conclusion that the heaven moves and that the earth does not than one is entitled to draw from phrases like 'God repented' the conclusion that God can actually change His mind like a human being.[11] In view of the fact that it is sometimes said or implied that this interpretation of the relevant Scriptural assertions was invented by theologians only when the Copernican hypothesis had been verified and could no longer be rejected, it is interesting to note the clear statement of it by Nicholas Oresme in the fourteenth century.

Furthermore, one can give positive reasons in support of the hypothesis that the earth rotates. For example, it is reasonable to suppose that a body which receives influence from another body should itself move to receive this influence, like a joint being roasted at the fire. Now, the earth receives heat from the sun. It is reasonable, then, to suppose that the earth moves in order to receive this influence.[12] Again, if one postulates the rotation of the earth one can 'save the appearances' much better than on the opposite hypothesis, since if one denies the earth's movement one has to postulate a great number of other movements in order to explain the empirical data.[13] Nicholas draws attention to the fact that Heraclitus Ponticus (Heraclides of Pontus) had put forward the hypothesis of the earth's movement; so it was not a new idea. Nevertheless, he himself ends by rejecting this hypothesis, 'notwithstanding the reasons to the contrary, for they are conclusions which are not evidently conclusive'.[14] In other words, he is not prepared to abandon the common opinion of the time for a hypothesis which has not been conclusively proved.

Nicholas had a critical mind and he was certainly no blind adherent of Aristotle. He saw that the problem was one of 'saving the appearances'; and he asked which hypothesis would account for the empirical data in the most economical manner. It appears to me to be fairly clear that, in spite of his eventual acceptance of the commonly held opinion, he considered the hypothesis of the earth's daily rotation on its axis to meet all requirements better than the opposite hypothesis. The same could not be said about Albert of Saxony, however, who rejected the theory of the earth's rotation on the ground that it did not save the appearances. Like Francis of Meyronnes, he seems to have thought that the theory claimed that all the movements of the heavenly bodies could be eliminated if the earth were regarded as rotating; and he pointed out that the movements of the planets could not be eliminated in this way. Buridan also rejected the theory of the earth's rotation, though he discussed it quite sympathetically. It was Nicholas Oresme who saw clearly that the theory would only eliminate the diurnal rotation of the 'fixed' stars and would still leave the planets in motion. Some of the reasons he proposed in favour of the theory were good reasons, but others were not; and it would be an extravagance to depict Nicholas as having given a clearer and profounder exposition of the hypothesis of the earth's movement than the astronomers of the Renaissance, as Pierre Duhem was inclined to do. It is obvious, however, that men like Albert of Saxony and Nicholas Oresme can properly be called the precursors of the Renaissance physicists, astronomers and mathematicians. In so calling them Duhem was quite justified.

4. One of the questions discussed in the *Du ciel et du monde* is whether there could be other worlds besides this one. According to Nicholas, neither Aristotle nor anyone else has shown that God could not create a plurality of worlds. It is useless to argue from the unicity of God to the unicity of the world: God is not only one and unique but also infinite, and if there were a plurality of worlds none of them would be, as it were, outside the divine presence and power.[15] Again, to say that if there were another world, the element of earth in the other world would be attracted to this earth as to its natural place is no valid objection: the natural place of the element of earth in the other world would be in the other world and not in this.[16] Nicholas concludes, however, that although no sufficient proofs have been adduced by Aristotle or anyone else to show that there could not be other worlds in addition to this one, there never has been, is not and never will be any other corporeal world.[17]

5. The existence of a certain interest in scientific study during the thirteenth century has been mentioned earlier in

this chapter; and the conclusion was then drawn that the scientific work of the succeeding century cannot be ascribed simply to the association of some of the fourteenth-century physicists with the Ockhamist movement. It is true, of course, that certain philosophical positions maintained by Ockham himself or by other followers of the *via moderna* were calculated to influence the conceptions of scientific method and of the status of physical theories. The combination of a 'nominalist' or conceptualist view of universals with the thesis that one cannot argue with certainty from the existence of one thing to the existence of another thing would naturally lead to the conclusion that physical theories are empirical hypotheses which can be more or less probable but which cannot be proved with certainty. Again, the emphasis laid by some philosophers on experience and observation as the necessary basis of our knowledge of the world might well encourage the view that the probability of an empirical hypothesis depends on the extent of its verification, that is, on its ability to explain or account for the empirical data. One might perhaps be tempted to suggest that the philosophy of the nominalist movement could have led to the conclusion that physical theories are empirical hypotheses which involve a certain amount of 'dictation' to nature and *a priori* construction, but which depend for their probability and utility on the extent to which they can be verified. A theory is constructed on the basis of empirical data, it might have been said, but it is a mental construction on the basis of those data. Its object, however, is to explain the phenomena, and it is verified in so far as it is possible to deduce from it the phenomena which are actually observed in ordinary life or which are obtained by artificial and purposive experiment. Moreover, that explanatory theory will be preferable which succeeds in explaining the phenomena with the least number of assumptions and presuppositions and which thus best satisfies the principle of economy.

But it is one thing to say that conclusions of this sort might have been suggested by the new movement in philosophy during the fourteenth century, and it is another thing to say that they were actually drawn. On the one hand, philosophers like Ockham do not seem to have shown any particular interest in questions of scientific theory and method as such, while on the other hand the physicists appear to have been more interested in their actual scientific research and speculations than in reflection on the underlying theory and method. This is, after all, only what one would expect. Reflection on scientific method and theory can hardly reach a high degree of development until physical science has itself progressed to a considerable extent and has reached a stage which prompts and stimulates reflection on the method employed and its theoretical presuppositions. We certainly do find in the thought of the fourteenth-century physicists some elements of the scientific theory which might have been suggested by contemporary philosophical developments. For example, Nicholas Oresme clearly regarded the function of any hypothesis about the world's rotation as being that of 'saving the appearances' or accounting for the observable data, and he clearly regarded as preferable the hypothesis which best satisfied the principle of economy. But the fourteenth-century physicists did not make in any very clear manner that kind of distinction between philosophy and physical science which the philosophy of the Ockhamist movement would appear to facilitate. As we have seen, the affiliations of the several physicists with the nominalist movement in philosophy were not by any means always as close as has sometimes been imagined. Moreover, the use of the principle of economy, as found in the physical speculations of Nicholas Oresme, for example, was already known in the thirteenth century. Robert Grosseteste, for instance, realized quite well that the more economical hypothesis is to be preferred to the less economical. He also realized that there is something peculiar about a mathematical explanation in astronomical physics, in that it does not provide knowledge of causes in a metaphysical sense. One has, then, to be careful in ascribing to the exclusive influence of the Ockhamist movement ideas in fourteenth-century science which, in the abstract, might perhaps have been the result of that movement. The idea of a scientific theory involving *a priori* mental construction could hardly arise except in a post-Kantian intellectual climate; and even the idea of physical theories as being concerned with 'saving the appearances' does not seem to have received special attention from or to have been specially developed by fourteenth-century nominalists.

It is true, however, that one can see a new view of the world coming to birth in the fourteenth century and that this was facilitated by the adoption of the theory of impetus in the explanation of movement. As we have seen, according to this theory celestial dynamics were explained on the same principle as terrestrial dynamics. Just as a stone continues to move after it has left the hand of the thrower, because a certain impetus has been imparted to it, so the celestial bodies move in virtue of an impetus originally imparted to them by God. On this view the first mover, God, appears as efficient rather than as final cause. By saying this I do not mean to imply that men like Nicholas Oresme and Albert of Saxony denied that God is final as well as efficient cause: I mean rather that the impetus theory which they adopted facilitated a shift of emphasis from the Aristotelian idea of God causing the movements of the heavenly bodies by 'drawing' them as final cause to the idea of God as imparting at creation a certain impetus in virtue of which these bodies, encountering no resistance, continued to move. This view might easily suggest that the world is a mechanical or quasi-mechanical system. God set the machine going, as it were, when He created it, after which it continues working on its own without further divine 'interference' save the activity of conservation and concurrence. If this idea were developed, God's function would appear to be that of a hypothesis for explaining the source of movement in the universe. And it would be natural to suggest that consideration of final causes should be excluded from physical science in favour of consideration of efficient causes, as Descartes, for example, insisted.

It must be repeated that I am not attempting to father all the ideas mentioned above on the physicists of the fourteenth century. They were concerned with the problem of motion as a particular problem rather than with drawing broad conclusions from it. And they were certainly not deists. None the less, one can see in the adoption of the impetus theory a step on the road towards a new conception of the material world. Or it might be better to say that it was a step on the road towards the development of physical science as distinct from metaphysics. It facilitated the growth of the idea that the material world can be considered as a system of bodies in motion in which impetus or energy is transmitted from body to body while the sum of energy remains constant. But it is one thing to state that the world, as considered by the physicist, can be regarded in this light, and it is another thing to say that the physicist, in his capacity as physicist, can give an adequate account of the world as a whole. When Descartes later insisted on the exclusion of consideration of final causes by what we would call the physical scientist and the astronomer, he did not say (nor did he think) that consideration of final causes has no place in philosophy. And the physicist-philosophers of the fourteenth century certainly did not say anything of the kind. It is conceivable that reflection on their scientific theories could have prompted them to make a clearer distinction between the world of the physicist and the world of the philosopher than they actually did; but in point of fact the idea that there is a rigid distinction between science and philosophy was an idea of much later growth. Before this idea could develop, science itself had to attain a very much richer and fuller development. In the thirteenth and fourteenth centuries we see the beginnings of empirical science in Christian Europe but only the beginnings. Still, it is as well to realize that the foundations of modern science were laid in mediaeval times. And it is as well also to realize that the development of empirical science is in no way alien in principle to the Christian theology which formed the mental background in the Middle Ages. For if the world is the work of God it is obviously a legitimate and worth-while object of study.

Chapter Eleven

MARSILIUS OF PADUA

Church and State, theory and practice – Life of Marsilius – Hostility to the papal claims – The nature of the State and of law – The legislature and the executive – Ecclesiastical jurisdiction – Marsilius and 'Averroism' – Influence of the Defensor pacis.

1. The standard political idea of the Middle Ages was the idea of the two swords, of Church and Empire as two intrinsically independent Powers. In other words, the normal mediaeval theory, as presented by St. Thomas, was that Church and State were distinct societies, the former being concerned with man's supernatural well-being and his attainment of his last end, the latter with man's temporal well-being. As man has but one final end, a supernatural end, the Church must be considered superior to the State in point of value and dignity; but that does not mean that the Church is a glorified State enjoying direct jurisdiction in the temporal affairs of particular States, for, on the one hand, the Church is not a State and, on the other hand, each of them, the Church and the State, is a 'perfect' society.[1] All authority of man over man comes ultimately from God; but God wills the existence of the State as well as that of the Church. States existed before the Church, and the institution of the Church by Christ did not abrogate the State or subordinate the State, in the conduct of its own affairs, to the Church.

This view of Church and State is part and parcel of the harmonious philosophical structure achieved in the thirteenth century and associated especially with the name of St. Thomas Aquinas. But it is obvious enough that in practice a harmony of two Powers is inherently unstable, and in point of fact the disputes between papacy and empire, Church and

State, loom large on the stage of mediaeval history. The Byzantine emperors had not infrequently attempted to interfere in purely doctrinal questions and to settle these questions by their own decisions; the western emperors did not attempt to usurp the teaching function of the Church, but they frequently quarrelled with the papacy over questions of jurisdiction, investiture and so forth, and we find first one side, then the other, gaining ground or giving ground, according to circumstances and according to the personal strength and vigour of the leaders on either side and their personal interest in advancing and maintaining practical claims. But we are not concerned here with the inevitable frictions and practical disputes between popes and emperors or kings: we are concerned only with the wider issues of which these practical disputes were, in part, the symptoms. (I say 'in part' because in the concrete historical life of the Middle Ages disputes between Church and State were in practice inevitable, even when no fundamentally conflicting theories about the relations of the two Powers were involved.) Whether one calls these wider issues 'theoretical' or 'practical' depends largely on one's point of view; it depends, I mean, on whether or not one regards political theory as simply an ideological reflection of concrete historical developments. I do not think, however, that any simple answer to the question is feasible. It is an exaggeration to say that theory is always simply the pale reflection of practice, exercising no influence on practice; and it is an exaggeration to say that political theory is never the reflection of actual practice. Political theory both reflects and influences practice, and whether one should emphasize the active or the passive element can be decided only by unprejudiced examination of the case under discussion. One cannot legitimately affirm *a priori* that a political theory like that of Marsilius of Padua, a theory which emphasized the independence and sovereignty of the State and which formed the antithesis to Giles of Rome's theoretical justification of the attitude of Pope Boniface VIII, was no more than the pale reflection of economic and political changes in the concrete life of the later Middle Ages. Nor is one entitled to affirm *a priori* that theories like that of Marsilius of Padua were the chief factor responsible for the practical disturbance of the harmonious balance between the Powers in so far as there ever was a harmonious balance in the sphere of practice–and for the emergence of sharply defined national entities with claims which amounted to that of complete autonomy. If one states either of these positions *a priori*, one is stating a theory which itself needs justification, and the only justification which could possibly be given would have to take the form of an examination of the actual historical data. In my opinion there are elements of truth in both theories; but it is not possible in a history of philosophy adequately to discuss the problem how far a given political theory was an ideological epiphenomenon of concrete historical changes or how far it played a part in actively influencing the course of history. In what follows, then, I wish to outline the ideas of Marsilius of Padua without committing myself to any decided opinion concerning the actual influence of these ideas or their lack of it. To form a decided opinion in virtue of a preconceived general theory is not, I think, a proper proceeding; and to discuss an actual example in sufficient detail is not possible in a general work. If, then, I expound Marsilius' ideas in a rather 'abstract way', this should not be taken to mean that I discount the influence of actual historical conditions in the formation of these ideas. Nor should incidental remarks concerning the influence of historical conditions on Marsilius' thought be taken to mean that I subscribe to the Marxist thesis concerning the nature of political theory. I do not believe in general *a priori* principles of interpretation to which the facts of history have to be fitted; and this holds for the anti-Marxist as well as for the Marxist theories.

2. It is uncertain in what year Marsilius of Padua was born. It would seem that he gave himself to the study of medicine; but in any case he went to Paris, where he was rector of the university from September 1312 until May 1313. The subsequent course of events is by no means clear. It appears that he returned to Italy and studied 'natural philosophy' with Peter of Abano from 1313 to the end of 1315. He may then have visited Avignon, and it appears from bulls of 1316 and 1318 that he was offered benefices at Padua. At Paris he worked on the *Defensor pacis*, with the collaboration of his friend John of Jandun, the book being finished on June 24th, 1324. His enmity towards the papacy and the 'clericals' must have begun at a considerably earlier date, of course; but in any case the book was denounced, and in 1326 Marsilius of Padua and John of Jandun fled from Paris and took refuge at Nuremberg with Ludwig of Bavaria, whom Marsilius accompanied to Italy, entering Rome in his entourage in January 1327. In a papal bull of April 3rd, 1327,

Marsilius and John were denounced as 'sons of perdition and fruits of malediction'. The presence of Marsilius at his court was an obstacle to the success of Ludwig's attempts at reconciliation, first with John XXII, then with Benedict XII; but Ludwig had a high opinion of the author of the *Defensor pacis*. The Franciscan group did not share this opinion, and Ockham criticized the work in his *Dialogus*, a criticism which led to the composition of the *Defensor minor*. Marsilius also published his *De iurisdictione imperatoris in causis matrimonialibus*, which was designed to serve the emperor in a practical difficulty concerning the projected marriage of his son. Marsilius maintained that the emperor could, on his own authority, dissolve an existing marriage and also dispense from the impediment of consanguinity. These two works were composed about 1341–2. A discourse of Clement VI, dated April 10th, 1343, asserts that the 'heresiarchs', Marsilius of Padua and John of Jandun, were both dead; but the exact date of Marsilius' death is unknown. (John of Jandun died considerably earlier than Marsilius.)

3. In his book on Marsilius of Padua[2] Georges de Lagarde finds the key to his mentality, not in a passion for religious reformation nor in a passion for democracy, but in an enthusiastic love for the idea of the lay State or, negatively, in a hatred of ecclesiastical interference in State affairs, that is to say, in a hatred of the doctrines of papal supremacy and of independent ecclesiastical jurisdiction. This is, I think, quite true. Possessed by an ardent enthusiasm for the autonomous State, the idea of which he supported by frequent references to Aristotle, Marsilius set out to show that the papal claims and the ecclesiastical jurisdiction laid down in the Canon Law involve a perversion of the true idea of the State and that they have no foundation in the Scriptures. His examination of the natures of Church and State and of their mutual relations leads him to a theoretical reversal of hierarchy of Powers: the State is completely autonomous and supreme.

But Marsilius was not simply pursuing an abstract theory. It appears that at one time he permitted himself to be lured from the quiet paths of science by the invitations of the Duke of Verona, Can Grande della Scala, and by Matteo Visconti of Milan. In any case his sympathies lay with the Ghibelline party, and he considered that the papal policy and claims were responsible for the wars and miseries of northern Italy. He lays at the door of the popes, who have disturbed the peace with their excommunications and interdicts, the responsibility for the wars, the violent deaths of thousands of the faithful, the hatred and contention, the moral corruption and crimes, the devastated cities and uncared for countryside, the churches abandoned by their pastors, and the whole catalogue of evils which afflict the Italian City-States.[8] He may, no doubt, have exaggerated the situation: but the point I wish to make is that Marsilius was not simply theorizing in the abstract; his starting-point was a concrete historical situation, and his interpretation of this concrete situation reflected itself in his political theory. Similarly, in his account of the State as it ought to be we see an idealized reflection of the contemporary north-Italian republic, just as the Platonic and Aristotelian political theories were, to a greater or less extent, the idealization of the Greek City-State. The ideal of the empire, which is so prominent in Dante's political thought, is without any real effect on Marsilius' thought.

When, therefore, in the first *Dictio* of the *Defensor pacis* Marsilius discusses the nature of the State and draws on the teaching of Aristotle, it must be remembered that his thought is not moving in the purely abstract sphere but that it reflects his interpretation of and his enthusiasm for the Italian City-State. It may even be that the more abstract passages and the more Aristotelian parts are due to the influence of his collaborator, John of Jandun. Again, when in the second *Dictio* he discusses the Scriptural foundation, or lack of foundation, of the papal claims and of the independent ecclesiastical jurisdiction demanded by the Canon Law, it must be remembered that there is no real evidence that he had ever studied Civil Law and that his knowledge of Canon Law and of papal pronouncements did not, in spite of what some writers have maintained, amount to much more than knowledge of a Collection of Canons of the pseudo-Isidore and the bulls of Boniface VIII, Clement V and John XXII. He may have been acquainted with the Decree of Gratian; but the passages which are adduced as evidence of a knowledge of Gratian are too vague to serve as a proof of anything which could truly be called 'knowledge'. When Marsilius fulminated against the papal claims, he had primarily in mind the papal supremacy as conceived by Boniface VIII and those who shared his outlook. This is not to say, of course, that Marsilius did not deliver a general attack on the Church and its claims; but it is as well to remember that this attack had its roots in enmity towards the specific claims of specific ecclesiastics. When one reads in the third and concluding *Dictio* the summary of Marsilius' position, one should bear in mind both the historical situation which gave rise to and was reflected in his theoretical statements and the abstract theory which, though historically conditioned, had its influence in inculcating a certain general mentality and outlook.

4. The first *Dictio* begins with a quotation from Cassiodorus in praise of peace. The quotations from classical writers and from the Bible cause perhaps a first impression of abstraction and antiquity; but very soon, after remarking that Aristotle has described almost all the causes of strife in the State, Marsilius remarks that there is another cause, which neither Aristotle nor any of his contemporaries or predecessors saw or could see.[4] This is a covert reference to Marsilius' particular reason for writing; and thus the actuality of the book makes itself felt at once, despite the borrowings from former writers.

The account of the nature of the State as a perfect or self-sufficing community which is brought into being for the sake of life but exists for the sake of the good life,[5] and the account of the 'parts' of the State[6] depend on Aristotle; but Marsilius adds an account of the priestly 'part' or order.[7] The priesthood is, then, part of the State, and though Christian revelation has corrected error in teaching and provided a knowledge of the salutary truth, the Christian priesthood remains none the less a part of the State. Marsilius' fundamental 'Erastianism' is thus asserted very early in the *Defensor pacis*.

Leaving out of account the cases where God directly appoints the ruler, one can reduce the different types of government to two fundamental types, government which exists by consent of the subjects and government which is contrary to the will of the subjects.[8] The latter type of government is tyrannical. The former type does not necessarily depend on election; but a government which depends on election is superior to a government which does not depend on election.[9] It may be that non-hereditary rule is the best form of elective government, but it does not follow that this form of government is best suited for any particular State.

Marsilius' idea of law, which next comes up for discussion in the *Defensor pacis*, involved a change from the attitude of thirteenth-century thinkers like St. Thomas. In the first place law has its origin, not in the positive function of the

State, but in the need of preventing quarrels and strife.[10] Statute law is also rendered necessary with a view to preventing malice on the part of judges and arbiters.[11] Marsilius gives, indeed, several definitions of law. For example, law is the knowledge or doctrine or universal judgment concerning the things which are just and useful to the State's life.[12] But knowledge of these matters does not really constitute law unless a coercive precept is added touching their observance. In order that there should be a 'perfect law' there must be knowledge of what is just and useful and of what is unjust and harmful; but the mere expression of such knowledge is not law in the proper sense unless it is expressed as a precept backed up by sanctions.[13] Law is, therefore, a preceptive and coercive rule, fortified by sanctions applicable in this life.[14]

It would seem to follow from this that law concerns the objectively just and useful, that is to say, what is just and useful in itself, with a logical priority to any positive enactment and that Marsilius implicitly accepts the idea of natural law. So he does to a certain extent. In the second *Dictio*[15] he distinguishes two meanings of natural law. First, it may mean those statutes of the legislator on the rightness and obligatory character of which practically all people agree; for example that parents are to be honoured. These statutes depend on human institution; but they are called natural laws inasmuch as they are enacted by all nations. Secondly, 'there are certain people who call "natural law" the dictate of right reason in regard to human acts, and natural law in this sense they subsume under divine law'. These two senses of natural law, says Marsilius, are not the same; the phrase is used equivocally. In the first case natural law denotes the laws which are enacted in all nations and are practically taken for granted, their rightness being recognized by all: in the second case it denotes the dictates of right reason, which include dictates not universally recognized. From this it follows that 'certain things are licit according to human law which are not licit according to divine law, and conversely'.[16] Marsilius adds that licit and illicit are to be interpreted according to divine rather than human law when the two conflict. In other words, he does not simply deny the existence of natural law in the sense in which St. Thomas would understand it; but he pays little attention to the concept. His philosophy of law represents a transition stage on the way to the rejection of natural law in St. Thomas's sense.

That there is a shift of emphasis and a change in attitude

is clear from the fact, already indicated, that Marsilius was unwilling to apply the word 'law' in a strict sense to any precept which is not fortified by sanctions applicable in this life. It is for this reason that he refused to allow that the law of Christ (*Evangelica Lex*) is law properly speaking: it is rather a speculative or operative doctrine, or both.[17] He speaks in the same strain in the *Defensor minor*.[18] Divine law is compared with the prescriptions of a doctor, it is not law in the proper sense. As natural law in the sense of the Thomist philosophy is expressly said by Marsilius to be reckoned under divine law, it, too, cannot be said to be law in the same sense that the law of the State is law. Thus, although Marsilius does not deny outright the Thomist conception of natural law, he implies that the standard type of law is the law of the State, and his doctrine points towards the conclusion that the law of the State is autonomous and supreme. As Marsilius subordinated Church to State, it would seem that he tended towards the idea that it is the State alone which can judge whether or not a given law is consonant with the divine law and is an application of it; but, on the other hand, as he reserved the name of law in the proper sense to the positive law of the State and refused it to divine law and to natural law in the Thomist sense, one might equally well say that his thought tended towards the separation of law and morality.

5. Law in the proper sense being human law, the law of the State, who precisely is the legislator? The legislator or first efficient cause of law is the people, the totality of citizens, or the more weighty part (*pars valentior*) of the citizens.[19] The more weighty part is estimated according to quantity and quality of persons: it does not necessarily mean a numerical majority, but it must, of course, be legitimately representative of the whole people. It can be understood either in accordance with the actually obtaining customs of States or it may be determined according to the opinions expressed by Aristotle in the sixth book of the *Politics*.[20] However, since there are practical difficulties in the way of the multitude's drawing up the laws, it is suitable and useful that the drawing up of laws should be entrusted to a committee or commission, which will then propose the laws for acceptance or rejection by the legislator.[21] These ideas of Marsilius reflect in large part the theory, if not always the practice, of the Italian republic.

The next point for consideration is the nature, origin and

scope of executive power in the State, the *pars principans*. The office of the prince is to direct the community according to the norms set by the legislator; his task is to apply and enforce the laws. This subordination of the prince to the legislator is best expressed when the executive power is conferred on each successive prince by election. Election is, in itself at least, preferable to hereditary succession.[22] In each State there should be a supreme executive power, though it does not necessarily follow that this power should be in the hands of one man.[23] Supremacy means that all other powers, executive or judicial, must be subordinate to the prince; but the supremacy is qualified by the assertion that if the prince transgresses the laws or fails seriously in the duties of his office he should be corrected, or if necessary removed from office, by the legislator or by those appointed by the legislature for this task.[24]

Marsilius' dislike of tyranny and his preference for the election of the executive reflect his concern with the well-being of the Italian City-State, while the concentration of supreme executive and judicial power in the hands of the prince reflects the general consolidation of power in the European States. It has been maintained that Marsilius envisaged a clear separation of powers; but though he separated the executive from the legislative power, he subordinated the judiciary to the executive. Again, it is true that he admitted in a sense the sovereignty of the people; but the later theory of the social contract has no clear explicit foundation in Marsilius' political theory. The subordination of the executive power to the legislature is supported by practical considerations touching the good of the State rather than by a philosophic theory of the social contract.

6. In discussing the nature of the State Marsilius has in view, of course, his coming attack on the Church. For example, the concentration of executive and judicial power, without exception, in the hands of the prince is designed to deprive the Church of all 'natural' foundations to its claims. It remains to be seen if the Church can support her claims from the data of revelation; and this subject is considered in the second part of the *Defensor pacis*. The transition from the first to the second part[25] consists of the statements that the State can function and that its parts can discharge their proper tasks only if the State is in a condition of peace and tranquillity; that it cannot be in this condition if the

prince is interfered with or suffers aggression; and that the Church has in fact disturbed the peace by its interference with the rights of the Holy Roman Emperor and of other persons.

After considering various definitions or meanings of the words 'Church', 'temporal', 'spiritual', 'judge' and 'judgment' Marsilius proceeds to argue[26] that Christ claimed no temporal jurisdiction when He was in this world but subjected Himself to the civil power, and that the Apostles followed Him in this. The priesthood, then, has no temporal power. Marsilius goes on in the following chapters to minimize the 'power of the keys' and sacerdotal jurisdiction. As to heresy, the temporal legislator may make it a crime with a view to securing the temporal well-being of the State; but to legislate on this point and to exercise coercion belongs to the State, not to the Church.[27]

After an excursus on absolute poverty, from which he draws the conclusion that Church endowments remain the property of the donor, so that the Church has only the use of them,[28] Marsilius proceeds to attack the divine institution of the papacy. It would be out of place to enter upon a discussion of Marsilius' attempt to disprove the papal claims by reference to the Scriptures; nor does space permit any detailed consideration of his conciliar theory, but it is important to note, first that Marsilius assumes that the Scriptures alone are the rule of faith, and secondly that decisions of General Councils are not regarded by him as having any coercive force unless ratified by the temporal legislator. Canon Law is dismissed as having no weight. A historical treatment of papal encroachments leads up to a consideration of the dispute between John XXII and Ludwig of Bavaria.[29] Mention is made of the state of affairs in Italy and of the excommunication of Matteo Visconti.

In the third part Marsilius gives a brief summary of the conclusions he has reached in the *Defensor pacis*. He makes it quite clear that he is primarily concerned, not with the furtherance of democracy nor with any particular form of government, but rather with the rejection of papal supremacy and ecclesiastical jurisdiction. Moreover, the whole course of the work shows that Marsilius was not content simply with rejecting ecclesiastical interference in temporal matters; he went on to subordinate the Church to the State in all matters. His position was not that of one protesting against the encroachments of the Church on the sphere of the State while admitting the Church as a 'perfect society', autonomous in spiritual affairs: on the contrary, his position was frankly 'Erastian' and, at the same time, of a revolutionary character. Previté-Orton is obviously quite correct when he says that, in spite of disproportions in the work, there is unity of purpose and idea in the *Defensor pacis*. 'Everything is subordinated to the main aim, that of the destruction of papal and ecclesiastical power.' In the first part of the work, that which deals with the nature of the State, those themes are discussed and those conclusions are drawn which will serve as foundation for the second part. On the other hand, Marsilius was not animated by a hatred against papal supremacy and ecclesiastical jurisdiction for hatred's sake: as we have seen, his actual starting-point was what he regarded as the deplorable condition of northern Italy. He speaks on occasion about the empire, of course, and he apparently envisages the emperor as ratifying decisions of General Councils; but he was interested above all in the City-State or republic, which he considered to be supreme and autonomous in matters spiritual and temporal. There is, indeed, some excuse for regarding him as a forerunner of Protestantism; his attitude towards the Scriptures and towards the papacy shows as much; but it would be a great mistake to regard his attack on the papacy and on ecclesiastical jurisdiction as having proceeded from religious convictions or zeal. One can, of course, admit that in the course of his writing Marsilius became a 'religious controversialist'; but his religious controversy was undertaken, not for the sake of religion, but in the interests of the State. What characterizes him is his conception of the completely autonomous State. He admitted divine law, it is true; but he also admitted that human law may conflict with divine law, and in this case all subjects of the State, clerics and laymen, must obey human law, though one passage, mentioned earlier, seems to imply that if a law of the State obviously contradicts the law of Christ, the Christian should follow the latter. But since the Church, according to Marsilius, has no fully independent authority to interpret the Scriptures, it would scarcely be possible for the Christian to appeal to the teaching of the Church. In spite of its roots in contemporary history Marsilius' political theory looks forward to conceptions of the nature and function of the State which are modern in character, and which have scarcely brought happiness to mankind.

7. It has been maintained that Marsilius' political theory

is 'Averroistic' in character. Speaking of the *Defensor pacis* Étienne Gilson remarks that it is 'as perfect an example of political Averroism as one could wish'.[30] This Averroism consists in the application to politics of the Averroistic dichotomy between the sphere of faith and the sphere of reason. Man has two ends, a natural end, which is served by the State, utilizing the teaching of philosophy, and a supernatural end, served by the Church, utilizing the data of revelation. As the two ends are distinct, the State is completely independent, and the Church has no title to interfere in political affairs. However, although Gilson stresses the Averroism of John of Jandun, he admits that the *Defensor pacis* is due principally to Marsilius of Padua and that what one actually knows of the Averroism of Marsilius 'does not go beyond an application of the theoretic separation of reason and faith to the domain of politics, where he transmutes it into a strict separation of the spiritual and the temporal, of the Church and the State'.[31]

Maurice De Wulf, on the other hand, held that any collaboration of John of Jandun in the *Defensor pacis* has to be excluded, on the ground of the work's unity of plan and homogeneity of style, and was of the opinion that, although Marsilius had been in contact with Averroistic circles, he was influenced much more by the political writings of Aristotle.[32] The Church is not a true society, at least it is not a 'perfect society' since it has no temporal sanctions at its disposal wherewith to enforce its laws. The Church is little more than an association of Christians who find their true unity in the State; and, though the priesthood is of divine institution, the Church's task, as far as this world is concerned, is to serve the State by creating the moral and spiritual conditions which will facilitate the work of the State.

De Wulf's view of the matter, apart from his rejection of any collaboration on the part of John of Jandun, seems to me to be more in accordance with the tone and spirit of the *Defensor pacis* than the idea that the work is of specifically Averroistic inspiration. Marsilius thought that the Church's claims and activity hindered and disturbed the peace of the State, and he found in the Aristotelian conception of the autonomous and self-sufficing State the key to the solution of the problem, provided that the Church was subordinated to the State. It seems to me that Marsilius was animated much more by regard for what he considered to be the welfare of the State than by theoretical considerations concerning the end of man. Nevertheless, this in no way excludes an Averroistic influence on Marsilius' thought and, after all, Averroism was, or professed to be, integral Aristotelianism. Averroes was regarded as the 'Commentator'. Marsilius was influenced by Peter of Abano and was in touch with John of Jandun; and both of these men were animated by the Averroistic veneration for Aristotle. There was really no homogeneous doctrine or set of doctrines which one can call 'Averroism'; and if it is true that 'Averroism' was less a doctrine than an attitude, one can perfectly well admit the 'Averroism' of Marsilius without being thereby compelled to conclude that his inspiration was derived from the Averroists rather than from Aristotle.

8. The *Defensor pacis* was solemnly condemned on April 27th, 1327; but it does not appear that the work was really studied by Marsilius' contemporaries, even by those who wrote against it, though Clement VI affirmed that he, when a cardinal, had submitted the work to a profound examination and had discovered therein 240 errors. Clement VI made this assertion in 1343, and we do not possess his publication. In 1378 Gregory XI renewed the condemnations of 1327; but the fact that the majority of the copies of manuscripts were made at the beginning of the fifteenth century seems to confirm the supposition that the *Defensor pacis* was not widely circulated in the fourteenth century. Those who wrote against the work in the fourteenth century tended to see in it little more than an attack on the independence of the Holy See and the immunity of the clergy: they did not realize its historical importance. In the following century the Great Schism naturally gave an impetus to the diffusion of Marsilius' theories; and these ideas exercised their long-term influence more as a 'spirit' than as precisely the ideas of Marsilius of Padua. It is significant that the first printed edition of the *Defensor pacis* was published in 1517 and that the work was apparently utilized by Cranmer and Hooker.

Chapter Twelve

SPECULATIVE MYSTICISM

Mystical writing in the fourteenth century – Eckhart – Tauler – Blessed Henry Suso – Ruysbroeck – Denis the Carthusian – German mystical speculation – Gerson.

1. One is accustomed perhaps to think of the sixteenth century, the century of the great Spanish mystics, as the period which was particularly distinguished for mystical writings. It may, indeed, well be that the works of St. Teresa and St. John of the Cross are the supreme achievements of mystical theology, the theoretical exposition, so far as this is possible, of the experimental knowledge of God; but we must remember that there had been writers on mysticism from early Christian times. We have only to think of St. Gregory of Nyssa and of the Pseudo-Dionysius in the Patristic age, of St. Bernard and of Hugh and Richard, of St. Victor in the twelfth century, and of St. Bonaventure and St. Gertrude in the thirteenth century. And in the fourteenth and fifteenth centuries there was a remarkable flowering of mystical writings. This fact is attested by the works of writers like Eckhart (1260–1327), Tauler (*c.* 1300–61), Bl. Henry Suso (*c.* 1295–1366), Ruysbroeck (1293–1381), St. Catherine of Siena (1347–80), Richard Rolle of Hampole (*c.* 1300–49), Walter Hilton (d. 1396), John Gerson (1363–1429), Denis the Carthusian (1402–71), St. Catherine of Bologna (1413–63) and St. Catherine of Genoa (1447–1510). It is with these mystical writings of the fourteenth and early part of the fifteenth centuries that I am concerned in this chapter; but I am concerned with them only in so far as they seem to be relevant to the history of philosophy; I am not concerned with mystical theology as such. This means that I shall confine my attention to philosophic speculation which appears to have been

influenced by reflection on the mystical life; and this in turn means in effect that special consideration will be given to two themes, namely the relation of finite being in general and that of the human soul in particular to God. More concretely, it is writers like Eckhart rather than writers like Richard Rolle whose thought will be discussed. In a work on mystical theology as such, attention would have to be paid to writers who cannot be dealt with here; but in a work on the history of philosophy, attention can be paid only to those who can reasonably be thought of as 'philosophers' according to some traditional or normal use of the term. I do not mean to imply, however, that the writers whom I propose to discuss in this chapter were primarily interested in theory. Even Eckhart, who was much more given to speculation than Henry Suso, for example, was deeply concerned with the practical intensification of religious life. This practical orientation of the mystical writers is shown partly by their use of the vernacular. Eckhart used both German and Latin, his more speculative work being in the latter language; Henry Suso also used both languages; Tauler preached in German; Ruysbroeck wrote in Flemish; and we possess a large collection of Gerson's French sermons, though he wrote mainly in Latin. A profound affective piety, issuing in a desire to draw others to closer union with God, is characteristic of these mystics. Their analyses of the mystical life are not so detailed and complete as those of the later Spanish mystical writers; but they form an important stage in the development of mystical theology.

One might reasonably be inclined to see in the flowering of mystical writing in the fourteenth century a reaction against logical and abstract metaphysical studies, against what some people call 'objective thinking', in favour of the one thing needful, salvation through union with God. And that there was such a reaction seems to be true enough. On the one hand there were the older philosophical traditions and schools; on the other hand there was the *via moderna*, the nominalist movement. The wranglings of the schools could not transform the heart; nor did they bring a man nearer to God. What more natural, then, than that the religious consciousness should turn to a 'philosophy' or pursuit of wisdom which was truly Christian and which looked to the work of divine grace rather than to the arid play of the natural intellect? The remarks of Thomas à Kempis on this matter are well known and have often been quoted. For example,

'I desire to feel compunction rather than to know its definition'; 'a humble rustic who serves God is certainly better than a proud philosopher who, neglecting himself, considers the movement of the heavens'; 'what is the use of much quibbling about hidden and obscure matters, when we shall not be reproved at the Judgment for being ignorant of them?'; 'and what do genera and species matter to us!'[1] Thomas à Kempis (1380–1471) belonged to the Brethren of the Common Life, an association founded by Gerard Groot (1340–84), who had been strongly influenced by the ideas of Ruysbroeck. The Brethren were of importance in the educational field, and they devoted special attention to the religious and moral upbringing of their charges.

But it was not only Scholastic aridities and academic wranglings about abstract questions which influenced, by way of reaction, the mystical writers; some of them seem to have been influenced by the Ockhamist tendency to deny the validity of the traditional natural theology and to relegate all knowledge of God, even of His existence, to the sphere of faith. The answer to this was found by the mystics, or by some of them, in an extension of the idea of experience. Thus, though Henry Suso did not deny the validity of a philosophical approach to God, he tried to show that there is a certitude based on interior experience, when this accords with the revealed truths of faith. And, indeed, had not Roger Bacon, who insisted so much on the experimental method in the acquisition of knowledge, included spiritual experience of God under the general heading of experience? The mystics in their turn saw no reason for confining 'experience' to sense-experience or to consciousness of one's internal acts.

From the philosophical point of view, however, the chief point of interest concerning the mystical writers is their speculative rationalization of religious experience, particularly their pronouncements concerning the relation of the soul to God and, in general, of creatures to God. As is not uncommon with mystical writers of earlier and also later times, some of them made statements which were certainly bold and which were likely to arouse the hostile attention of theologians who regarded the literal sense of such statements. The chief offender in this respect was Eckhart, a number of whose propositions were subsequently condemned, though Henry Suso, his disciple, defended his orthodoxy. There has also been controversy concerning statements made by Ruysbroeck and Gerson. In what follows I shall give particular, if brief, consideration to this speculative aspect of the mystics' writings. Though certain statements, especially in Eckhart's case, are unorthodox if understood in an absolutely literal sense, I do not consider that the writers in question had any intention of being unorthodox. Many of their suspect propositions can be paralleled in earlier writers and are to be seen in the light of the neo-Platonic tradition. In any case I consider that the attempt which has been made in certain quarters to find a new 'German theology' in Eckhart and his disciples is a vain attempt.

2. Meister Eckhart was born about 1260 at Hochheim near Gotha. Joining the Dominican Order he studied and then lectured at Paris. After having been Provincial of Saxony and later Vicar-General of the Order, he returned to Paris in 1311, where he lectured until 1314. From Paris he moved to Cologne; and it was the archbishop of that city who in 1326 instituted an inquiry into Eckhart's doctrine. Eckhart appealed to the Holy See; but in 1329, two years after his death, 28 propositions taken from his later Latin writings were condemned by Pope John XXII.

In the *Quaestiones Parisienses*[2] Eckhart raises the question whether in God being (*esse*) and understanding (*intelligere*) are the same. His answer is, of course, in the affirmative; but he proceeds to maintain[3] that it is not because God is that He understands, but that He is because He is intellect and understanding. Understanding or intellection is 'the foundation of His being' or existence. St. John did not say: 'In the beginning was being, and God was being'; he said: 'In the beginning was the Word, and the Word was with God, and the Word was God.' So, too, Christ said: 'I am the Truth.' Moreover, St. John also says that all things were made through the Word; and the author of the *Liber de causis* accordingly concludes that 'the first of created things is being'. It follows that God, who is creator, is 'intellect and understanding, but not being or existence' (*non ens vel esse*). Understanding is a higher perfection than being.[4] In God, then, there is neither being nor existence, formally speaking, since God is the cause of being. Of course, if one likes to call understanding 'being', it does not matter; but in this case it must be understood that being belongs to God because He is understanding.[5] 'Nothing which is in a creature is in God save as in its cause, and it is not there formally. And so, since being belongs to creatures, it is not in God save as in its cause; and thus there is not being in

God but the purity of being.'[6] This 'purity of being' is understanding. God may have said to Moses, 'I am who am'; but God was then speaking like someone whom one meets in the dark and questions as to his identity, and who, not wishing to reveal himself, answers, 'I am who I am.'[7] Aristotle observed that the power of vision must itself be colourless, if it is to see every colour. So God, if He is the cause of all being, must Himself be above being.[8]

In making *intelligere* more fundamental than *esse* Eckhart certainly contradicted St. Thomas; but the general notion that God is not being, in the sense that God is super-being or above being, was a commonplace of the neo-Platonic tradition. The doctrine can be found in the writings of the Pseudo-Dionysius, for example. As we have seen, Eckhart cites the author (in a remote sense) of the *Liber de causis*, namely Proclus; and it is very likely that he was influenced by Theodoric (or Dietrich) of Freiberg (*c.* 1250–*c.* 1311), another German Dominican, who made copious use of Proclus, the neo-Platonist. The neo-Platonic side of the teaching of Albert the Great lived on in the thought of Dominicans like Theodoric of Freiberg, Berthold of Moosburg and Meister Eckhart, though it must be added that what for St. Albert was a relic, as it were, of the past, became for some later thinkers a principal and exaggerated element of their thought. In his (unpublished) commentary on Proclus' *Elementatio theologica* Berthold appealed expressly to Albert the Great.

It has been held that, after having maintained in his earlier works that God is *intelligere* and not *esse*, Eckhart changed his view and later maintained that God is *esse*. This was the opinion of Maurice De Wulf, for example. Others, however, like M. Gilson, will not admit a change of doctrine on Eckhart's part. That Eckhart declared that God is *esse*, existence, is certain. Thus, in the *Opus tripartitum*[9] his first proposition is, *Esse est Deus*. 'God and existence are the same.'[10] And he alludes to the words in the book of Exodus, 'I am who am.' 'God alone is properly speaking being (*ens*), one, true and good.'[11] 'To anyone who asks concerning God what or who He is, the reply is: Existence.'[12] That this sounds like a change of front can hardly be denied; but Gilson argues that Eckhart always emphasized the unity of God and that for him real unity is the property of intelligent being alone; so that the supreme unity of God belongs to Him because He is, above all things, intellect, *intelligere*. Eckhart was certainly understood as seeking a unity in God transcending the distinction of Persons; and one of the condemned propositions (24) runs as follows. 'Every distinction is alien to God, whether in Nature or in Persons. Proof: the Nature itself is one, this one thing, and any of the Persons is one and the same thing as the Nature.' The statement and condemnation of this proposition means, of course, that Eckhart was understood by the theologians who examined his writings as teaching that the distinction of Persons in the Godhead is logically posterior to the unity of Nature in such a way that unity transcends trinity. Henry Suso defended Eckhart by observing that to say that each of the divine Persons is identical with the divine Nature is the orthodox doctrine. This is perfectly correct. The examining theologians, however, understood Eckhart to mean that the distinction of Persons from one another is a secondary 'stage', as it were, in the Godhead. But I am not concerned with the orthodoxy or unorthodoxy of Eckhart's trinitarian doctrine: I wish merely to draw attention to the emphasis he laid on the unity of the Godhead. And it is Gilson's contention that this perfect unity belongs to God, according to Eckhart's constant opinion, in virtue of God's being primarily *intelligere*. The pure divine essence is *intelligere*, which is the Father, and it is from the fecundity of this pure essence that there proceed the Son (*vivere*) and the Holy Spirit (*esse*).

The truth of the matter seems to be that there are various strands in Eckhart's thought. When he comments on the words, 'I am who am', in the *Expositio libri Exodi*, he observes that in God essence and existence are the same and that the identity of essence and existence belongs to God alone. In every creature essence and existence are distinct, and it is one thing to ask about the existence of a thing (*de annitate sive de esse rei*) and another to ask about its quiddity or nature. But in the case of God, in whom existence and essence are identical, the fit reply to anyone who asks who or what God is, is that God exists or is. 'For existence is God's essence.'[13] This doctrine is obviously the Thomist doctrine, learnt and accepted by the Dominican. But in the very passage mentioned Eckhart speaks of the 'emanation' of Persons in the Godhead and uses the very neo-Platonic expression *monas monadem gignit*. Moreover, the tendency to find in God a unity without distinction, transcending the distinction of Persons, a tendency to which I have referred above, is also of neo-Platonic inspiration, as is also the doctrine that God is above being. On the other hand, the notion that *intelligere* is the supreme divine perfection seems to be original: in the Plotinian scheme the One is above intellect. Probably it is not possible to harmonize these different strands perfectly; but it is not necessary to suppose that when Eckhart stressed the identity of existence and essence in God he was consciously renouncing his 'former' view that God is *intelligere* rather than *esse*. In the *Expositio libri Genesis* he says: 'the nature of God is intellect, and for Him to be is to understand'; *natura Dei est intellectus, et sibi esse est intelligere.*[14]

However, whether he changed his opinion or not, Eckhart made some rather bold statements in connection with the characterization of God as existence, *esse*. For example, 'outside God there is nothing, inasmuch as it would be outside existence'.[15] God is creator but He does not create 'outside' Himself. A builder makes a house outside himself, but it is not to be imagined that God threw, as it were, or created creatures outside Himself in some infinite space or vacuum.[16] 'Therefore God created all things, not to stand outside Himself or near and beside Himself, like other craftsmen, but He called (them) from nothingness, that is, from non-existence, to existence, which they found and received and had in Him. For He Himself is existence.'[17] There is nothing outside the first cause; for to be outside the first cause would mean being outside existence; since the first cause is God, and God is being and existence. The doctrine that 'outside' God there is nothing is certainly susceptible of an orthodox interpretation: if, that is to say, it is taken as tantamount to the denial of the creature's independence of God. Moreover, when Eckhart declares that, though creatures have their specific natures from their forms, which make them this or that kind of being, their *esse* does not proceed from the form but from God, he might seem to be simply insisting on the facts of divine creation and divine conservation. But he goes further than this and declares that God is to the creature as act to potency, as form to matter, and as *esse* to *ens*, implying apparently that the creature exists by the existence of God. Similarly he says that nothing so lacks distinction as that which is constituted and that from which and through which and by which it is constituted and subsists; and he concludes that nothing so lacks distinction (*nihil tam indistinctum*) as the one God or Unity and the multiplicity of creatures (*creatum numeratum*).

Now, if these propositions are taken in isolation, it is no wonder that Eckhart should be regarded as teaching a form of pantheism. But there is no justification for taking these texts in isolation, if we wish, that is to say, to discover what Eckhart meant. He was accustomed to use antinomies, to state a thesis and give reasons for it, and then to state an antithesis and give reasons for it. Obviously both sets of statements must be taken into consideration if Eckhart's meaning and intention are to be understood. For example, in the case in point the thesis is that nothing is so distinct from the created as God is. One of the reasons given is that nothing is so distant from anything as is the opposite of that thing. Now, 'God and the creature are opposed as the One and Unnumbered is opposed to number, the numbered and the numerable. Therefore nothing is so distinct (as God) from any created being.' The antithesis is that nothing is so 'indistinct' from the creature as God is; and reasons are given for saying this. It is pretty clear that Eckhart's line of thought was as follows. It is necessary to say that God and creatures are utterly different and opposed; but if one *simply* says this, one is implying what is not true; at least one is stating what is not the whole truth; for the creature exists only by and through God, without whom it is nothing at all.

For an understanding of Eckhart's antinomies one can profitably consult Otto Karrer's *Meister Eckhart*,[18] where he cites texts and appends explanatory notes. Karrer may endeavour in an exaggerated manner to assimilate Eckhart's teaching to that of St. Thomas, but his remarks serve to correct an exaggerated view of Eckhart's departures from St. Thomas. For example, Eckhart states that God alone is and that creatures are nothing and also that God is not being; that all creatures are God and also that all creatures are nothing; that no things are so unlike as Creator and creature and that no things are so like as Creator and creature; that God is in all things and also that God is above all things; that God is in all things as their being and also that God is outside all things. That God alone is and that creatures are nothing means simply that in comparison with God creatures are as nothing. In the Augustinian *Soliloquies*[19] occurs the statement that 'only of the Immortal can one really say that He is', and St. Anselm asserts[20] that in a certain sense God alone is. The statement that all creatures are God refers primarily to their eternal presence in God, in the divine intellect, while the statement that they are nothing means that they are nothing apart from God. The doctrine that God and creatures are both like and unlike implies the theory of analogy and it has its roots in the Pseudo-Dionysian *Divine Names*.[21] St. Thomas affirmed[22] that the creature is like God but that God should not be said to be like the creature. God as immanent is in all things by 'power, presence and essence', but He is also above all things, or transcends all things, since He is their creator out of nothing and in no way depends on them. Thus, in his ninth German sermon[23] Eckhart says: 'God is in all creatures . . . and yet He is above them.' In other words, there is no adequate reason for finding pantheism in his thought, even though a considerable number of statements, taken in isolation, would seem to imply that he was a pantheist. What draws one's attention in his thought is the bold way in which he juxtaposes his theses and antitheses rather than the isolated statements, which are frequently commonplaces of mediaeval philosophy and can be discovered in Augustine or the Pseudo-Dionysius or the Victorines or even St. Thomas. As Karrer observes, one can find apparent antinomies even in St. Thomas. For instance, in the *Summa theologica*[24] St. Thomas says that God is above all things (*supra omnia*) and yet in all things (*in omnibus rebus*); that God is in things and yet that all things are in God; that nothing is distant from God and yet that things are said to be distant from God. One condemned proposition of Eckhart begins, 'all creatures are one pure nothingness'; and to say that his intentions were not heterodox is not, of course, to question the legitimacy of the ecclesiastical action which was taken, since it is obvious enough that the propositions in question could easily be misinterpreted, and what was condemned was the proposition as it stood taken in its literal or natural sense but not necessarily as the author understood and meant it. The proposition in question was condemned as 'badly sounding, rash and suspected of heresy', and Rome could hardly judge of it in any other way when it was presented for theological comment and judgment. To realize this, one has only to read the following passage in the fourth German sermon.[25] 'All creatures are a pure nothing. I do not say that they are little or something; they are a pure nothing.' But he goes on to explain what he means. 'All creatures have no being, as their being depends on the presence of God. If God turned away from creatures for one moment, they would be reduced to nothing.' The historian of philosophy, however, is concerned with the author's intended meaning, not with the theological 'note' to be attached to isolated propositions; and it is, I think, to be regretted that some historians have apparently allowed the boldness of some of Eckhart's propositions to blind them both to the general context and meaning and to the history of the propositions in question.

Eckhart also made some strange statements concerning the act of creation. In the *Expositio libri Genesis* he says, with reference to the statement that God created 'in the beginning', that this 'beginning' is the 'now' of eternity, the indivisible 'now' (*nunc*) in which God is eternally God and the eternal emanation of the divine Persons takes place.[26] He goes on to say that if anyone asks why God did not create the world before He did, the answer is that He could not do so; and He could not do so because He creates the world in the same 'now' in which He is eternally God. It is false to imagine that God awaited, as it were, a moment in which to create the world. To put the matter crudely, in the same 'now' in which God the Father exists and generates His coeternal Son He also creates the world. At first hearing at least this sounds as though Eckhart meant to teach that creation is from eternity, that it is coeternal and bound up with the generation of the Son. Indeed, the first three condemned propositions show clearly that the examining theologians understood him in this sense.

It may be, of course, that Eckhart meant the eternity of creation to refer to the object of the creative act, the actual world, and not only to the act of creation as it is in God. This is certainly the natural interpretation of many of the statements he makes. But in this case are we also to take with absolute literalness his statement that 'creation' and every work of God is simultaneously perfected and finished in the very beginning of creation?[27] If so, would not this imply that there is no time and that the Incarnation, for instance, took place at the beginning of creation? It seems to me that Eckhart was thinking of creation as the work of God who is not in time. God created in the beginning, he says, 'that is, in Himself', since God Himself is the *Principium*.[28] For God there is no past or future; for Him all things are present. So He may rightly be said to have completed His work at the moment of creation. God is the beginning and end of all things, 'the first and the last'; and since God is eternal, existing in one eternal 'now', He must be conceived as eternally creating all things in that eternal 'now'. I am not suggesting that Eckhart's statements, taken as they stand, were correct from the theological point of view; but he seems to me to have been looking at the creation of the world from what one might call God's point of view and to have been insisting that one should not imagine that God created the world 'after' a time in which there was no world. As to the connection of creation with the generation of the Son, Eckhart was thinking of the words of St. John:[29] 'All things were made by him (the Word): and without him was made nothing that was made.' Coupling these words with the statement contained in the first verse of the first chapter of Genesis, 'In the beginning God created heaven and earth', and understanding 'beginning' with reference to God, that is to say, as referring to God's eternal 'now', he says that God created the world simultaneously with the generation of the Son, by whom 'all things were made'. This would certainly seem to imply that there was no beginning of time and to amount to a denial of creation in time; but in the *Expositio libri Genesis*,[30] after referring to the Platonic Ideas or *rationes rerum* and saying that the Word is the *ratio idealis*, he goes on to quote Boethius and says that God created all things *in ratione et secundum rationem idealem*. Again, the 'beginning' in which God created heaven and the earth is the *intellectus* or *intelligentia*. It is possible, then, that Eckhart did not mean that the object of the creative act, the actual world, is eternal, but rather that God eternally conceived and willed creation in and through the Word. This, in any case, is what he later said he had meant. 'Creation, indeed, and every act of God is the very essence of God. Yet it does not follow from this that if God created the world from eternity, the world on this account exists from eternity, as the ignorant think. For creation in the passive sense is not eternal, just as the created itself is not eternal.'[31] Eckhart obviously utilized sayings like that of St. Albert the Great: 'God created from eternity, but the created is not from eternity,'[32] and of St. Augustine: 'In the eternal Word dost Thou speak eternally all that Thou speakest; and yet not all exists at once and from eternity that Thou effectest in speaking.'[33]

We seem perhaps to have strayed far from Eckhart the mystic. But the mystic aims at union with God, and it is not unnatural that a speculative mystic like Eckhart should emphasize the immanence of God in creatures and their dwelling in God. He did not deny God's transcendence; he affirmed it. But he certainly used exaggerated expressions and ambiguous expressions in stating the relations of creatures in general to God. A like boldness and proneness to exaggeration can be seen in his statements concerning the relation of the human soul in particular to God. In the human soul there is an element, which he called *archa* and which is uncreated. This element is the intelligence.[34] In virtue of *intelligere* the soul is deiform, since God Himself is *intelligere*. But the supreme mystical union with God does not take place through the activities of love and knowledge, which are activities of the soul and not the essence of the soul: it takes place in the innermost recess of the soul, the 'spark' or *scintilla animae*, where God unites the soul to Himself in a hidden and ineffable manner. The intellect apprehends God as Truth, the will as the Good: the essence of the soul, however, its citadel (*bürgelin*), is united with God as *esse*. The essence of the soul, also called its 'spark' (*vünkelin* or *scintilla*) is simple; it is on it that the image of God is stamped; and in the mystical union it is united with God as one and simple, that is to say, with the one simple divine essence transcending the distinction of Persons.[35] Eckhart thus preaches a mystical union which reminds one of Plotinus' 'flight of the alone to the Alone', and one can see the parallelism between his psychology and his metaphysic. The soul has a simple, unitary ground or essence and God has a simple essence transcending the distinction of Persons: the supreme mystical union is the union of the two. But this doctrine of a ground of the soul which is superior to the intelligence as a power does not necessarily mean that the soul's presence is not, in a higher sense, intellect. Nor does the doctrine that the ground of the soul is united with God as *esse* necessarily mean that the *esse* is not *intelligere*. In other words, I do not think that the mystical teaching of Eckhart necessarily contradicts Gilson's view that the statement that God is *esse* involves no break with the earlier statements that God is *intelligere*. The Sermons seem to make it clear that Eckhart did not change his opinion. He speaks of the ground of the soul as intellect.

Of the union mystically effected between God and the soul Eckhart speaks in an extremely bold way. Thus in the German sermon on the text, 'the just shall live for evermore; and their reward is with the Lord',[36] he declares that 'we are wholly transformed and changed into God'. And he goes on to say that, just as the bread is changed into the Body of

Christ, so is the soul changed into God in such a way that no distinction remains. 'God and I we are one. By knowledge I take God into myself; by love I enter into God.' Just as fire changes wood into itself, 'so we are transformed into God'. So too in the following sermon[37] Eckhart says that just as the food which I eat becomes one with my nature so do we become one with the divine nature.

Not unnaturally, statements of this kind did not pass unnoticed. The statement that there is something uncreated in the soul was censured, and the statement that we are wholly transformed into God in a manner similar to that of the transformation of bread into Christ's Body was condemned as heretical. In his self-justification Eckhart admitted that it is false to say that the soul or any part of it is uncreated; but he protested that his accusers had overlooked his having declared that the supreme powers of the soul were created in and with the soul.[38] In point of fact Eckhart had implied that there is something uncreated in the soul, and it is not to be wondered at that his words led to trouble; but he maintained that by 'uncreated' he meant 'not created *per se*, but concreated' (with the soul). Moreover, he had said not that the soul is uncreated but that if the whole soul were essentially and totally intellect, it would be uncreated. It is, however, difficult to see how he could maintain this, unless by 'intellect' he meant the ground of the soul, which is the image of God. In this case he may have meant that the soul, if totally and essentially the image of God (*imago Dei*), would be indistinguishable from the Word. This seems to be its probable meaning.

As to the statement that 'we are transformed and changed into God', Eckhart admits that it is an error.[39] Man, he says, is not the 'image of God, the unbegotten Son of God; but he is (made) to the image of God'. He goes on to say that just as many hosts on many altars are turned into the one Body of Christ, though the accidents of each host remain, so 'we are united to the true Son of God, members of the one head of the Church who is Christ'. In other words, he admits that his original statements were exaggerated and incorrect, and that the comparison of the union of the soul with God to transubstantiation is an analogy, not a parallel. As a matter of fact, however, though Eckhart's statements in his sermons concerning mystical union with God were obviously *male sonantes* as they stood, they are by no means exceptional among mystical writers, even among some whose orthodoxy has never seriously been called in question. Phrases like man becoming God or the transformation of the soul into God can be found in the works of writers of unquestioned orthodoxy. If the mystic wishes to describe the mystical union of the soul with God and its effects, he has to make use of words which are not designed to express any such thing. For example, in order to express the closeness of the union, the elevation of the soul and the effect of the union on the soul's activity, he employs a verb like 'transform' or 'change into'. But 'change into' denotes such processes as assimilation (of food), consumption of material by fire, production of steam from water, heat from energy, and so on, whereas the mystical union of the soul with God is *sui generis* and really requires an altogether new and special word to describe it. But if the mystic coined a brand new word for this purpose, it would convey nothing at all to anyone who lacked the experience in question. Therefore he has to employ words in more or less ordinary use, even though these words inevitably suggest pictures and parallels which do not strictly apply to the experience he is attempting to describe. There is nothing to be surprised at, then, if some of the mystic's statements, taken literally, are inadequate or even incorrect. And if the mystic is also theologian and philosopher, as Eckhart was, inexactitude is likely to affect even his more abstract statements, at least if he attempts to express in theological and philosophical statements an experience which is not properly expressible, employing for this purpose words and phrases which either suggest parallels that are not strict parallels or already possess a defined meaning in theology and philosophy.

Moreover, Eckhart's thought and expression were influenced by a number of different sources. He was influenced, for example, by St. Thomas, by St. Bonaventure, by the Victorines, by Avicenna, by the Pseudo-Dionysius, by Proclus, by the Christian Fathers. He was, too, a deeply religious man who was primarily interested in man's attitude to and experience of God: he was not primarily a systematic philosopher, and he never systematically thought through and rendered consistent the ideas and phrases which he had found in various authors and the ideas which occurred to him in his own meditations on the Scriptures. If, then, it is asked whether certain statements made by Eckhart are theologically orthodox when taken in isolation and according to their 'natural' meaning, the answer can hardly be any other than a negative answer. Eckhart lived at a time when exactitude and accuracy of expression were expected; and the fact that he made his bold and exaggerated statements in sermons, the hearers of which might easily misunderstand his real intentions, renders the theological censure of certain propositions easily understandable. On the other hand, if it is asked whether Eckhart intended to be heterodox and whether he intended to found a 'German theology', the answer must also be in the negative. Disciples like Henry Suso warmly defended the Master against charges of heresy; and a man like Suso would never have done this had he seen any reason to doubt Eckhart's personal orthodoxy. To my mind it seems absurd either to make of Eckhart a 'German thinker' in revolt against Catholic orthodoxy or to attack the theologians who took exception to certain of his statements as though there were nothing in these statements to which they were entitled to take exception.

3. John Tauler was born at Strasbourg about the year 1300 and entered the Dominican Order at an early age. He did his studies at Paris; but it is clear that he was already more attracted to the mystical writers and to the writers influenced by neo-Platonism than to the logical investigations of contemporary philosophers or the purely abstract metaphysical speculations of the Schoolmen. He is famous as a preacher rather than as a theologian or a philosopher, and his preaching seems to have been especially concerned with the reformation and deepening of the spiritual life of religious and clergy. At the time of the Black Death he ministered heroically to the sick and dying. His writings present an orthodox Catholic and Christocentric mysticism, in distinction from the heretical and pantheistic mystical doctrines which were strenuously propagated at the time by various associations. He died in the city of his birth in the year 1361.

In Tauler's writings we find the same psychological doctrine of the 'spark' or 'foundation' of the soul as in the writings of Eckhart. The image of God resides in this apex or highest part of the soul, and it is by retreating within himself, transcending images and figures, that a man finds God. If a man's 'heart' (*Gemüt*) is turned towards this foundation of the soul, that is to say, if it is turned towards God, his faculties of intellect and will function as they ought; but if his 'heart' is turned away from the foundation of the soul, from the indwelling God, his faculties, too, are turned away from God. In other words, between the foundation of the soul and the faculties Tauler finds a link, *das Gemüt*, which is a permanent disposition of the soul in regard to its foundation or apex or 'spark'.

Tauler not only utilized the writings of St. Augustine, St. Bonaventure and the Victorines, but also those of the Pseudo-Dionysius; and he seems to have read some Proclus. He was also strongly influenced by Eckhart's teaching. But, whereas Eckhart not infrequently spoke in such a way that his orthodoxy was called in question, it would be superfluous to raise any such question in regard to Tauler, who insists on the simple acceptance of revealed truths and whose thought is constantly Christocentric in character.

4. Henry Suso was born at Constance about the year 1295. He entered the Dominican Order and did his studies at Constance (perhaps partly at Strasbourg), after which he went to Cologne. There he made the personal acquaintance of Eckhart, for whom he retained a lasting admiration, affection and loyalty. Returning to Constance he spent some years there, writing and practising extraordinary mortifications and penances; but at the age of forty he began an apostolic life of preaching not only in Switzerland but also in Alsace and the Rhineland. In 1348 he changed his convent at Constance for that at Ulm (driven thereto by calumnies) and it was at Ulm that he died in January, 1366. He was beatified by Gregory XVI in 1831.

Suso's chief concern as writer was to make known the soul's path to the highest union with God: he was above all a practical mystical writer. The more speculative part of his thought is contained in *The Little Book of Truth* (*Büchlein der Wahrheit*) and in the last eight chapters of his autobiography. *The Little Book of Eternal Wisdom* (*Büchlein der ewigen Weisheit*) is a book of practical mysticism. Suso wrote a Latin version of it, the *Horologium Sapientiae*, which is not a translation but a development. Some letters and at least two certainly authentic sermons have also been preserved.

Suso warmly defended Eckhart against the charge of confusing God and creatures. He himself is perfectly clear and decisive about the distinction between them. He says indeed that creatures are eternally in God and that, as in God, they are God; but he carefully explains what he means by this. The ideas of creatures are eternally present in the divine mind; but these ideas are identical with the divine essence; they are not forms distinct from one another or from the divine essence. Further, this being of creatures in God is quite distinct from the being of creatures outside God: it is only through creation that 'creatures' exist. One cannot attribute creatureliness to creatures as they are in God. However, 'the creatureliness of any nature is nobler and more useful to it than the being which it has in God'.[40] In all this Suso was not saying anything different from what St. Thomas had taught. Similarly he expressly teaches that creation is a free act of God.[41] He certainly uses the Pseudo-Dionysian (that is to say, neo-Platonic) idea of the overflowing of the divine goodness; but he is careful to observe that this overflowing takes place as a necessary process only within the Godhead, where it is 'interior, substantial, personal, natural, necessary without compulsion, eternal and perfect'.[42] The overflowing in creation is a free act on God's part and is distinct from the eternal procession of the divine Persons. There is, then, no question of pantheism in Suso's thought.

A similar freedom from pantheistic tendencies is clear in Suso's doctrine of the soul's mystical union with God. As with Eckhart and Tauler, the mystical union is said to take place in the 'essence' of the soul, the 'spark' of the soul. This essence or centre of the soul is the unifying principle of the soul's powers, and it is in it that the image of God resides. Through the mystical union, which takes place by supernaturally impressed knowledge and love, this image of God is further actualized. This actualization is called the 'birth of God' (*Gottesgeburt*) or 'birth of Christ' (*Christusgeburt*) in the soul, by means of which the soul is made more like to and more united with the Deity in and through Christ. Suso's mysticism is essentially Christocentric. He speaks of the soul's 'sinking into' God; but he emphasizes the fact that there is not, and never can be, a complete ontological identification of the ground or essence of the soul with the divine Being. Man remains man, even if he becomes deiform: there is no pantheistic absorption of the creature in God.[43] As I have said, Suso was strongly influenced by Eckhart, but he was always careful to bring his teaching into clear harmony with the doctrines of Catholic Christianity. It would, indeed, be preferable to say that his mystical teaching sprang from the Catholic tradition of spirituality, and that, as far as Eckhart is concerned, Suso interpreted the latter's teaching in an orthodox sense.

It has been said that Suso's thought differed from Eckhart's in regard to its direction. Eckhart preferred to start with God: his thought moved from the simple divine essence to the Trinity of Persons, especially to the Word or *Logos*, in which he saw the archetype of creation, and so to creatures in the Word. The union of the soul with God appeared to him as a return of the creature to its dwelling-place in the Word, and the highest mystical experience of the soul is the union of its centre with the simple centre or essence of the Godhead. Suso, however, was less speculatively inclined. His thought moved from the human person to the latter's dynamic union with Christ, the God-Man; and he emphasized strongly the place of the Humanity of Christ in the ascent of the soul to God. In other words, though he often used more or less the same phrases that Eckhart used, his thought was less neo-Platonic than Eckhart's, and he was more strongly influenced than was Eckhart by the affective spirituality and the Christocentric 'bride-mysticism' of St. Bernard.

5. John Ruysbroeck was born in 1293 at the village of Ruysbroeck near Brussels. After some years spent at the latter city he became Prior of the Augustinian convent of Groenendael (Green Valley) in the forest of Soignes near Brussels. He died in 1381. His writings include *The Adornment of the Spiritual Marriage* and *The Book of the Twelve Beguines*. He wrote in Flemish.

Ruysbroeck, who was strongly influenced by the writings of Eckhart, insists on the original presence of the creature in God and on the return to that state of unity. One can distinguish in man a threefold unity.[44] 'The first and highest unity of man is in God.' Creatures depend on this unity for their being and preservation, and without it they would be reduced to nothing. But this relationship to God is essential to the creature and it does not, of itself, make a man really good or bad. The second unity is also natural: it is the unity of man's higher powers in as much as these spring from the unity of his mind or spirit. This fundamental unity of spirit is the same as the first type of unity, the unity which depends on God; but it is considered in its activity rather than in its essence. The third unity, also natural, is the unity of the senses and of the bodily activities. If in regard to the second natural unity the soul is called 'spirit', in regard to the third it is called 'soul', that is, as vital principle and principle of sensation. The 'adornment' of the soul consists in the supernatural perfection of the three unities; the first through the moral perfection of the Christian; the second through the theological virtues and the gifts of the Holy Spirit; the third through mystical and inexpressible union with God. The highest unification is 'that most high unity in which God and the loving spirit are united without intermediary'.

Like Eckhart Ruysbroeck speaks of 'the most high and superessential Unity of the Divine Nature'. The words recall the writing of the Pseudo-Dionysius. With this supreme Unity the soul, in the highest activity of the mystical life, can become united. But the union transcends the power of reason; it is accomplished by love. In it the ground of the soul is, as it were, lost in the ineffable abyss of the Godhead, in the Essential Unity to which 'the Persons, and all that lives in God, just give place'.[45]

Not unnaturally, Ruysbroeck's doctrine was attacked, particularly by Gerson. However, that he did not intend to teach pantheism Ruysbroeck made clear in *The Mirror of Eternal Salvation* and in *The Book of the Twelve Beguines*. He was defended by Jan van Schoonhoven (d. 1432), himself a mystic, and Denis the Carthusian did not hesitate to borrow from his writings.

6. Denis the Carthusian, who was born at Rychel in 1402 and died as a Carthusian of Roermond in 1471, does not belong chronologically to the period which is being treated in the first part of this work. For the sake of convenience, however, I shall say a few words about him here.

The 'ecstatic Doctor' had done his higher studies at Cologne, and, for a mystical writer, he was surprisingly interested in Scholastic themes. He composed commentaries on the *Sentences* of Peter Lombard and on Boethius, as well as on the writings of the Pseudo-Dionysius, and he wrote a summary of the orthodox faith according to the works of St. Thomas, a manual of philosophy and theology (*Elementatio philosophica et theologica*) and other theological works. In addition, there are his purely ascetical and mystical treatises. It is clear that he was at first a devoted follower of St. Thomas; and his hostility not only towards the nominalists but also towards the Scotists seems to have continued throughout his life. But he gradually moved from the camp of the Thomists to that of the followers of St. Albert, and he was much influenced by the writings of the Dominican Ulric of Strasbourg (d. 1277), who had attended St. Albert's lectures at Cologne. Not only did Denis reject the real distinction between essence and existence, which he had at first defended; but he also abandoned the Thomist view of the rôle of the 'phantasm' in human knowledge. Denis restricted the necessity of the phantasm to the lower levels of knowledge and maintained that the soul can know without recourse to the phantasm its own activity, angels and God. Our knowledge of the divine essence, however, is negative; the mind comes to realize clearly the incomprehensibility of God. In this emphasis on negative but immediate knowledge of God Denis was influenced by the Pseudo-Dionysius and by the writings of Ulric of Strasbourg and other followers of St. Albert. The Carthusian Doctor is a remarkable example of the combination of mystical with Scholastic interests.

7. The German mystics of the Middle Ages (I include Ruysbroeck, although he was a Fleming) drew their mysticism from its roots in the Christian Faith. It is not a question of enumerating sources, of showing the influence of the Fathers, of St. Bernard, of the Victorines, of St. Bonaventure or of trying to minimize the neo-Platonic influences on expression and even on idea, but of realizing the mystics' common belief in the necessity of supernatural grace which comes through Christ. The Humanity of Christ may play a larger part in the thought of Suso, for example, than in that of Eckhart; but the latter, in spite of all his exaggerations, was first and foremost a Christian. There is, then, no real support for the attempt which has been made to discover in the writings of the German mediaeval mystics like Eckhart, Tauler and Suso a 'German mysticism', if by this is meant a mysticism which is not Catholic but one proceeding from 'blood and race'.

On the other hand, the German mystics of the fourteenth century do represent an alliance of Scholasticism and mysticism which gives them a stamp of their own. Grabmann remarked that the combination of practical mysticism and of speculation is ultimately a continuation of St. Anselm's programme, *Credo, ut intelligam*. However, although the speculation of the German mystics grew out of the currents of thought which had inspired the mediaeval Scholastics and which had been systematized in various ways in the thirteenth century, their speculation must be seen in the light of their practical mysticism. If it was partly the circumstances of the education of this or that mystical writer which moulded the framework of his speculation and influenced his choice of theoretic ideas, it was also partly his practical mystical life and his reflection on his spiritual experience which influenced the direction of his speculation. It would be a mistake to think that the doctrine of the *scintilla animae*, the spark of the soul or the essence or ground or apex of the soul, was no more than a stock idea which was adopted mechanically from predecessors and passed on from mystic to mystic. The term *scintilla conscientiae* or *synderesis* occurs in St. Jerome[46] and it reappears in, for example, St. Albert the Great, who means by it a power existing in all men which admonishes them of the good and opposes evil. St. Thomas, who refers to St. Jerome,[47] speaks of synderesis metaphorically, as the *scintilla conscientiae*.[48] The mystics certainly meant something else than synderesis when they spoke of the spark or ground of the soul; but, even granting that, practically all the expressions by which they characterized the ground of the soul were already to be found, according to Denifle, in the writings of Richard of St. Victor. No doubt Denifle's contention is true; but the German mystics made the idea of the ground or spark of the soul one of their leading ideas, not simply because they found it in the writings of a revered predecessor, but because it fitted in with their experience of a mystical union with God transcending the conscious play of acts of intelligence and will. As found in their predecessors, the idea doubtless suggested to them this close union; but their meditation on the idea went hand in hand with their experience.

Possibly certain German writers have gone too far in finding in the combination of speculation with practical mysticism a distinguishing mark of the German mystics. It serves to differentiate them from some mystics, it is true, who were more or less innocent of theoretic speculations; but a similar combination can be seen in the case of the Victorines in the twelfth century and, indeed, in that of Gerson himself, though Gerson had scant sympathy for the line of speculation adopted by Eckhart and Ruysbroeck, as he interpreted it at least. However, there is an added characteristic which is connected with the fact that Eckhart, Tauler and Suso were all members of the Dominican Order, the Order of Friars Preachers. They disseminated mystical doctrine in their sermons, and attempted, as I have already mentioned, to deepen in this way the general spiritual life, particularly among religious. No doubt one could make a similar observation about St. Bernard, for example, but, particularly in the case of Eckhart, there is a speculative flavour and framework, due to the intervening development of mediaeval philosophy, which is not to be found in St. Bernard's sermons. Moreover, the Germans are more 'rugged', less flowery. The German speculative mysticism is so closely connected with Dominican preaching that it enables one to speak, in this sense, of the 'German mysticism' of the Middle Ages, provided that one does not mean to imply that the German Dominicans were attempting to establish a German religion or a German *Weltanschauung*.

8. John Gerson, who was born in 1363, succeeded Peter d'Ailly as chancellor of the university of Paris in 1395.[49] He has been accounted a nominalist; but his adoption of certain nominalist positions did not proceed from adherence to the nominalist philosophy. He was a theologian and mystical writer rather than a philosopher; and it was in the interests of faith and of theology that he tended in certain matters towards nominalist doctrine. Gerson's chancellorship fell in the period of the Great Schism (1378–1417) and he took a prominent part in the work of the Council of Constance. Much distressed not only at the state of the Church, but also at the condition of university studies and the propagation of doctrines which had, it seemed to him, led to or facilitated the rise of theories like those of Hus, he sought to apply a remedy, not through a dissemination of nominalism as such but through a recall of men to the right attitude towards God. The conflict of systems of philosophy and the curiosity and pride of theologians had, he thought, been responsible for much evil. In his *De modis significandi propositiones quinquaginta* Gerson maintained that the various branches of study had become confused to the detriment of truth, logicians trying to solve metaphysical problems by the *modus significandi* proper to logic, metaphysicians and logicians endeavouring to prove revealed truths or to solve theological problems by methods which are not fitted for dealing with the object of theology. This confusion, thought Gerson, had led to a state of anarchy in the intellectual world and to untrue conclusions. Furthermore, the pride of the Scholastic theologians had engendered curiosity and the spirit of novelty or singularity. Gerson published two lectures *Contra vanam curiositatem in negotio fidei*, against vain curiosity in the matter of faith, in which he drew attention to the part played in Scholastic disputes by love of one's own opinions, envy, the spirit of contention and contempt for the uneducated and the uninitiated. The root fault is the pride of the natural reason which endeavours to exceed its bounds and to solve problems which it is incapable of solving.

It is from this angle that one should regard Gerson's attack on realism. The notion of ideas in God involves a confusion, first of logic with metaphysics, and then of metaphysics with theology. Secondly, it implies that God is not simple, since the realists tend to speak of these *rationes ideales* in God as though they were distinct; and some even speak as though creatures pre-existed in God, that is to say, as though the divine ideas were creatures existing in God. Thirdly, the doctrine of divine ideas, employed in explaining creation, serves only to limit the divine freedom. And why do philosophers and theologians limit the divine freedom? From a desire of understanding that which cannot be understood, a desire which proceeds from pride. The thinkers of the Platonic tradition also speak of God, not primarily as free, but as the Good, and they utilize the principle of the natural tendency of goodness to diffuse itself in order to explain creation. But by doing so they tend to make creation a necessary effect of the divine nature. Again, realist metaphysicians and theologians insist that the moral law in no way depends on the divine will, thus restricting the divine liberty, whereas in point of fact 'God does not will certain actions because they are good; but they are good because He wills them, just as others are bad because He prohibits them.'[50] 'Right reason does not precede the will, and God does not decide to give law to a rational creature because He has first seen in His wisdom that He ought to do so; it is rather the contrary which takes place.'[51] It follows that the moral law is not immutable. Gerson adopted this Ockhamist position in regard to the moral law because he considered that it was the only position consonant with God's liberty. The Platonizing philosophers and theologians, he thought, had abandoned the principle of belief, of humble subjection, for the pride of the understanding. Moreover, he did not fail to draw attention to the realist aspects of the thought of John Hus and of Jerome of Prague; and he drew the conclusion that the pride of the understanding manifested by the realists leads in the end to open heresy.

Thus Gerson's attack on realism, though it involved him in some positions which were actually held by the nominalists, proceeded rather from religious preoccupations than from any particular enthusiasm for the *via moderna* as such. 'Repent and believe the Gospel'[52] was the text on which Gerson built his two lectures against vain curiosity in the matter of faith. The pride which had invaded the minds of university professors and lecturers had made them oblivious to the need for repentance and to the simplicity of faith.

This point of view is obviously more characteristic of a man whose concern is the soul's attitude towards God than of a man who is passionately interested in academic questions for their own sake. Gerson's hostility towards the metaphysics and theology of the realists certainly bears some analogy to Pascal's hostility towards those who would substitute for the God of Abraham and Isaac and Jacob the 'God of the philosophers'.

If we look at the matter from this point of view, it is not surprising to find Gerson expressing his amazement that the Franciscans had abandoned St. Bonaventure for *parvenus* in the intellectual world. St. Bonaventure's *Itinerarium mentis in Deum* he regarded as a book beyond all praise. On the other hand, if we consider Gerson's hostility towards realism, his attacks on Ruysbroeck and his attempt to connect realism with the heresies of John Hus and Jerome of Prague, his enthusiasm for St. Bonaventure might well appear somewhat startling when it is remembered that St. Bonaventure laid great stress on the Platonic doctrine of ideas in its Augustinian form and roundly condemned Aristotle for 'execrating' the ideas of Plato. Gerson's conviction was that the theologians of his time had neglected the Bible and the Fathers, the true sources of theology, in favour of pagan thinkers and of importations from metaphysics which impaired the simplicity of faith. He regarded, however, the Pseudo-Dionysius as the disciple and convert of St. Paul, and considered the Dionysian writings to form part of the well-spring of true wisdom. St. Bonaventure he revered as a man who had consistently drunk of these undefiled waters and who had concerned himself above all with the true wisdom, which is the knowledge of God through Jesus Christ.

In spite, then, of his attack on realism, Gerson's mystical doctrine was deeply influenced by the teaching of the Pseudo-Dionysius. M. André Combes, in his most interesting study of Gerson's relation to the writings and thought of the Pseudo-Dionysius,[53] after showing the authenticity of the *Notulae super quaedam verba Dionysii de Caelesti Hierarchia* and arguing that the work should precede the first lecture against 'vain curiosity' in the *Opera* of Gerson, makes it clear that Gerson was never simply a 'nominalist' and that his ideas were never simply identical with those of Peter d'Ailly (1350–1420), his 'master'. In fact, as M. Combes has shown, Gerson borrowed from the Pseudo-Dionysius not merely an arsenal of terminology, but also the important doctrine of the 'return'. Creatures proceed from God and return to God. How is this return accomplished? By each nature performing those acts which are proper to it. Strictly speaking, says Gerson (in his *Sermo de die Jovis sancta*), it is only the rational creature who returns to God, though Boethius said that all things return to their beginning or principle. But the important point about Gerson's doctrine of the 'return' is the emphasis he lays on the fact that it does not mean an ontological merging of the creature with God. As he regarded the Pseudo-Dionysius as a personal disciple of St. Paul, he was convinced that the Dionysian teaching was perfectly 'safe'. But, realizing that it could be misinterpreted, he considered that the theologian must elucidate the Areopagite's true meaning; and he himself utilized the writings of Hugh of St. Victor and of St. Albert the Great. From this two relevant and important points emerge. First, Gerson by no means condemned or rejected the Scholastic theology as such, which he considered necessary for the right interpretation of the Scriptures, of the Fathers and of St. Paul's disciple. Secondly, when he attacked Ruysbroeck, he was not attacking him for drawing on the teaching of the Pseudo-Dionysius but for misinterpreting and perverting that doctrine. Of course, we know that the Pseudo-Dionysius was not a disciple of St. Paul and that he drew copiously on Proclus; but the point is that Gerson interpreted the Pseudo-Dionysius as if he were not a Platonist. This explains how he could show at the same time a marked hostility towards the Platonizers and a marked predilection for the Pseudo-Dionysius.

Gerson accepted the threefold division of theology given by the Pseudo-Dionysius, symbolic theology, theology in the proper sense, and mystical theology. The threefold division is to be found in St. Bonaventure's *Itinerarium mentis in Deum*;[54] but Gerson seems to have drawn the distinction from the Pseudo-Dionysius' writings rather than from St. Bonaventure: at least he consulted the former and cites him as his authority. Mystical theology, he says, is the experimental knowledge of God, in which love, rather than the abstract speculative intellect, is at work, though the highest intellectual function is also involved. The *intelligentia simplex* and the *synderesis* or highest affective power are operative in mystical experience, which is not a rejection but a realization of the highest powers of the soul. Mystical union affects the foundation of the soul; but it is a union which does not dissolve the human personality in the Godhead. Mystical theology, at least if it is understood as mysticism itself rather than as the theory of mysticism, is the crown of theology, because it approaches nearest to the beatific vision, which is the final end of the soul.

The presence of this threefold division in Gerson's thought helps to make it clear that, while emphasizing the primacy of mystical theology, he did not reject theology in the ordinary sense. Nor did he reject philosophy. Whether his bent of mind might have led him to reject all but mystical theology had it not been for the Pseudo-Dionysius, St. Bonaventure and St. Albert is another and not very profitable question. He certainly laid stress on the Scriptures and the teaching of the Fathers and he certainly thought that theologians would do well to pay more attention to those sources; he certainly thought, moreover, that speculative theology contaminated by unwarranted importations from suspect philosophers encouraged pride and vain curiosity; but there is no real evidence for saying either that he rejected all Scholastic development of Scriptural and Patristic teaching or that he rejected a philosophy which observed its due limits. In some ways Gerson is the most interesting representative of the movement of speculative mysticism in the late Middle Ages. He shows us that the movement was primarily inspired by the desire for remedying the evils of the time and for deepening men's religious life: it was by no means a mere counterblast to nominalist scepticism. As for Gerson's own nominalism, it is truer to say that he adopted and exploited certain nominalist positions in the service of his own primary aim rather than that he was a nominalist. To say that Gerson was a nominalist philosopher who at the same time happened to be a mystic would be to give a false impression of his aims, his theoretical position and his spirit.

Appendix One

Honorific titles applied to philosophers treated of in this volume.

DURANDUS:	Doctor modernus, *later* Doctor resolutissimus.
PETRUS AUREOLI:	Doctor facundus.
WILLIAM OF OCKHAM:	Venerabilis inceptor.
ANTOINE ANDRÉ:	Doctor dulcifluus.
FRANCIS DE MARCIA:	Doctor succinctus.
JOHN OF MIRECOURT:	Monachus albus.
GREGORY OF RIMINI:	Doctor authenticus.
JOHN RUYSBROECK:	Doctor admirabilis.
DENIS THE CARTHUSIAN:	Doctor ecstaticus.
JOHN GERSON:	Doctor christianissimus.
JACOB BÖHME:	Philosophus teutonicus.
FRANCIS SUÁREZ:	Doctor eximius.

Appendix Two

A SHORT BIBLIOGRAPHY

General Works

BOEHNER, PH., O.F.M. *Medieval Logic*. Manchester, 1952.

BRÉHIER, E. *La philosophie du moyen âge*, nouvelle édition corrigée. Paris, 1949.

Histoire de la philosophie. Tome 1, *L'antiquité et le moyen âge*. Paris, 1943. (A treatment of Renaissance philosophy is included in this volume.)

BURCKHARDT, J. *The Civilization of the Renaissance*. London, 1944.

CARLYLE, R. W. and A. J. *A History of Mediaeval Political Theory in the West*. 6 vols. London, 1903–36.

CASSIRER, E. *Individuum und Kosmos in der Philosophie der Renaissance*. Berlin, 1927.

COPLESTON, F. C. *Mediaeval Philosophy*. London, 1952.

CROMBIE, A. C. *Augustine to Galileo. The History of Science, A.D. 400–1650*. London, 1952. (Unfortunately this work appeared when the present volume was already in proof.)

CURTIS, S. J. *A Short History of Western Philosophy in the Middle Ages*. London, 1950.

DEMPF, A. *Die Ethik des Mittelalters*. Munich, 1930.

Metaphysik des Mittelalters. Munich, 1930.

DE WULF, M. *Histoire de la philosophie médiévale*. Tome 3, *Aprés le treizième siècle*. Louvain, 1947 (6th edition).

DILTHEY, W. *Gesammelte Schriften*, vol. 2 (for Renaissance). Berlin and Leipzig, 1919.

FRISCHEISEN-KÖHLER, M. and MOOG, W. *Die Philosophie der Neuzeit bis zum Ende des XVIII Jahrhunderts*. Berlin,

1924. (This is the third volume of the revised Ueberweg and covers the Renaissance period.)

GEYER, B. *Die patristische und scholastische Philosophie*. Berlin, 1928. (This is the second volume of the revised edition of Ueberweg.)

GILSON, É. *La philosophie au moyen âge*. Paris, 1944. (2nd edition, revised and augmented.)

The Unity of Philosophical Experience. London, 1938.

Being and Some Philosophers. Toronto, 1949.

L'être et l'essence. Paris, 1948.

GRABMANN, M. *Die Philosophie des Mittelalters*. Berlin, 1921.

Mittelalterliches Geistesleben. 2 vols. Munich, 1926 and 1936.

HAURÉAU, B. *Histoire de la Philosophie scolastique*. 3 vols. Paris, 1872–80.

HAWKINS, D. J. B. *A Sketch of Mediaeval Philosophy*. London, 1946.

HIRSCHBERGER, J. *Geschichte der Philosophie. I, Altertum und Mittelalter*. Freiburg i. B., 1949.

PICAVET, F. *Esquisse d'une histoire générale et comparée des philosophies médiévales*. Paris, 1907 (2nd edition).

Essais sur l'histoire générale et comparée des théologies et des philosophies médiévales. Paris, 1913.

POOLE, R. L. *Illustrations of the History of Medieval Thought and Learning*. London, 1920 (2nd edition).

ROMEYER, B. *La philosophie chrétienne jusqu'à Descartes*. 3 vols. Paris, 1935–7.

RUGGIERO, G. DE. *La filosofia del Cristianesimo*. 3 vols. Bari.

Rinascimento, Riforma e Contrariforma. Bari, 1937.

VIGNAUX, P. *La pensée au moyen âge*. Paris, 1938.

Chapter Two: Durandus and Petrus Aureoli

Texts

DURANDUS

In 4 libros Sententiarum. Various sixteenth-century editions (of 3rd redaction), beginning with the Paris edition of 1508.

Durandi de S. Porciano O.P. Quaestio de natura cognitionis et Disputatio cum anonymo quodam necnon Determinatio Hervaei Natalis O.P. J. Koch (edit.). Münster, 1929; 2nd edition 1929 (Opuscula et textus, 6).

Durandus de S. Porciano, Tractatus de habitibus. Quaestio 4: De subiectis habituum, addita quaestione critica anonymi cuiusdam. J. Koch (edit.). Münster, 1930. (Opuscula et textus, 8).

PETRUS AUREOLI

In 4 libros Sententiarum. Rome, 1596.

Studies

DREILING, R. *Der Konzeptualismus in der Universalienfrage des Franziskanererzbischofs Petrus Aureoli (Pierre d'Auriole).* Münster, 1913 (Beiträge, 11, 6).

KOCH, J. *Jakob von Metz, O.P.* Archives d'histoire doctrinale et littéraire du moyen âge, 1929–30 (pp. 169–232).

Durandus de Sancto Porciano O.P. Forschungen zum Streit um Thomas von Aquin zu Beginn des 14 Jahrhunderts, Erster Teil, Literargeschichtliche Grundlegung. Münster, 1927 (Beiträge 26, 1).

KRAUS, J. *Die Universalienlehre des Oxforder Kanzlers Heinrich von Harclay in ihrer Mittelstellung zwischen skotistischen Realismus und ockhamistischen Nominalismus.* Divus Thomas (Fribourg, Switzerland), vol. 10 (1932), pp. 36–58 and 475–508 and vol. 11 (1933), pp. 288–314.

PELSTER, F. *Heinrich von Harclay, Kanzler von Oxford, und seine Quästionen.* Miscellanea F. Ehrle, vol. 1, pp. 307–56. Rome, 1924.

TEETAERT, A. *Pierre Auriol.* Dictionnaire de théologie catholique, vol. 12, cols. 1810–81. Paris, 1934.

Chapters Three–Eight: William of Ockham

Texts

Super quattuor libros sententiarum subtilissimae quaestiones. Lyons, 1495.

Quodlibeta septem. Paris, 1487; Strasbourg, 1491.

Expositio aurea et admodum utilis super artem veterem. Bologna, 1496.

Summa totius logicae. Paris, 1948, and other editions, especially: *Summa Logicae. Pars prima.* Ph. Boehner, O.F.M. (edit.). St. Bonaventure, New York, and Louvain, 1951.

Summulae in libros Physicorum. Bologna, 1495 and other editions.

Quaestio prima principalis Prologi in primum librum sententiarum cum interpretatione Gabrielis Biel. Ph. Boehner, O.F.M. (edit.). Paderborn, 1939.

The Tractatus de successivis, attributed to William Ockham. Ph. Boehner, O.F.M. (edit.). St. Bonaventure (New York), 1944.

The Tractatus de praedestinatione et de praescientia Dei et de futuris contingentibus of William Ockham. Ph. Boehner, O.F.M. (edit.). St. Bonaventure (New York), 1945. (This edition also contains a 'Study on the Mediaeval Problem of a Three-valued logic' by the editor.)

Ockham: Selected Philosophical Writings. Ph. Boehner, O.F.M. (edit.). London, 1952.

Gulielmi de Occam Breviloquium de potestate papae (critical edition). L. Baudry (edit.). Paris, 1937.

Gulielmi de Ockham Opera politica, vol. 1. J. O. Sikes (edit.). Manchester, 1940.

Studies

ABBAGNANO, N. *Guglielmo di Ockham.* Lanciano, 1931.

AMANN, E. *Occam.* Dictionnaire de théologie catholique, vol. 11, cols. 864–904. Paris, 1931.

BAUDRY, L. *Guillaume d'Occam. Sa vie, ses œuvres, ses idées sociales et politiques. I, L'homme et les œuvres.* Paris, 1949.

BOEHNER, PH., O.F.M. *Ockham's Theory of Truth.* Franciscan Studies, 1945, pp. 138–61.

Ockham's Theory of Signification. Franciscan Studies, 1946, pp. 143–70.

CARRÉ, H. M. *Realists and Nominalists* (pp. 101–25). Oxford, 1946.

GIACÓN, C. *Guglielmo di Occam.* 2 vols. Milan, 1941.

GUELLUY, R. *Philosophie et théologie chez Guillaume d'Ockham.* Louvain, 1947.

HAMANN, A., O.F.M. *La doctrine de l'église et de l'état chez Occam.* Paris, 1942.

HOCHSTETTER, E. *Studien zur Metaphysik und Erkenntnislehre des Wilhelms von Ockham.* Berlin, 1937.

LAGARDE, G. DE. *Naissance de l'esprit laïque au déclin du moyen âge.*

Cahier IV: *Ockham et son temps.* 1942.

V: *Ockham. Bases de départ.* 1946.

VI: *Ockham. La morale et le droit.* 1946.

MARTIN, G. *Wilhelm von Ockham. Untersuchungen zur Ontologie der Ordnungen*. Berlin, 1949.

MOODY, E. A. *The Logic of William of Ockham*. London, 1935.

VIGNAUX, P. *Nominalisme*. Dictionnaire de théologie catholique, vol. 11, cols. 748–84. Paris, 1931.

ZUIDEMA, S. U. *De Philosophie van Occam in zijn Commentaar op de Sententiën*. 2 vols. Hilversum, 1936.

Chapter Nine: The Ockhamist Movement: John of Mirecourt and Nicholas of Autrecourt.

Texts

JOHN OF MIRECOURT

BIRKENMAIER, A. *Ein Rechtfertigungsschreiben Johanns von Mirecourt*. Münster, 1922 (Beiträge, 20, 5).

STEGMÜLLER, F. *Die zwei Apologien des Jean de Mirecourt*. Recherches de théologie ancienne et médiévale, 1933, pp. 40–79, 192–204.

NICHOLAS OF AUTRECOURT

LAPPE, J. *Nikolaus von Autrecourt*. Münster, 1908 (Beiträge, 6, 1). (This contains correspondence between Nicholas and Bernard of Arezzo and between Nicholas and Giles.)

O'DONNELL, J. R. *Nicholas of Autrecourt*. Mediaeval Studies, 1 (1939), pp. 179–280. (This contains an edition of the *Exigit*.)

Studies

LANG, A. *Die Wege der Glaubensbegründung bei den Scholastikern des 14 Jahrhunderts*. Münster, 1931 (Beiträge, 30, 1–2).

LAPPE, J. See above.

MICHALSKI, C. *Les courants philosophiques à Oxford et à Paris pendant le XIVe siècle*. Bulletin de l'Académie polonaise des Sciences et des Lettres, 1920 (separately, Cracow, 1921).

Les sources du criticisme et du scepticisme dans la philosophie du XIVe siècle. Cracow, 1924.

Le criticisme et le scepticisme dans la philosophie du XIVe siècle. Bulletin de l'Académie polonaise des Sciences et des Lettres, 1925 (separately, Cracow 1926).

Les courants critiques et sceptiques dans la philosophie du XIVe siècle. Cracow, 1927.

O'DONNELL, J. R. *The Philosophy of Nicholas of Autrecourt and his appraisal of Aristotle*. Mediaeval Studies, 4 (1942) pp. 97–125.

RITTER, G. *Studien zur Spätscholastik*, 2 vols. Heidelberg, 1921–2.

VIGNAUX, P. *Nominalisme*. Dictionnaire de théologie catholique, vol. 11, cols. 748–84. Paris, 1931.

Nicholas d'Autrecourt, *ibid*., cols. 561–87.

WEINBERG, J. R. *Nicholas of Autrecourt. A Study in 14th-century Thought*. Princeton, 1948.

Chapter Ten: The Scientific Movement

Texts

BURIDAN

Johannis Buridani Quaestiones super libros quattuor de caelo et mundo. A. E. Moody (edit.). Cambridge (Mass.), 1942.

Quaestiones super octo libros physicorum Aristotelis. Paris, 1509.

In metaphysicen Aristotelis quaestiones. Paris, 1480, 1518.

Summulae logicae. Lyons, 1487.

Quaestiones et decisiones physicales insignium virorum Alberti de Saxonia, Thimonis, Buridani. Paris, 1516, 1518. (Contains Buridan's *Quaestiones in libros de Anima* and his *Quaestiones* on Aristotle's *Parva naturalia*.)

ALBERT OF SAXONY

Quaestiones super artem veterem. Bologna, 1496.

Quaestiones subtilissimae Alberti de Saxonia super libros Posteriorum. Venice, 1497.

Logica. Venice, 1522.

Sophismata Alberti de Saxonia. Paris, 1489.

Quaestiones in libros de caelo et mundo. Pavia, 1481.

Subtilissimae quaestiones super octo libros physicorum. Padua, 1493.

Quaestiones in libros de generatione (contained in work mentioned last under *Buridan*).

MARSILIUS OF INGHEN

Quaestiones Marsilii super quattuor libros sententiarum. Strasbourg, 1501.

Abbreviationes super VIII libros. Venice, 1521.
Egidius cum Marsilio et Alberto de generatione. Venice, 1518.

NICHOLAS OF ORESME
Maistre Nicole Oresme: Le livre du ciel et du monde. A. D. Menut and A. J. Denomy (edit.). Mediaeval Studies, 1941 (pp. 185–280), 1942 (pp. 159–297), 1943 (pp. 167–333). (This Text and Commentary has been published separately. Date unstated.)

Studies

BOCHERT, E. *Die Lehre von der Bewegung bei Nicolaus Oresme*. Münster, 1934 (Beiträge, 31, 3).
DUHEM, P. *Le système du monde: histoire des doctrines cosmologiques de Platon à Copernic*. 5 vols. Paris, 1913–17.
Études sur Léonard de Vinci. 3 vols. Paris, 1906–13.
HASKINS, C. H. *Studies in the History of Mediaeval Science*. Cambridge (Mass.), 1924.
HEIDINGSFELDER, G. *Albert von Sachsen*. Münster, 1926 (Beiträge 22, 3–4).
MAIER, A. *Das Problem der intensiven Grösse in der Scholastik*. Leipzig, 1939.
Die Impetustheorie der Scholastik. Vienna, 1940.
An der Grenzen von Scholastik und Naturwissenschaft. Studien zur Naturphilosophie des 14 Jahrhunderts. Essen, 1943.
Die Vorläufer Galileis im 14 Jahrhundert. Rome, 1949.
MICHALSKI, C. *La physique nouvelle et les différents courants philosophiques au XIVe siècle*. Bulletin de l'Académie polonaise des Sciences et des Lettres, 1927 (separately, Cracow, 1928).
MOODY, E. A. *John Buridan and the Habitability of the Earth*. Speculum, 1941, pp. 415–25.
RITTER, G. *Studien zur Spätscholastik*. Vol. 1, *Marsilius von Inghen und die okkamistische Schule in Deutschland*. Heidelberg, 1921.
SARTON, G. *Introduction to the History of Science*. 3 vols. Washington, 1927–48.
THORNDIKE, L. A *History of Magic and Experimental Science*. Vols. 3–4, *The fourteenth and fifteenth centuries*. New York, 1934.

Chapter Eleven: Marsilius of Padua

Texts

The Defensor Pacis of Marsilius of Padua. C. W. Previté-Orton (edit.). Cambridge, 1928.

Marsilius von Padua, Defensor Pacis. R. Scholz (edit.). Hannover, 1933.

Studies

CHECCHINI, A. and BOBBIO, N. (edit.). *Marsilio da Padova, Studi raccolti nel VI centenario della morte.* Padua 1942.

GEWIRTH, A. *Marsilius of Padua. The Defender of Peace.* Vol. 1, *Marsilius of Padua and Medieval Political Philosophy.* New York, 1951.

LAGARDE, G. DE *Naissance de l'esprit laïque au déclin du moyen âge.* Cahier II: *Marsile de Padoue.* Paris, 1948.

PREVITÉ-ORTON, C. W. *Marsiglio of Padua.* Part II: *Doctrines.* English Historical Review, 1923, pp. 1–18.

Chapter Twelve: Speculative Mysticism

Texts

ECKHART

Meister Eckhart. Die deutschen und lateinischen Werke herausgegeben im Auftrage der Deutschen Forschungsgemeinschaft. Stuttgart, 1936 (in course of publication).

Magistri Eckhardi Opera latina auspiciis Instituti Sanctae Sabinae ad codicum fidem edita. Leipzig.

I. *Super oratione dominica.* R. Klibansky (edit.). 1934.

II. *Opus tripartitum:* Prologi. H. Bascour, O.S.B. (edit.). 1935.

III. *Quaestiones Parisienses.* A. Dondaine, O.P. (edit.). 1936.

Eine lateinische Rechtfertigungsschrift des Meister Eckhart. A. Daniels (edit.). Münster, 1923 (Beiträge, 23, 5).

Meister Eckhart. Das System seiner religiösen Lehre und Lebensweisheit. Textbuch aus den gegrückten und ungedrückten Quellen mit Einführung. O. Karrer (edit.). Munich, 1926.

TAULER

Die Predigten Taulers. F. Vetter (edit.). Berlin, 1910.

Sermons de Tauler. 3 vols. E. Hugueny, P. Théry and A. L. Corin (edit.). Paris, 1927, 1930, 1935.

BL. HENRY SUSO

Heinrich Seuse. Deutsche Schriften. K. Bihlmeyer (edit.). 2 vols. Stuttgart, 1907.

L'œuvre mystique de Henri Suso. Introduction et traduction. 4 vols. B. Lavaud, O.P. Fribourg, Switzerland, 1946–7.

Blessed Henry Suso's Little Book of Eternal Wisdom. R. Raby (translator). London, 1866 (2nd edition).

The Life of Blessed Henry Suso by Himself. T. F. Knox (translator). London, 1865.

RUYSBROECK

Jan van Ruusbroec. Werke. Nach der Standardschrift von Groenendal herausgegeben von der Ruusbroec–Gesellschaft in Antwerpen. 2nd edition. 4 vols. Cologne, 1950.

GERSON

Johannis Gersonii opera omnia. 5 vols. M. E. L. Du Pin (edit.). Antwerp, 1706.

Jean Gerson, Commentateur Dionysien. Les Notulae super quaedam verba Dionysii de Caelesti Hierarchia. A. Combes. Paris, 1940.

Six Sermons français inédits de Jean Gerson. L. Mourin (edit.). Paris, 1946.

Studies

BERNHART, J. *Die philosophische Mystik des Mittelalters von ihren antiken Ursprungen bis zur Renaissance*. Munich, 1922.

BIZET, J. A. *Henri Suso et le déclin de la scolastique*. Paris, 1946.

BRIGUÉ, L. *Ruysbroeck*. Dictionnaire de théologie catholique, vol. 14, cols. 408–20. Paris, 1938.

BÜHLMANN, J. *Christuslehre und Christusmystik des Heinrich Seuse*. Lucerne, 1942.

COMBES, A. *Jean de Montreuil et le chancelier Gerson*. Paris, 1942.

CONNOLLY, J. L. *John Gerson, Reformer and Mystic*. Louvain, 1928.

DELLA VOLPE, G. *Il misticismo speculativo di maestro Eckhart nei suoi rapporti storici*. Bologna, 1930.

DEMPF, A. *Meister Eckhart. Eine Einführung in sein Werk.* Leipzig, 1934.

DENIFLE, H. *Das geistliche Leben. Deutsche Mystiker des 14 Jahrhunderts.* Salzburg, 1936 (9th edition by A. Auer).

HORNSTEIN, X. DE *Les grands mystiques allemands du XIVe siècle. Eckhart, Tauler, Suso.* Lucerne, 1920.

WAUTIER D'AYGALLIERS, A. *Ruysbroeck l'Admirable.* Paris, 1923.

NOTES

CHAPTER ONE

[1] The use of the phrase 'indirect power' involves an interpretation of Thomas's doctrine.

CHAPTER TWO

[1] i.e. Hervaeus Natalis, who became Master-General of the Dominicans in 1318.

[2] The relation is a *modus essendi ad aliud, qui est ipse respectus relationis.* 1 *Sent.* (A), 33, 1.

[3] *Relatio est alia res a suo fundamento, et tamen non facit compositionem. Ibid.*

[4] *Relata realia ex natura sui fundamenti habent inter se necessariam coexigentiam ratione fundamenti. Ibid.* (A), 31, 1. *In creaturis realis relatio requirit dependentiam in relato. Ibid.* (A), 30, 2.

[5] *Quaestio de natura cognitionis* (ed. J. Koch), p. 18.

[6] 1 *Sent.* (A), 13, 1, and 33, 1.

[7] 1 *Ibid.* (C), 33, 1.

[8] 2 *Sent.*, 3, 7, 8.

[9] *Ibid.*, 9, 3, 3, p. 114, a A. Pagination is given according to the 1596 edition (Rome).

[10] *Ibid.*

[11] *Ibid.*, p. 115, a F.

[12] *Ibid.*, 3, 2, 4, p. 30, c F.

[13] *Ibid.*, p. 66, b D.

[14] *Ibid.*, 9, 2, 3, p. 109, b A B.

[15] *Ibid.*, 11, 4, 2, pp. 142–5.

[16] 1 *Sent.*, 9, 1, p. 319, a B.

[17] *La philosophie au moyen âge*, p. 632.

[18] 1 *Sent.*, 9, 1, p. 320, a B.

[19] *Ibid.*, p. 321, b B C.

[20] *Die patristische und scholastische Philosophie*, p. 526.

[21] 1 *Sent.*, 9, 1, p. 321, a D E.

[22] *Ibid.*, b B.

[23] *Ibid.*, 23, 2, p. 539, a F–b A.

[24] *Prologus in Sent.*, 5, p. 66, a D.

[25] *Ibid.*, a F.

[26] *Ibid.*, a E.

[27] 1 *Sent.*, 35, 4, 2, p. 816, b C–E.

[28] *Prologus in Sent.*, prooemium, 3, p. 25, a F. Petrus Aureoli is here arguing that it is possible for an act of intuition to exist in the absence of the object. This view was also held by Ockham. The remark about keeping close to experience is incidental in the context; but it is none the less significant and enunciates a principle.

[29] *Der Konzeptualismus . . . des Franziskanererzbischofs Petrus Aureoli*, p. 197.

[30] 2 *Sent.*, 16, 1, 1, p. 218, b.

[31] *Ibid.*, p. 219, a B.

[32] *Ibid.*, 12, 2, 1, p. 174, b D.

[33] *Ibid.*, 15, 1, 1, p. 223, a F.

[34] *Ibid.*, 15, 1, 2, p. 223, b A–C.

[35] *Ibid.*, b E–F.

[36] *Ibid.*, p. 224, b D–F.

[37] *Ibid.*, 15, 1, 2, p. 226, a E–F.

[38] *Ibid.*, p. 226, a F–b B.

[39] *Ibid.*, 19, 1, p. 246, b D.

[40] *Ibid.*, p. 247, a.

[41] 1 *Sent.*, 38, 3, p. 883, b C–D.

[42] *Ibid.*, p. 888, a B.

[43] *Ibid.*, p. 889, b A.

[44] *Ibid.*, 39, 3, p. 901, a C.

[45] *Ibid.*, a F–b A.

[46] *Ibid.*, p. 902, a F–b B.

[47] On this subject see J. Koch: *Durandus de S. Porciano O.P.*, in *Beiträge zur Gesch. des Mittelalters*, 26, 1, pp. 199 ff., Münster i. W., 1927.

[48] *Ibid.*, pp. 340–69.

CHAPTER THREE

[1] As he seems to have been ordained subdeacon in February 1306, he was most probably born before 1290; according to P. Boehner, about 1280.

[2] P. Boehner follows Pelster in interpreting *inceptor* in the strict sense, that is to say, as meaning someone who had fulfilled all the requirements for the doctorate, but who had not taken up his duties as an actual professor. If this interpretation is accepted it is easy to explain how the *Venerabilis Inceptor* could sometimes be called *doctor*, and even *magister*; but the word *inceptor* should not, I think, be so explained as to imply that the man to whom it was applied was, or might be, an actual doctor. The word was used for a candidate for the doctorate, a 'formed bachelor', and though Ockham was qualified to take the doctorate, he does not appear to have actually taken it. As to his honorific title, *Venerabilis Inceptor*, the first word was applied to him as founder of 'nominalism', while the second, as we have seen, referred simply to his position at the time his studies at

Oxford came to an end. Incidentally, there is no evidence whatever that he ever studied at Paris or took the doctorate there.

[3] The word *ordinatio* was used to denote the text or the part of a text which a mediaeval lecturer actually wrote or dictated with a view to publication.

[4] *Tractatus de successivis*, edit. Boehner, p. 29.

[5] See E. Iserloh: *Um die Echtheit des Centiloquium; Gregorianum*, 30 (1949), 78–103.

[6] See, for example, Georges de Lagarde (cf. *Bibliog.*), IV, pp. 63–6; V, pp. 7 ff.

CHAPTER FOUR

[1] Ed. Bochenski, p. 1.

[2] Edited by P. Boehner, O.F.M. The Franciscan Institute, St. Bonaventure, N.Y. and E. Nauwelaerts, Louvain. *Pars prima*, 1951.

[3] Edited by P. Boehner, O.F.M. *Ibid.*, 1951.

[4] 1 *Sent.*, 2, 8, Q.

[5] *Summa totius logicae*, 1, 63.

[6] *Quodlibet*, 4, 19.

[7] 1 *Sent.*, 2, 4, D.

[8] *Ibid.*, 2, 6, B.

[9] *Ibid.*, 2, 8, Q.

[10] *Ibid.*, 2, 6, E E. *Respondeo quod conveniunt (Socrates et Plato) aliquibus, quia seipsis, et quod Socrates convenit cum Platone non in aliquo sed aliquo, quia seipso.*

[11] *Expositio aurea*, 3, 2, 90, R.

[12] See vol. II, p. 154.

[13] *Quodlibet*, 4, 19.

[14] *Ibid.*

[15] *Summa totius logicae*, 1, 12.

[16] Cf. *S.T.*, 1, 76, 2, *ad* 4; 1, 85, 2.

[17] 1 *Sent.*, 2, 4, M.

[18] *Ibid.*

[19] *Ibid.*, 2, 4, O.

[20] *Summa totius logicae*, 3, 2.

[21] *Ibid.*

[22] *Ibid.*

[23] 1 *Sent.*, 2, 6, D.

CHAPTER FIVE

[1] 1 *Sent.*, 3, 2, F.

[2] *Prol. Sent.*, 1, 2.

[3] *Ibid.*

[4] 1 *Sent.*, 27, 3, K.

[5] *Quodlibet*, 1, 13.

[6] *Ibid.*, 1, 14.

[7] *Ibid.*

[8] 2 *Sent.*, 15, E.
[9] *Quodlibet*, 1, 13.
[10] *Ibid.*, 6, 6.
[11] *Ibid.*
[12] *Ibid.*, 5, 5.
[13] *Ibid.*
[14] *Ibid.*
[15] *Ibid.*, 6, 6.
[16] 1 *Sent.*, 41, 1, E.
[17] 2 *Sent.*, 2, H.
[18] Cf. *Expositio aurea*, 2, 64, V.
[19] 1 *Sent.*, 30, 1, S.
[20] *Ibid.*, 30, 1, R.
[21] *Expositio aurea*, 2, 64, R.
[22] 1 *Sent.*, 30, 5.
[23] 2 *Sent.*, 2, G.
[24] 1 *Sent.*, 35, 5, N.
[25] 2 *Sent.*, 3, B.
[26] 1 *Sent.*, 1, 3, N.
[27] *Ibid.*, 41, 1, F.
[28] 2 *Sent.*, 9, C, D, E.
[29] *Tractatus de successivis*, ed. Boehner, p. 47.
[30] *Ibid.*, p. 46.
[31] This treatise is a compilation; but it is a compilation from Ockham's authentic writings. See p. 58.
[32] 2, 9.
[33] Cf. *Tractatus de successivis*, ed. Boehner, pp. 41–2.
[34] For the Aristotelian definitions of place and time see, for example, the first volume of this history, *Greece and Rome*, Vol. I, Part II, pp. 63–65.
[35] 2 *Sent.*, 12 D.
[36] *Tractatus de successivis*, ed. Boehner, p. 111.
[37] *Ibid.*, p. 119.
[38] *Ibid.*, p. 37.

CHAPTER SIX

[1] *Prol. Sent.*, 9, N.
[2] *Ibid.*
[3] *Ibid.*, D, D.
[4] 3 *Sent.*, 9, T.
[5] 1 *Sent.*, 3, 1, E.
[6] *Quodlibet*, 2, 7; *Summa totius logicae*, 3, 2.
[7] 1 *Sent.*, 2, 9, P.
[8] *Ibid.*, X.
[9] *Ibid.*, P.
[10] 3 *Sent.*, 9, R.
[11] *Ibid.*, Q.
[12] *Ibid.*, R.
[13] *Ibid.*, E.

[14] *Expositio aurea*, 2, 39, V.
[15] 1 *Sent.*, 3, 1, D.
[16] *Ibid.*, F.
[17] 1 *Sent.*, 3, 4, D, F.
[18] This principle is that whatever is moved is moved by another (*quidquid movetur ab alio movetur*).
[19] Cf. *Quodlibet*, 7, 22–3.
[20] *Ibid.*, 4, 2.
[21] *Summulae in libros physicorum*, 2, 6.
[22] 2 *Sent.*, 3, NN; *Quodlibet*, 4, 1.
[23] 1 *Sent.*, 1, 4, E.
[24] *Quodlibet*, 2, 1.
[25] 1 *Sent.*, 2, 10, O.
[26] *Ibid.*
[27] *Quodlibet*, 1, 1.
[28] 1 *Sent.*, 35, 2, C.
[29] *Prol. Sent.*, 2, D, D.
[30] 1 *Sent.*, 2, 9, P.
[31] *Ibid.*, R.
[32] *Ibid.*, 3, 2, F.
[33] *Ibid.*, M.
[34] Cf. 1 *Sent.*, 35, 5, C.
[35] In other words, Ockham considered that the upholders of the theory had been misled by language, confusing words or names with things.
[36] 1 *Sent.*, 35, 5, E.
[37] *Ibid.*, G.
[38] *Ibid.*, E.
[39] *Ibid.*, G.
[40] *Ibid.*
[41] *Ibid.*
[42] *Ibid.*
[43] *Ibid.*
[44] Cf. 1 *Sent.*, 35, 5, E.
[45] *Ibid.*, M.
[46] 1 *Sent.*, 35, 2, D.
[47] *Ibid.*
[48] *Ibid.*, 38, 1, L.
[49] *Ibid.*, 38, 1, M.
[50] St. Thomas held that future contingent events are present to God in virtue of His eternity and that He knows them as present.
[51] Ed. Boehner, p. 15.
[52] *Ibid.*
[53] 2, 32.
[54] 4, 4.
[55] 1 *Sent.*, 45, 1, C.
[56] *Ibid.*, G.
[57] *Ibid.*, 42, 1, G.

CHAPTER SEVEN

[1] *Quodlibet*, 1, 12.
[2] *Ibid.*, 1, 10.
[3] *Ibid.*, 2, 1.
[4] 2 *Sent.*, 22, H.
[5] *Quodlibet*, 2, 10.
[6] 2 *Sent.*, 26, E.
[7] *Ibid.*
[8] *Ibid.*, D.
[9] *Ibid.*, 9, C C.
[10] 4 *Sent.*, 7, F.
[11] 2, 10.
[12] *Quodlibet*, 2, 10; 2 *Sent.*, 22, H.
[13] *Quodlibet*, 2, 11.
[14] *Ibid.*, 2, 10.
[15] See Vol. 2, Part II, of this history, pp. 171–4.
[16] *Quodlibet*, 2, 10.
[17] 2 *Sent.*, 24, L.
[18] *Ibid.*, K.
[19] *Ibid.*, 25, O.
[20] *Ibid.*, A A.
[21] 1 *Sent.*, 25, J.
[22] *Quodlibet*, 4, 11.
[23] 3 *Sent.*, 1, B; cf. 1 *Sent.*, 23, 1, C.
[24] 1 *Sent.*, 25, 1, J.
[25] *Ibid.*, 23, 1, C.
[26] *Ibid.*, 1, 3, U.
[27] *Quodlibet*, 1, 16.
[28] *Ibid.*
[29] 3 *Sent.*, 10, H.
[30] 1 *Sent.*, 1, 4, S.
[31] *Ibid.*, E.
[32] *Ibid.*, 1, 6, P.
[33] 3 *Sent.*, 10, D.
[34] Cf. 3 *Sent.*, 4, M; 3 *Sent.*, 10, D; 4 *Sent.*, 12, C.
[35] 3 *Sent.*, 13, U.
[36] 2 *Sent.*, 5, H.
[37] On Scotus's moral theory, see Vol. 2, Part II, of this history, pp. 268–74.
[38] 2 *Sent.*, 19, P.
[39] 4 *Sent.*, 9, E–F.
[40] 3 *Sent.*, 12, AAA.
[41] 2 *Sent.*, 19, O.
[42] Cf. *Opus nonaginta dierum*, c. 95.
[43] 1 *Sent.*, 41, K.

[44] 3 *Sent.*, 12, NN. For the reference to Aristotle's *Ethics*, cf. *Nicomachean Ethics*, 1107, a.

[45] *Ibid.*, 12, CCC.

[46] 3 *Sent.*, CCC–DDD.

[47] Cf. *Nicomachean Ethics*, 1105, a b.

[48] 3 *Sent.*, 13, O.

[49] On this subject, see the following chapter.

[50] 3 *Sent.*, 13, C.

[51] *Ibid.*, 12, CCC.

CHAPTER EIGHT

[1] *Opus nonaginta dierum*, c. 14.

[2] *Dialogus*, 22, 6.

[3] Cf. *Opus nonaginta dierum*, c. 2.

[4] *Dialogus*, 1, 3, 2, 24.

[5] 1, 13.

[6] *Dialogus*, 2, 3, 1, 27.

[7] *Ibid.*, 2, 3, 2, 6.

[8] *Opus nonaginta dierum*, 2, 4.

[9] Ockham did not deny papal supremacy as such; he rejected what he called 'tyrannical' supremacy.

CHAPTER NINE

[1] *Recherches de théologie ancienne et médiévale* (1933), pp. 40–79, 192–204.

[2] 2, 3, concl. 3.

[3] 1 *Sent.*, 19, concl. 6, *ad* 5.

[4] *Beiträge zur Geschichte der Philosophie des Mittelalters*, VI, 2. References to 'Lappe' in the following account of Nicholas's philosophy are references to this edition, dated 1908.

[5] *Mediaeval Studies*, vol. 1, 1939, pp. 179–280. References to the *Exigit* in the following pages are references to this edition.

[6] Lappe, p. 4.

[7] *Ibid.*, 6*, 33.

[8] *Ibid.*, 15–16.

[9] Cf. *Exigit*, p. 235.

[10] Lappe, 9*, 15–20.

[11] *Ibid.*, 13*, 9–12.

[12] *Exigit*, p. 237.

[13] Lappe, 34*, 7–9.

[14] *Ibid.*, 12*, 20–3.

[15] *Ibid.*, 13*, 19–20.

[16] p. 225.

[17] Lappe, 31*, 16–17.

[18] *Ibid.*, 33*, 12–14.

[19] *Ibid.*, 33*, 18–19.

[20] *Exigit*, p. 185.
[21] Lappe, 39*, 8.
[22] Cf. *Exigit*, pp. 181–2.
[23] Lappe, 41*, 31–4.
[24] *Ibid.*, 40*, 26–33.

CHAPTER TEN

[1] Theodoric's explanation of the shape of the bow was correct, though he failed to explain the colours.
[2] 2 *Sent.*, 18, J.
[3] *Ibid.*, 9, E.
[4] 12, 9.
[5] *Timaeus*, 56a.
[6] 62d., p. 280.
[7] 140a, p. 273. References are to the edition by A. D. Menut and A. J. Denomy.
[8] 140d–141a, p. 275.
[9] 141b, p. 276.
[10] *Josue*, 10, 13.
[11] 141d–142a, pp. 276–7.
[12] 142b, p. 277.
[13] 143c–d, p. 278.
[14] 144b, p. 279.
[15] 38b–c, p. 243.
[16] 38a–b, p. 243.
[17] 39b–c, p. 244.

CHAPTER ELEVEN

[1] A 'perfect' society is a self-sufficing society, possessing in itself all the means required for attaining its end.
[2] *Naissance de l'esprit laïque*; Cahier II, *Marsile de Padoue.*
[3] *Def. pacis*, 2, 26, 19.
[4] 1, 3.
[5] 1, 4.
[6] 1, 5.
[7] 1, 5–6.
[8] 1, 9, 5.
[9] 1, 9, 7.
[10] 1, 5, 7.
[11] 1, 11.
[12] 1, 10, 3.
[13] 1, 10, 5.
[14] 2, 8, 5.
[15] 12, 7–8.
[16] 2, 12, 9.
[17] 2, 9, 3.
[18] 1, 4.

[19] 1, 12, 3.
[20] 1, 12, 4.
[21] 1, 13, 8.
[22] 1, 15, 3; cf. 1, 16.
[23] 1, 17, 2.
[24] 1, 18.
[25] 1, 19.
[26] 2, 4.
[27] 2, 10.
[28] 2, 14.
[29] 2, 26.
[30] *La philosophie au moyen âge* (1944), p. 592.
[31] *Ibid.*, p. 691.
[32] *Histoire de la philosophie médiévale,* tome III (1947), p. 142.

CHAPTER TWELVE

[1] *Imitation of Christ*, 1, 1; 1, 2; 1, 3.
[2] Ed. A. Dondaine, O.P., 1936, p. 1.
[3] p. 3.
[4] p. 5.
[5] p. 7.
[6] *Ibid.*
[7] pp. 7–8.
[8] p. 9.
[9] *Prologus generalis*; ed. H. Bascour, O.S.B., 1935.
[10] p. 12.
[11] p. 21.
[12] p. 22.
[13] Meister Eckhart, *Die lateinischen Werke: erster Band*, fasc. 2, pp. 98–100, Stuttgart-Berlin, 1938.
[14] *Ibid.*, fasc. 1, p. 52, Stuttgart-Berlin, 1937.
p. 52, Stuttgart-Berlin, 1937.
[15] *Opus tripartitum, Prologus generalis*; ed. H. Bascour, O.S.B., p. 18.
[16] *Ibid.*, p. 16.
[17] *Ibid.*
[18] Munich, 1926.
[19] 1, 29.
[20] *Proslog.*, 27, and *Monol.*, 31.
[21] 9, 6.
[22] *Summa theologica*, 1, 4, 3, *ad* 4.
[23] Meister Eckhart, *Die deutschen Werke: erster Band, Meister Eckhart's Predigten*, fasc. 2, p. 143.
[24] 1, 8, 1, *ad* 1 ff.
[25] *Op. cit.*, fasc. 1, pp. 69–70.
[26] Meister Eckhart, *Die lateinischen Werke: erster Band*, fasc. 1, p. 50, Stuttgart-Berlin, 1937.
[27] *Opus tripartitum, Prologi*, p. 18; ed. H. Bascour, O.S.B.

[28] *Ibid.*, p. 14.
[29] 1, 3.
[30] *Die lateinischen Werke: erster Band*, fasc. 1, pp. 49–50.
[31] Cf. Daniels, *Eine lateinische Rechtfertigungsschrift des Meister Eckhart*, p. 10, n. 8. *Beiträge*, 23, 5, Münster i. W., 1923.
[32] Commentary on the *Celestial Hierarchy* of the Pseudo-Dionysius, 4.
[33] *Conf.*, 11, 7.
[34] Cf. twelfth German sermon, pp. 197–8. Cf. p. 189, n. 3.
[35] Cf. Meister Eckhart, *Die deutschen Werke: erster Band, Meister Eckhart's Predigten*, fasc. 1, pp. 24–45. Stuttgart-Berlin, 1936.
[36] *Wisdom* 6, 16; *op. cit.*, fasc. 2, pp. 99–115.
[37] *Op. cit.*, p. 119.
[38] Daniels, p. 5, n. 4; p. 17, n. 6.
[39] *Ibid.*, p. 15, n. 1.
[40] *Book of Truth*, 332, 16.
[41] *Vita*, 21–4, p. 178.
[42] *Ibid.*, 178, 24–179, 7.
[43] Cf. *Vita*, 50 and 51, p. 176.
[44] *Adornment*, 2, 2.
[45] *Ibid.*, 3, 4.
[46] *P.L.*, 25, 22 AB.
[47] *De Veritate*, 16, 1, obj. 1.
[48] *Ibid.*, 17, 2, *ad* 3.
[49] Gerson died in 1429. For chronological details, see *La vie et les œuvres de Gerson* by P. Glorieux (Archives d'histoire doctrinale et littéraire du moyen âge, t. 18, pp. 149–92; Paris, 1951).
[50] *Opera*, 3, col. 13.
[51] *Ibid.*, col. 26.
[52] *St. Mark* 1, 15.
[53] *Jean Gerson, Commentateur Dionysien*, Paris, 1940.
[54] 1, 7.